Treadwell Gold

AN ALASKA SAGA OF RICHES AND RUIN

SHEILA KELLY

University of Alaska Press
Fairbanks

University of Alaska Press
P.O. Box 756240
Fairbanks, AK 99775-6240

ISBN 978-1-60223-075-0 (cloth), 978-1-60223-118-4 (paper), 978-1-60223-102-3 (e-book)

Library of Congress Cataloging-in-Publication Data for the cloth edition:
Kelly, Sheila, 1942–
     Treadwell gold : an Alaska saga of riches and ruin / by Sheila Kelly.
      p. cm.
  Includes bibliographical references and index.
  ISBN 978-1-60223-075-0 (alk. paper)
   1. Douglas Island (Alaska)—History, Local—20th century.   2. Treadwell
(Alaska)—History.   3. Extinct cities—Alaska—Douglas Island.   4. Douglas
Island (Alaska)—Gold discoveries.   5. Douglas Island (Alaska)—Social life and
customs—20th century.   6. Gold miners—Alaska—Douglas Island—History—
20th century.   7. Gold mines and mining—Alaska—Douglas Island—
History—20th century.   I. Title.
  F912.D75K45 2010
  979.8'4—dc22

2009035477

Cover design by Dixon Jones

This publication was printed on acid-free paper that meets the minimum
requirements for ANSI / NISO Z39.48–1992 (R2002) (Permanence of Paper for
Printed Library Materials).

We gratefully acknowledge the Rasmuson Foundation for a grant to support the
publication of this book.

To Raymond, Marion, and Honorah Kelly
and all the children who grew up in Treadwell

Contents

Prologue

W HO HAS HEARD OF TREADWELL? The boom and bust of these great gold mines in southeast Alaska is a gripping story, an important part of American history, and a formative part of my own family. But mention the name, and most people draw a blank.

As a child, I knew Treadwell as an obscure reference my father would make when telling his six children about how things were in the "old" days when he and his two sisters, Marion and Honorah (Honey), were growing up in Alaska during the first quarter of the twentieth century.

My first visit to Alaska was in 1958, when I was sixteen. I spent an unforgettable summer in Ketchikan with Aunt Honey and Uncle Chester (Archie) Archbold, who was assistant superintendent of the South Tongass National Forest. I was there when President Eisenhower signed the Alaska Statehood Act on July 7, 1958, so I was certified as an honorary citizen of the state. I had already fallen in love with the place, not surprising considering I was just one generation removed from the pioneer Kelly family that had settled there in 1899. But I would not return until decades later.

After my father and his sister Honey died in the late 1970s, their surviving sister, Marion, began regaling me with amazing tales. I wished then that I had paid more attention to Dad's stories that started, "When I was a boy . . ." Later, as the twentieth century (and my own half century) drew to a close, I became hungry for family history. I knew ours happened to include a unique American frontier experience, the dramatic story of a hard-rock gold-mining town.

The Kelly hometown was Treadwell, Alaska, on Douglas Island across Gastineau Channel from Juneau. While my family history intrigued me,

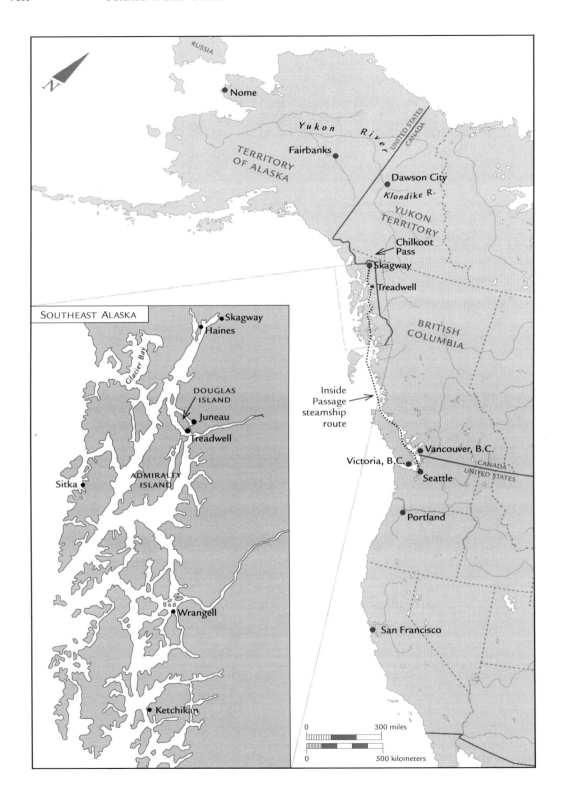

what pulled me deeper into the story was learning that over the course of four decades, starting in 1882, this little town achieved fame as the largest hard-rock gold-mining operation in the world, creating far more wealth than the flash-in-the-pan Klondike Gold Rush. As early as 1890, the first U.S. Census taken in Alaska proclaimed that Treadwell, "as the first enterprise to attract large capital, [marked] the turning point in Alaska's fortunes."[1]

My hours of conversation with Aunt Marion, along with a one-hundred-page hand-written memoir left by Honey, launched me on what became a multidecade quest. Based on the Kelly sisters' recollections, I published an article, "A Childhood in Treadwell," in the *Alaska Journal* in 1985 and a second article, "Honey and Arch, An Alaskan Love Story," in 1986. Over several years, I went to Juneau and scoured the files of local newspapers, the *Douglas Island News* and the *Alaska Daily Empire*, searching for details about my family. I tracked down, interviewed, and shared photo albums with people who had lived in Treadwell during that time, including Irving Anderson, son of the Swedish hoist operator August Anderson, and Robert Kinzie Jr. and Philip Bradley Jr., sons of superintendents. At first, I wanted to know only what they could tell me about my father's family.

Then something happened. Maybe it was those hours I spent in the Alaska State Library immersed in the treasure trove of fine historical photos of Treadwell taken by well-known Alaska photographers W. H. Case, H. H. Draper, Lloyd Winter, Percy Pond, and E. A. Hegg. Their black-and-white masterpieces showed the mud-smudged miners at work half a mile down in the dark tunnels, or dressed up in suits and seated five hundred strong for a fine meal at the boardinghouse. I was enthralled with the artistic quality of photographs of giant boilers and hoists. I smiled at the images of workers' clapboard cottages and the families in their Sunday best for Fourth of July festivities. The portraits of Tlingit Indian women selling their exquisite woven baskets at steamship docks fascinated me. The scenes of the spectacular mine cave-in shocked and saddened me. As I pursued my research and heard stories firsthand from my family and their friends who lived through it all, I began to identify with the place and the people. I felt pride in the fact that Treadwell is credited with opening up development, and even tourism, on the great northern frontier. The town became a compelling character, not just the background. I found that Treadwell is mentioned in book chapters, guidebooks, memoirs, and thousands of websites, but there was no book that gave the whole fascinating story.

When I went to Douglas Island for the first time in September 1996, I stood on what is now known as Sandy Beach, formed from the fine sand tailings left over from processing millions of tons of ore to release the gold. The town was gone. All that was left is remnants of buildings along the Treadwell Mine Historic Trail in a public park that skirts Gastineau Channel.

Near the beach, the start of the trail is marked by a timber structure, twelve feet high by five feet wide, housing five twelve-foot steel rods with giant hammers on the ends. This battery of five "stamps" was the first miniature mill brought to Douglas Island in 1882 by John Treadwell to pulverize the ore from the newly discovered lode. The town that sprung up here eventually boasted 960 of these stamps pounding twenty-four hours a day, producing both the enormous wealth and the thunderous noise that were trademarks of Treadwell.

The path wound two miles through acres of dense alders, cottonwood, mountain ash, and a few Sitka spruce. The temperate rainforest had reclaimed the site with bracken, cow parsnip, Indian rhubarb, blueberries, salmonberries, and gray currants. Dog walkers and the high school cross-country team using the trail paid little attention to the crumbling remains in the adjacent woods.

John Treadwell's original five-stamp mill now marks the start of the Treadwell historic trail on Douglas Island. (Photo by Andy Mills. Courtesy of Paulette Simpson.)

Scattered along the trail were a few wooden markers with cryptic labels: "The Vaults," "300 Mill," "Assay Office," "New Office Building," and "Cave-in." Back in the underbrush I stumbled on rusting hulks of steam boilers, ore cars, odd-shaped rollers and metal scraps, railway tracks that disappeared, and jumbles of cable drums. Behind them loomed moss-covered Mayan-like ruins of massive concrete foundations, the crumbling evidence that this was once the site of a great enterprise.

I carried a 1914 map of the town at its heyday, showing all the mines, the hoists, the narrow-gauge railroad tracks and trestles, and the two hundred buildings that supported the mines and housed the miners and their families, including my grandparents, father, and aunts. I veered off the marked path and climbed through the tangled understory to find the site of the Kelly family cottage in a residential section known as Treadwell Heights. I watched and listened for family ghosts, trying to get a feeling for both the house that once stood there and the surrounding town. The gurgling rush of the stream behind me would have been lost in the industrial cacophony of early Treadwell. I imagined the ore cars Aunt Marion had talked about screaming by on a railway trestle that rose right in front of me leading to the 300 Mill just to the left of their house.

Looking out through the trees to Gastineau Channel, I saw south-bound ducks flying by. Then a white behemoth floated past like a beast from *Jurassic Park*. The SS *Star Princess*, last of the summer season's nine hundred cruise-ship voyages, turned into Juneau. At 951 feet and carrying twenty-seven hundred passengers, the ship was four times as long and carried twenty times as many passengers as the vessels that plied this channel in 1905. At the turn of the century, steamships were the only form of transportation for families, businesspeople, and adventurous excursionists who dared come north.

Looking across the channel at Mount Roberts behind Juneau, I saw a dust of the powdered-sugar snow locals called "termination dust" that announced summer was over and winter on its way. The warm September day's cloudless azure sky gave no hint of the Takus, those fierce winter winds noted in regional history and fatal to Treadwell—and still feared today. Dependable as the tides, the Takus come right off the Juneau Icefield that has blanketed the mountains of the Coastal Range for thousands of years.

Leaving what I had determined to be my ancestral home site, I went deeper into the forest to unmarked areas with more building remnants and machine skeletons. Two concrete pillars were the only remains of the assay office, where the quality of gold was determined and these immovable posts provided the unwavering base for finely calibrated gold scales. Behind a cyclone fence, I saw the Glory Hole, a huge open pit where mining began with the daily retorts of blasting filling the air to tear thousands of tons of ore from the lode. Farther along, down a grassy draw among the brambles, was a round concrete structure that looked like a giant UFO crumbling in the trees. This was the central ore bin, one of the many Treadwell innovations designed to speed up the processing of high volumes of ore. Up another hill I spotted a concrete building with bars on the windows and two vaults inside—the refinery, where wide-eyed Treadwell children once witnessed white-hot liquid gold pouring into brick molds.

I found parts of giant gears and cable intact in the shell of the hoist house of the cyanide plant. The shack still showed a faded red paint with green trim.

Back at the beach, I looked out into the channel over the double row of rotting pilings that had once been the busiest wharf in Alaska. This was the staging area for the Treadwell story: Here ships unloaded the miners, machinery, coal and oil, engineers, tourists, and families that supported the burgeoning town. And these same ships headed back south loaded with Treadwell's precious export, a total of 206,000 pounds of gold bricks, most to be made into coins at the mint in San Francisco. On the wharf's far piling, a small square saltwater pump house perched, like the abandoned home of a giant bird. The machine shop where my grandfather worked centered on this wharf. When my grandmother died at twenty-nine, her body was sent by boat to her family plot in Oakland, California. From here Aunt Marion went back and forth on steamships to Seattle for polio treatments, later moving to San Francisco. My father went out from here to become a scholar, orator, and judge in Spokane. And Aunt Honey sailed out to Haines and then Petersburg to teach in Alaska's one-room schoolhouses.

I followed the water's edge to the site of the spectacular cave-in that had sounded the death knell for the town. Now it was a dimple in the shoreline, a quiet tree-lined cove, with saltwater wavelets gently lapping the shore. I stood there and envisioned the very different scenario that unfolded the night of April 21, 1917, when extraordinarily high tides in Gastineau Channel clawed at a crack in the mines' surface, then poured down into tunnels and shafts, flooding three of the town's four mines. By the next morning, Treadwell's most identifiable landmark was no longer the steep-sided Glory Hole, that yawning pit visible from some distance as a bold declaration that tons of riches had been gouged from the earth. The new draw in the little gold camp that achieved world fame was now the gaping sinkhole that had drowned the mines, swallowing a chunk of the town's buildings along with most of its future. The mills were silent and hundreds of workers left within days; my grandfather was one of the few who chose to stay on.

Moving away from the cave-in site, I backtracked along the shore to the area that had been the Treadwell Club, the town's social center that might be described as a country club. Octagonal white tiles dotted the tide line, remnants of the Turkish baths that were open twenty-four hours a day. A waterfront bank, sloughed off under the rusting train rails, exposed a town midden. I pocketed a thin mother-of-pearl shirt button, maybe worn to the Treadwell Firemen's Ball, which Marion told me was the grandest summer social occasion for Gastineau Channel residents. I dug up a white pottery cup and a perfectly oval bottomless vegetable dish from the site of the boardinghouse. Both were on the tables in a famous 1908 photograph of five hundred miners seated for the Fourth of July dinner. The button, the cup, and the vegetable dish held the story I wanted to capture, the everyday lives of those Treadwellians.

I used my own family—father, aunts, and grandparents—as the central thread in the story. Theirs is the perspective of a machinist and committed company man and his conservative Irish Catholic family. To fill out the dimensions of life in Treadwell, I searched for stories of other players. I was fortunate to get another firsthand account with colorful, heart-filled details from Irving Anderson about his big, boisterous Swedish Lutheran family. Irving's father, August Anderson, came to Treadwell as a Klondike adventurer–turned–corporate hoist operator and strikebreaker. Then I located Robert Kinzie Jr., Philip Bradley Jr., and Margaret Metzger Fordon, all children of Treadwell superintendents whose families enjoyed a more privileged way of life in the large elegant mansion that dominated the plaza of the company town. With passing time, it became impossible to interview people who had lived in Treadwell. I had to turn to books and articles for personal accounts from underground miners and workers' stories of struggles for better pay and working conditions. I also needed to know more about southeast Alaska's indigenous population, the Tlingit. They have been integral to the region for millennia, and they are part of the Treadwell story too.

My primary goal of bringing the town to life with a full cast of characters was limited by the demands of nonfiction. Since I couldn't add more characters, I decided the town itself should be given a leading role. Treadwell deserved to be recognized as the original catalyst for Alaska development. Just over a decade after the 1867 Alaska Purchase, the Treadwell mines began producing enormous wealth that preceded and outlasted the fevered Klondike Gold Rush. Treadwell created a base of jobs and commerce and drew thousands of adventuresome tourists curious to see a unique company town on the northern frontier. Aside from the fact that it is my own family history, Treadwell is a great story.

The tale has historic, economic, and geographic significance: The era bridged the nineteenth and twentieth centuries, from the Gay Nineties to the Roaring Twenties. The phenomenal success of this frontier enterprise fanned the industrial romance that celebrated America's capitalist prowess, while the distant location of Treadwell created a stream of commerce and tourism that defied the limitations of geography. In this multifaceted context, the personal stories share overlapping time periods and events of Treadwell life are repeated from the different perspectives.

As I was digging for pictures in family scrapbooks, I peeled off an early-twentieth-century photo of a small group of nicely dressed and properly hatted men and women, standing against a rough-hewn fence at the edge of a rock cliff. They seemed to be listening to a young boy at the front who was gesturing over the precipice. The faint penciled message on the back of the homemade postcard read. "Raymond Kelly, the guide, showing us the Glory Hole in Treadwell." I knew then how my story would start.

INTRODUCTION

⬖⬗⬖

Treadwell at Its Peak

*The Treadwell is the pride of Alaska. Its poetic
situation, romantic history, and admirable
methods should make it the pride of America.*
—*ALASKA YUKON* MAGAZINE, SEPTEMBER 1906

CIRCA 1912: AS THE SS *Cottage City* from San Francisco left
Stephen's Passage and headed north into Gastineau Channel along
Douglas Island, the passengers gathered at the rail. A steady thundering sound came down the channel. They were eight miles from their
destination, still forty minutes to go, but they could already hear it.

Ahead they could see the twin towns of Douglas (population 1,722)
and Treadwell (population 1,222).[1] Set against snow-capped green-mantled
mountains that rose three thousand feet, the mining town stretched
across two and a half miles of shoreline. A jumble of two hundred wooden
buildings spread for half a mile up barren treeless foothills. Long, low
warehouses lay at the feet of tall, narrow shaft houses, and slanted chutes
climbed the hillside. Smokestacks belched steam, and round orange oil
tanks dotted the shore like giant mushrooms. Barrackslike buildings
stood on pilings out over the water, and above the four mine sites were
clusters of cottages with green trim, lace curtains, and window boxes
ablaze with orange flowers. Huge sloping mounds of rock rubble rose

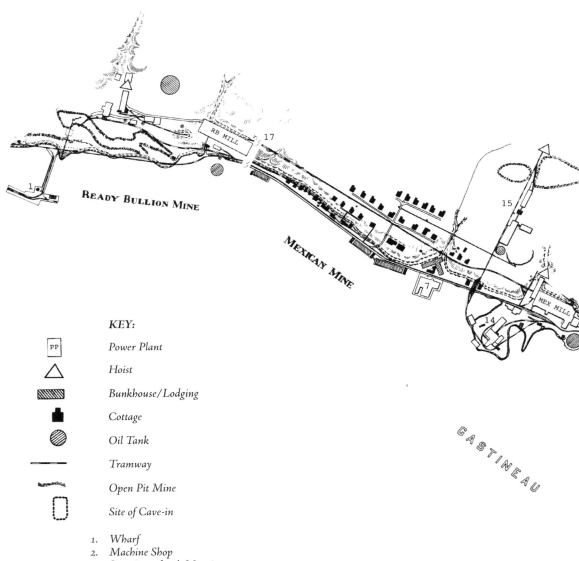

KEY:

PP	Power Plant
△	Hoist
▨	Bunkhouse/Lodging
■	Cottage
◉	Oil Tank
—	Tramway
⌇	Open Pit Mine
▢	Site of Cave-in

1.   Wharf
2.   Machine Shop
3.   Superintendent's Mansion
4.   Treadwell Store & Office
5.   Assay Office
6.   Plaza
7.   Dining Hall
8.   Treadwell Club
9.   Swimming Pool/Natatorium
10. Baseball Field
11. Central Crushing Plant
12. New School
13. Old School
14. Foundry
15. Cyanide Plant & Refinery
16. Kelly Cottage
17. Map shortened by 500 feet

TREADWELL
On Douglas Island

*The mine complex spread two miles along
the shoreline of Gastineau Channel*

Map adapted from Stone and Stone, *Hard Rock Gold*, 31-33

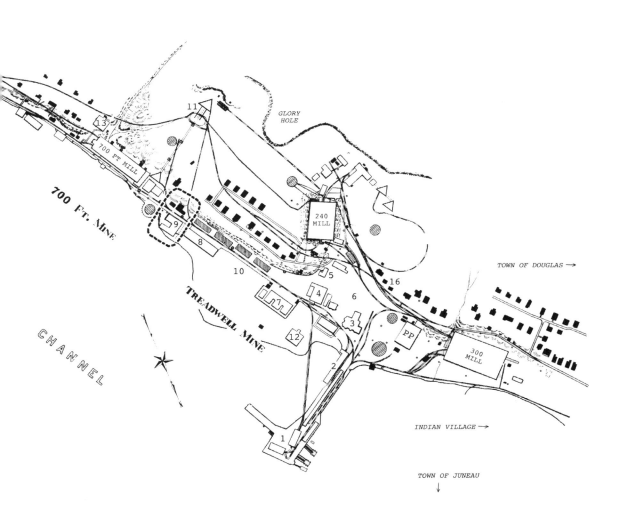

In 1916, Treadwell, Alaska, covered two miles along the eastern shore of Douglas Island on Gastineau Channel across from Juneau. The four mines extend from the Ready Bullion (far left) to the Teadwell (two large buildings of the 300 Mill visible at center). The Indian village stretches to the right along the beach to the town of Douglas.(Courtesy of the Alaska State Library, Winter and Pond Collection, P87-0348.)

up alongside the town's biggest buildings. Railroad tracks, trestles, and boardwalks with railings linked buildings and cottages. Up behind the town a huge open pit was gouged from the denuded hillside.

As the ship approached the dock, the roar reverberated off the mountains along the channel. This noise was Treadwell's auditory signature, coming from the town's five largest buildings filled with pounding hammers.

From their Pacific Coast Steamship Company travel brochure, the passengers learned that the amazing lode on which Treadwell sat was "unlimited." The gold did not come in nuggets, or even as dust. It was bound in rock at low concentrations. Producing one ounce of gold required eight and a half tons of ore. The extraction was complicated, requiring money, miners and machines, engineers and scientists. They all came together in the 1880s to create this new town on Alaska's frontier.

The boat pulled up to dock at Treadwell's deep-water pier, the only one in Alaska. Leaving the dock, the tourists glanced right to the shacks

of the Tlingit Indian village occupying the beach between Treadwell and Douglas. Then their attention landed on a grand three-story edifice on the left, with dormers and large bay windows, a glassed-in cupola, and a wraparound porch with a swing and filigreed wood railing, set in the middle of a tidy green patch of grass. A surprising sight in a mining camp, the Treadwell superintendent's home was more elegant than the newly built Alaska District Governor's residence across the channel in Juneau, where the capital had been moved from Sitka in 1906.

The curious sightseers were greeted by Jack (of all trades) Wilson, dressed in a khaki suit with matching belt, wide-brimmed Wild West hat, and a big badge that said "Jack." He was the mine watchman who gave tours, taught boxing to the local boys, and acted as the unofficial town sheriff. Raymond Kelly, enterprising preteen son of Treadwell Mining Company machinist Willy Kelly, tagged along as an apprentice guide. Raymond knew Treadwell, too. He had been born and raised there.

The first stop on the tour was the Glory Hole, that gaping pit everyone had seen from the boat. The visitors looked over the edge into a cavern 450 feet deep, 1,700 feet long, and 420 feet wide. The sides were a patchwork of white quartz and blue-black slate, with reddish splashes of iron. Most mine sites start with a Glory Hole, and the tourists wanted to know what that meant. Jack told them the origin of that name was debated: Some said it referred to that first easily accessible cache of high-grade ore. Others

Raymond Kelly guided tourists to view the Glory Hole, the site of the start of the Treadwell mines. (Courtesy of the Kelly Family Collection.)

said it honored those miners inevitably killed and "gone to glory" in such dangerous work. Treadwell's Glory Hole started with pit mining in 1882, at the site of John Treadwell's first claim. By 1906, over five million tons of ore had been blasted out and mining had moved underground, following the lode down and out under Gastineau Channel.

The size of the Glory Hole impressed the eye, but the magnitude of Treadwell's underground operation could only be imagined: miles of tunnels, going down over twenty-five hundred feet, three hundred men working a twelve-hour shift, blasting out cathedral-size rooms hundreds of feet high, with horses and mules pulling little trains loaded with ore to the shafts to be hauled up. Tourists didn't go underground without special permission and some miners had been upset when a party of Honolulu ladies descended to the twelve-hundred-foot level and "sang a number of their native airs." Miners considered it bad luck to have women underground.[2]

From their vantage point at the Glory Hole, tourists could see lines of miners with carbide lamps attached to their hats, swinging tin lunch pails, moving along a boardwalk on the way to the shafts.

Before going into the mill, Jack explained the steps in the gold-mining process so visitors could understand the grand machines they were seeing. The 300 Mill contributed the lion's share of the Treadwell roar. Raymond's family called this "our mill" because their house was just above it—cars carrying ore to the mill raced through their front yard, and in the winter he and his sisters sledded on the big hill made by rock waste from the mill. As the tour moved inside, Raymond pointed out the sign "Quiet, Men Working," although the noise was so deafening you could not hear a cannon fired twenty feet away.

Looking up in the middle of this immense building, the tourists saw the three hundred stamps: Each weighed around

Between 1882 and 1906, five million tons of ore were blasted out of the Glory Hole before mining operations moved underground. (Courtesy of the Alaska State Library, Winter and Pond Collection, P87-0348.)

a thousand pounds and fell seven inches onto an iron base, hammering away ninety-eight times a minute! Now the tourists understood how that noise carried all the way down the channel to meet their boat.

Housed in five buildings spread along the beach, 960 stamps pounded twenty-four hours a day, 363 days a year, stopping only on Christmas and the Fourth of July. The 300 Mill was the world's largest, 340 feet long and 85 feet wide, and the first ever built with a concrete foundation.

The 240 Mill next door imported massive fir trees from Washington State for a foundation. Jack pointed to the top of the stamps, where the Pelton waterwheels drove massive gears. The water that powered the mills flowed from the eighteen-mile-long "Treadwell Ditch," built between 1882

The 300 mill: The town of Treadwell had five stamp mills. This is the world's largest containing 300 stamps that fell on chunks of ore releasing free gold. (Courtesy of the Alaska State Library, Winter and Pond Collection, P87-0376.)

and 1889 by Chinese and Alaska Native laborers. This ingenious design gathered the gravity-driven, free-flowing water from numerous creeks in the mountains of central Douglas Island and brought it down through pipes, flumes, and culverts.[3] Raymond wanted them to know, too, that the Ditch up behind town was a great place to hike on trails that wound along lily ponds and blueberry bushes, through grass meadows and muskeg and great clumps of wild violets. This image contrasted with what they were walking past—the dead trees and blackened stumps that someone said "looked like Hell with the fire gone out."[4]

Jack continued with the story of why this site was one of the gold-mining wonders of the world. Plentiful amounts of ore and water were blessings of nature that made this site so profitable. To capture gold held for eons in masses of solid rock required drills and dynamite, chemicals and heat, money and men, technology and a dependable power source. "Hard-rock" mining was different from the Klondike, where the lone

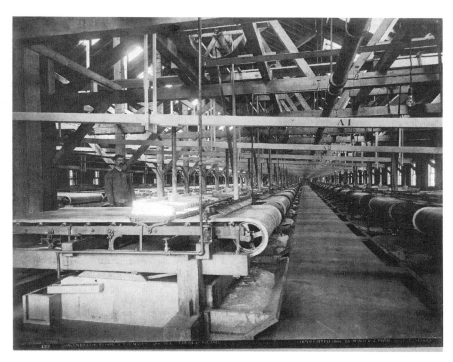

The vibrating vanner tables separated additional valuable ores from sandy waste. (Courtesy of the Michael and Carolyn Nore Collection.)

placer miner sifted through gravel in streambeds to find gold nuggets or fine gold dust.

As the stamps pulverized the ore, about half the gold was released and could be captured on mercury-coated plates. The light sand tailings left over were washed out to the beach. The remaining gold was held in the metal concentrates, the pyrites, and had to be extracted in several more steps using heat and chemicals. That all happened in the cyanide plant, the ski slope–shaped building on the south edge of town.[5]

The pyrite concentrates were put in sacks and piled into small railroad cars built and maintained by Raymond's dad, Willy Kelly, in the machine shop. Each morning strings of these cars climbed the inclined track to the cyanide plant.

Next door to the cyanide plant, tourists could see the refinery, a thick-walled concrete-fortified building with bars on the windows. In the refinery, gold precipitate was turned into liquid gold. Raymond told about the times he and his friends were allowed to watch as it was poured into brick-size bullion molds. The bricks were moved to the assay office for safekeeping until they could be shipped out. As the tourists strained to glimpse the piles of gleaming gold bricks, the men working there teased Raymond, saying, "If you can lift one you can have it." Each gold bar weighed eighty pounds and was worth $15,000.

Workers in the busy assay office ran over a hundred samples of ore in a day for both the mine and independent prospectors. Jack explained that free assays provided a way for the company to keep track of any gold discoveries in the area. The main job was daily testing of the ore from all the Treadwell mines, before, during and after milling, to track the efficiency of the process and determine the value. Raymond knew talk was going around that samples from the newer, deeper levels showed gradually decreasing gold content. He had heard that Superintendent Kinzie, his friend Robert's father, worried that the company stockholders would not be pleased. Every week the bricks were boxed up, wheeled by hand cart down to the pier, loaded on an outgoing steamer, and transported to the company office in San Francisco. Some went to the U.S. Mint in San Francisco, where the bricks were made into coins, some of them coming back up to Treadwell to be paid out in wages.

The Treadwell Club was open twenty-four hours a day, offering all workers access to a library, a theater, baths, bowling alleys, and other forms of recreation. (Courtesy of the Alaska State Library, Case and Draper Collection, P39-0888.)

The next stop was Raymond's favorite: the Treadwell Club, which looked like a barracks set on pilings out over the channel. But the inside was a surprise. Whoever heard of a country club for gold miners? But that's what it was. A plain one-story structure, 56 feet wide, 206 feet long, with 16-foot-high ceilings. Tourists wandered through, amazed to find a billiard room with five tables and an adjoining room for reading and letter writing, with 150 papers and magazines of the day, including many foreign publications in several languages. A small library had fifteen hundred volumes of classics, fiction, poetry, biography, history, and reference books, plus a children's section of over two hundred volumes. *

Stepping into the club's five-hundred-seat auditorium, the tourists marveled at the stage, "one of the finest in Alaska," Jack assured them. The floor was highly polished oak, suitable for dancing. Raymond's uncle Bobby Coughlin and his fiancée, Allie Bach, often won the prize for best dancers on the island.

Leaving the auditorium, the group passed a full-size bowling alley (one of two) and the darkroom. Photography was a popular hobby. Raymond developed his own pictures at home in the bathroom and he always brought some along for tourists to buy. The club, with ten bathrooms, a Turkish steam room, and barber shop with French mahogany walls and marble basins, was open and attended twenty-four hours a day. Everyone in Treadwell belonged. Dues of a dollar a month, deducted from wages, entitled each family to all the privileges. Jack noted the company's policy of free admission to all theatricals, concerts, and the latest innovation, "moving pictures."[6]

The tour group continued along the boardwalk to the natatorium, which housed a basketball court and a swimming pool, sometimes called "the tank." According to Jack, the tiled, steam-heated salt-water pool, with a big slide out over the shallow end, was "the finest on the Pacific Coast." Ladies swam on Friday, and children on Wednesday and Saturday. The company provided fluffy white towels with the company's red "T" monogram. There were swimming and diving lessons, competitions, and big water carnivals where the Treadwell band played. Raymond's uncle Milton Kelly was

Miners and managers participated in games of billiards together. Their uniforms identify the mines where they worked: 700, Ready Bullion, Mexican. (Courtesy of the Alaska State Library, Case and Draper Collection, P39-0975.)

The heated swimming pool adjacent to the Treadwell Club sponsored lessons, competitions, water polo, and festivals. (Courtesy of the Alaska State Library, Davis Collection, P117-118.)

a drummer. Raymond's friends, the Andersons and the Kinzies, took part in all the contests and festivities. But Raymond and his sisters, Marion and Honey, were no longer allowed there because a year earlier Marion had come down with polio, which their mother was sure was from the pool.

More gasps of surprise came as the group stepped inside the Treadwell store and office building, expecting to see a frontier trading post. The two-story emporium with a graceful curved stairway and wrought-iron railing boasted the largest stock of merchandise in Alaska: everything from bags of flour and provisions required by the grizzled Yukon prospector, to mincemeats, fancy pears, and fur boas the women of Treadwell wanted for Christmas holidays. An adjacent butcher shop was loaded with meat in the most modern refrigerated display cases. If the tour happened on payday, a line of men would be waiting outside the office for their wages, paid in stacks of twenty-dollar gold pieces, Treadwell's famous yellow money.

The company store offered a dazzling array of food, clothing, toys, and gifts brought in from the "Outside." (Courtesy of the Alaska State Library, Case and Draper Collection, P39-0902.)

Townspeople could purchase a variety of the best cuts of meat at low prices. A refrigerated case kept them fresh. (Courtesy of the Alaska State Library, Case and Draper Collection, P39-896.)

The company's two dining rooms could each seat four hundred to five hundred miners. Menus were comparable to those at a hotel. (Courtesy of the Alaska State Library, Case and Draper Collection, P39-0903.)

The tour moved on to the company boardinghouse, which, as Jack was quick to point out, happened to be the largest dining hall on the Pacific Coast. Double entry doors were flanked by an eight-foot-high mass of trailing orange nasturtiums planted and tended by the Japanese waiters. Inside the room, which was half the size of a football field, artificial palms were mounted in pots against sky blue walls. Long tables covered with white oilcloth were accompanied by benches with shelves underneath for hats and places for five hundred miners to sit and eat heartily. Another company boardinghouse down the beach at the Mexican mine seated an additional two hundred miners.

Since the mines operated round the clock, miners came up for a noon or midnight meal, and lunches were packed for them to take along to work. The meals were as good as those at any hotel in Douglas or Juneau. A typical menu offered salmon and roast beef, baked potatoes, corn, beans, tea and coffee, bread pudding, and blueberry pie.[7] The kitchens had all the modern equipment, including electric dishwashers, coffee

Up-to-date kitchens had the latest electrical appliances. The Treadwell baker was famous for his bread, pies, and doughnuts. (Courtesy of the Alaska State Library, Case and Draper Collection, P39-0900.)

pots, potato-peeling machines, and ice-cream makers. Raymond nodded to his friends on the kitchen staff who regularly saved scraps for his dog. Rover never went hungry. The whole beef the cooks used each day provided plenty of leftover parts and pieces.

From here Raymond pointed out his house set up on the hill. The company provided over one hundred steam-heated family cottages, with three or four bedrooms, for eleven dollars a month. Most of the underground miners were single men who lived in neatly furnished bunkhouses with comfortably sized rooms, electric lights, steam heat, and bedding, kept clean and orderly by janitors. Men of seventeen nationalities lived and worked in the town, including American, Norwegian, Danish, Austrian, Slovenian, Montenegrin, Scottish, Irish, German, French, Italian, Finnish, Russian, Japanese, and Alaska Native.

The tour group stopped at the plaza in front of the superintendent's house, where a huge American flag and the Treadwell company flag flew

To draw family men, the company provided roomy housing with electricity, steam heat, and bathrooms. Like all Treadwell buildings, the houses were painted red with green trim. (Courtesy of the Alaska State Library, Dexter Collection, P40-10.)

Tourists, who had expected to find people living in igloos, were surprised at the attractive decor. The foreman of the Ready Bullion mill and his family lived in this two-bedroom cottage in the Pines neighborhood. (Courtesy of the Alaska State Library, Mahaffy Collection, P238-7.)

over the only level spot in town. The company held its Fourth of July celebration here, and in winter they flooded the area for skating and sledding. The superintendent's residence (they didn't call it a mansion, though it really was) dominated the plaza. This home had a lawn and raspberry bushes along a picket fence. Raymond described the inside for the tourists, because he and his sisters often played here with Superintendent Kinzie's children.

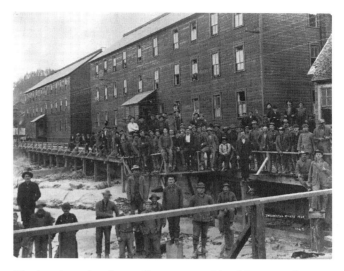

Single miners lived in well-maintained bunkhouses. The men crossed a boardwalk to reach the boardinghouse for meals. (Courtesy of the Alaska State Library, Dexter Collection, P40-28.)

The mansion's first floor had two living rooms and a playroom in the front, plus a big dining room for entertaining engineers and bankers from San Francisco, New York, and sometimes Europe.

The superintendent's residence was grander than the governor's mansion across the channel in Juneau, and company president F. W. Bradley disapproved of such opulence. (Courtesy of the Juneau-Douglas City Museum, 94.18.008.)

A staircase with a curved banister led upstairs to the bedrooms, sitting rooms, a bathroom with a clawfoot tub, a nursery, and a sewing room. The front room was for the governess. The top floor was a glassed-in cupola that commanded a view up and down Gastineau Channel, and the children were allowed to play there too.

———————

On the way back to the boat, Raymond pointed toward the company school, which most of the Treadwell children attended, including the Andersons and the Kinzies. There were fifty children in two classrooms, with two teachers. Raymond said that he and his sisters walked a mile into the town of Douglas to St. Ann's Catholic School. Treadwell had no churches (or saloons), but neighboring Douglas—just across a border that separated the two towns in name only—had seven churches and five saloons. His friends the Andersons went to the Swedish Lutheran Church. The Kellys and Kinzies attended Our Lady of the Mines Catholic Church. The Episcopal, Congregational, and Methodist churches all had active members, and the Quakers had both a school and services for Alaska Natives. The Greek Orthodox Church was known for festivals with the best food.

Someone asked about a hospital. The sisters of St. Ann ran one in Douglas, paid for by the mine. Injured miners were brought through Treadwell on train cars, then by stretcher to the hospital. Next to the hospital was the "dead house," a small shed big enough to hold one coffin awaiting funeral services. When Raymond was five, his birth mother lay there after she died of cancer. And a few years later, when the big explosion in the nearby Mexican mine killed thirty-nine miners, and the ore cars loaded with the wounded passed right by the Kellys' house on the way to the hospital, there wasn't enough room for them in the dead house or at St. Ann's Hospital.

———————

Back at the dock the tour group noticed the little square house set out on the end of the wharf. Some guessed that it was the shaft house, where men went down into the mine. No, said Jack, it was the saltwater pump

house. It lifted twenty-seven hundred gallons a minute from Gastineau
Channel, to be used for milling and fire protection during winter, when
fire danger was high and freshwater in the mountains was in snow pack
and could not be brought down the Treadwell Ditch.

The six-hundred-foot wharf was the thoroughfare that brought
in tourists and travelers, along with fresh flowers, ball gowns, boilers,
oranges, coal, and oil. The central export item—the prize commodity
shipped out and the reason for Treadwell's existence—were the canvas
bags weighted down with gleaming gold bricks.

Along the wharf, the tired tourists encountered a line of artisans,
craftspeople, and souvenir vendors. Local Tlingit women offered finely
woven baskets and carved canoes. The town children proffered long-
stemmed purple violets whose delicate perfume moved even mining engineers. Boys held out bits of sparkling pyrite passed off as fool's gold,
and girls presented luscious dusty blueberries gathered fresh from the
hills behind town by the Ditch. Raymond promoted his home-developed
picture postcards, plus the best-selling item—copies of the seventeen-
page illustrated booklet *Treadwell, An Alaskan Fulfillment* from the 1909
Alaska-Yukon-Pacific Exposition in Seattle, where Treadwell had star
billing and the gold exhibit dominated the Alaska pavilion.

The tourists went away impressed by the scale of the mine operation.
They were amazed at the town's cultural life, charmed by the precocious youngsters, and glad to
get away from that incessant
noise.

Laughing about what tour-
ists bought, the children compared their profits and headed
back to their ordinary life in
this extraordinary place, convinced that this noisy, gritty
company town was the best
possible place to grow up.

As the SS *Cottage City*
headed up to the next stop at
Glacier Bay, the tourists found

*Tlingit women sold woven baskets to tourists on the Tread-
well wharf. One tourist proclaimed, "Indian basketry is
poetry, music, art and life itself woven exquisitely together out
of dreams." (Higginson 1909, 93; Courtesy of the University of
Washington Libraries, Special Collections, NA 905.)*

the sentiments of proud Treadwellians summed up in the closing words of the booklet they had bought from Raymond Kelly:

> It seems then likely, since Science is holding her own so bravely in the struggle with Nature for possession of the hidden treasure of the hills, that for many years to come the mighty roar of Treadwell's stamps will still be heard, bearing with it, far beyond the limits of its farthest vibration, its cheery echo of prosperity and fulfillment.[8]

The accomplishments of Treadwell inspired awe, but for the tourists aboard the boat, the town's exuberant confidence brought up an inescapable and disturbing comparison—another technological wonder that was touted as the largest in the world and also representing man's victory over nature and the elements. Just a few months earlier, the crew of the *Titanic* had been speeding across the Atlantic, pushing the limits of the design of its unsinkable White Star Line flagship. Paying little attention to the massive icebergs drifting on the Labrador current after a mild arctic winter, the ship hit one and sank, with a loss of fifteen hundred lives. Two Treadwell residents barely escaped that disaster: the "Lucky Swede" who had a ticket but missed the boat, and a Chinese cook who survived and came back to work in the Mexican boardinghouse.

The adventuresome Alaska excursionists watched anxiously for icebergs as they approached Glacier Bay. Meanwhile, back in Treadwell the owners marched ahead in their pursuit of profit. Like the *Titanic* owners, they pushed the limits of the design of their amazing goose that laid golden eggs, dismissing the possibility that nature and the elements cannot always be conquered by men and technology.

ONE

Catalyst for Alaska Development

Treadwell's stimulative effect upon mining and tributary industries created a freight movement which enabled a steamship company to inaugurate regular trips and then blossom to . . . lucrative excursion service. —U.S. CENSUS, 1890

T HE TREADWELL STORY is an important chapter in the early history of an American Alaska, which began with Secretary of State William H. Seward's 1867 purchase of this large swath of land in the northwest corner of the continent from Russia. Americans called it "Seward's Folly," even though he got it for a bargain price—$7.2 million for 586,412 square miles, or about two cents per acre. The public mocked it as "Seward's Icebox," a remote and barren region, a frozen frontier of questionable value.

There was some basis for public skepticism. The new district could be accessed only by ocean, and ice blocked the western and northern parts of the vast territory for months each year. The Russian occupiers had concentrated on the limited seasonal fur trade, so there were few port facilities or navigational aids along a coast that was largely uncharted.

The most direct way from the lower United States to the southeast section of Alaska was a picturesque and perilous thousand-mile waterway

SEWARD'S FOLLY turned out to be a treasure chest at the very time the
United States needed mineral resources. "In a world which measured
progress by military strength and industrial capacity, the import of direct access
to mineral products was enormous."[1] With Alaska's potential riches in mind,
in 1872 Congress passed the Mining Law, stating that mineral prospecting and
mining were "the highest use of the new territory." "The mineral lands of the
public domain, both surveyed and unsurveyed, are hereby declared free and
open to exploration and occupation by all citizens." Prospecting became the
very duty of citizenship in the North.[2]

from Puget Sound to Glacier Bay. The Inside Passage wove through
narrow, winding, tide-swept channels, around forest-carpeted islands,
towering rocks, and unpredictable icebergs. The shores were subject to
peculiar currents and treacherous tides in unpredictable gales.

Travel to the area began slowly after the Purchase. In order to transport U.S. occupation troops, cargo, and mail, regular monthly boat services ran from United States ports to Sitka. Occasionally an intrepid
sightseer joined the trip, although an 1872 Appleton guidebook predicted
that "Alaska was not likely ever to be much frequented by travelers."[3] But

SCIENTIST AND NATURALIST John Muir was an early promoter of Alaska.
Commissioned by the U.S. government to reconnoiter southeast Alaska's
resources, Muir took his first trip in 1878, a one-hundred-mile journey in a thirty-foot
canoe with four Tlingit guides and a missionary. He documented flora and fauna
and the native villagers, noted the geology, and mapped the glaciers with scholarly
precision. While paddling up Gastineau Channel he noticed outcroppings of quartz
veins streaked with gold on Douglas Island. Familiar with geological deposits in his
home state of California, he predicted that this southeast Alaska panhandle area
could be a gold belt, "a second California."

On that trip, Muir was transported by the magnificence of the landscape. In the

as early as 1875, several steamship lines were making the trip, and the reports of unparalleled scenery lured the excursionist crowd, that wealthy leisure class ever in search of someplace new and different.

The mystique of Alaska struck a chord with adventurous tourists and entrepreneurs alike, and by the mid-1880s the skeptics had been won over by the twin lures of gold and tourism.

Treadwell lay in the middle of a mineral-rich belt that stretched over 125 miles along the coast of southeastern Alaska, from Berner's Bay in the north to Windham Bay in the south.

The first discovery in this area, in 1870, was placer gold that washed down from mountainous quartz veins and came to rest in the gravel beds of the streams. In 1880, prospectors Joe Juneau and Richard Harris, with the help of a man named Kaa wa.ee of the Auk Tlingit tribe, found gold in the coastal streams and in Silver Bow basin, behind the town that became Juneau. When word got out, crowds of eager gold seekers rushed to the area hoping to make a strike.

Wanderers and adventurers from all over the American West flocked northward, completing the march that had been going on since the 1848 California Gold Rush. Many hopeful miners learned about prospecting in California. From there, they trudged north through British Columbia and southeast Alaska to the Yukon. "Men with pans and picks slowly inch[ed] their way along the mountain backbone of North America from Sierra

tradition of Thoreau and Emerson, he exclaimed, "Forests and glaciers are the glory of Alaska. . . . To the lover of pure wildness Alaska is one of the most wonderful countries in the world. . . . Surely we must at length reach the very paradise of the poets, the abode of the blessed."[4]

Muir is seen as the father of the conservation movement, yet paradoxically, he helped push open the door to development of Alaska. He saw the material wealth to be extracted from the land and water and the spiritual riches to be gained from intact wilderness. His widely read writings drew more tourists, and the gold belt he noticed along Gastineau Channel rapidly developed into the largest hard-rock gold-mining operation in the world.

WITH A MORE PATRIOTIC THAN POETIC TONE, Civil War hero William Tecumseh Sherman exhorted tourists "to visit our own sublime regions in America before going to Europe." The United States' "imperial magnificence" was confirmed by the fact that no other nation in the world had a greater diversity of climate, from near tropical to arctic. Travel to the North became a civic duty among the privileged class. A sense of ownership prevailed. "An American would not be quite himself if he did not experience some glow of feeling in coming into a region however distant that belongs to his country and in part belongs to him."[5]

to the Stikine, through the canyons of the Fraser River, the snow fields of the Cassiars [along the coastal gold belt of Southeast Alaska], to the threshold of the sub arctic."[6] These men were in search of placer gold—that pure gold that could be recovered by hand, picked up in streams and gravel beds, ready to sell, with no additional treatment necessary.

By 1882, another kind of gold rush was under way across the Gastineau Channel from Juneau. At the Treadwell mine site on Douglas Island, the discovery of a huge lode of low-grade ore locked in quartz set in motion a gold-based enterprise that could only happen with capital, scientific expertise, and a skilled workforce. This site drew a different kind of speculator and required an infusion of money from stock sold on the Paris and London stock exchanges. A complex process was required to extract, capture, and refine the gold. With operations at such a grand scale, the Treadwell Company offered secure employment with dependable wages and a company town to live in.

But the appeal of this type of steady work of the modern-day wage slave was lost on the pick-and-shovel prospector. Placer mining was a poor man's shot at getting rich—on his own terms. He needed little or no capital to work a claim. His nature was to scorn the path of corporate mining. He wanted to be his own master, where the fruits of his labor—gold nuggets and dust—were his alone.

Prompted by gold discoveries in British Columbia and Alaska, in 1881 the Pacific Coast Steamship Company (PCSC) of San Francisco began to run three ships a month to southeast Alaska. The following year, the Treadwell mines began operation and the commerce and development that flourished there for four decades fueled enterprise and increased settlement in far reaches of the vast new territory of the North.

Unlike corporate hard-rock miners, the lone placer miner worked the cold river beds panning for gold nuggets and dust to call his own. (Courtesy of the Michael and Carolyn Nore Collection.)

The lure of gold and a fascination with America's industrial adventures easily enticed the leisure class to try this new destination. Steamship lines promised new experiences of breathtaking scenery, Native villages, and the Treadwell gold mines, "where fabulous riches lie underfoot, and man's ingenuity is tapping the treasure house with hard work and modern invention."[7]

The word was out. In 1884, two thousand excursionists made their way up the coast. In the first Alaska guidebook, author Eliza Scidmore held up the Treadwell mines as a local site as thrilling as glaciers and totem poles. In 1890, the steamships delivered five thousand curious tourists to the dock at Treadwell where 240 thumping stamps were at work. These

TOURISM PLAYED AN IMPORTANT ROLE in the spread of industrial capitalism in the late nineteenth century. Travelers "were both the buyers and the bought," purchasers of alluringly packaged experiences sold by the largest corporations of the period, the rail companies and their allied steamship companies. The Northern Pacific, Union Pacific, Canadian Pacific, and Great Northern railroads connected wealthy tourists from the East Coast with southeast Alaska–bound ships in Puget Sound and San Francisco. The increasing demand for luxuriously appointed and fast steamers fed expansion of all the fleets.[8]

BY 1888, the spreading fame of Treadwell had prompted one of the biggest mine swindles in history. The Bear's Nest claim was adjacent to John Treadwell's original Paris claim. The combination of proximity to the mythical Treadwell lode plus strategic planting of faked core samples had English and German investors lining up to buy it for a reported $2.5 million, the largest price to date for any Alaskan prospect. Promoters guaranteed it would stimulate capitalists to come to Alaska searching for other properties. Early reports from *Juneau City Mining Record* trumpeted "the rock is equally as good or better than the Treadwell." Work began on a 120-stamp mill and a tunnel. But less than a year later, the tunnel produced no paying ore and operations shut down. Debate raged over whether the failed venture was due to a swindle or incompetence. (John Treadwell's brother James was one of the sellers.) Later explorations found no paying ore, and the site was never mined.[9]

well-appointed floating hotels for the tourists joined marine traffic up and down the Inside Passage as steamships from around the world brought the coal and iron, food and clothing, managers, miners, and skilled workers required by the expanding venture. That year, commercial shipping topped thirty-five thousand tons, a level "far beyond that to be naturally expected of a region so remote and unknown as Alaska."[10]

The 1890 Census, which presented the first in-depth documentation of the United States' newest acquisition, credited the presence of the Treadwell mines for spurring the development of Alaska: "Treadwell's stimulative effect upon mining and tributary industries created a freight movement which enabled a steamship company to inaugurate regular trips and then blossom to . . . lucrative excursion service which has done more than any means toward . . . attracting capital for investments."

The growing population in Treadwell, Douglas, and Juneau welcomed the tourists coming up the Inside Passage. In 1890, the combined population at the Treadwell mine and the town of Douglas was only 402. In the next decade, the number of residents more than tripled to 1,347, and doubled again by 1910 to 2,944. By then, the mine had a payroll of 2,000 workers.[11]

The shipping industry was ripe for competition. In 1894, Charles Peabody incorporated the Alaska Steamship Company, ending the Pacific Coast Steamship Company monopoly. Expecting a bonanza from the ever-increasing stream of miners heading north, the two shipping lines engaged in a freight rate battle. Based on news leaking out of the Klondike, they knew they were competing for something big. They were right. When ships carrying tons of gold from the Klondike arrived back in Seattle and San Francisco in 1897,

The first hub of commerce in Alaska was the Treadwell wharf, where machinery, iron, coal, oil, foodstuffs, workers, and tourists poured in and shipments of gold bullion went out. (Courtesy of the Alaska State Library, Winter and Pond Collection, P87-339.)

the rush was on. During the summer and fall of 1897, more than eight thousand people headed for Alaska, and they were all frantically in search of passage by any mode available.

On July 11, 1897, Jack Carr, wearing gold nuggets for buttons, arrived in Juneau on his dogsled. He had sped out of Dawson, a remote part of the Canadian subarctic, thirty-five days earlier to be one of the first to take the news to the "Outside" of a bonanza gold strike in a place called the Klondike.[12]

The next week, on July 17, the *SS Portland*, crammed with newly rich prospectors, steamed into Seattle, and the *SS Excelsior* arrived in San Francisco with another load of jubilant Klondikers. The *Seattle Post-Intelligencer* headline shouted GOLD! GOLD! GOLD! ". . . a ton of gold onboard." Later a correction noted that the ship's cargo, in trunks and boxes, bottles and jars, bags and pockets, was closer to *two* tons of gold.[13]

Unlike earlier gold rushes, the Klondike stampede did not begin slowly and build up over time. Craziness erupted the instant the ships landed. Droves of workers from every trade and profession quit jobs, left families, and grabbed passage to Alaska and Canada on any seafaring

GOLD IS USUALLY FOUND in mineralized rock, the result of volcanic or other uprising from the earth's magma; such deposits are called *lode*. Often the rock closest to the surface has been eroded by temperature change and by the action of surface water. The resulting flecks, grains, and nuggets, usually washed into the bottoms of creeks or buried five to twenty feet down, is called *placer gold*. This gold can be easily taken by individual prospectors using a few simple tools: a pick, shovel, pan, and sluice box for running water over gravels, a method for melting the top layers of soil. Lode gold requires a considerable investment for tunneling, sinking shafts, blasting, and crushing. Development of lode deposits is capital and labor intensive, requiring significant investment and the contracting of a force of miners working for wages. Most of the gold in the creeks about Gastineau Channel was placer, which played out after a couple of years. The greater wealth was underground.[14]

mode possible. Ships going north had trouble coming back south because their crews had deserted to join the ranks of prospectors. Along the West Coast any commerce not related to the Klondike came to a standstill. Whalers and cannery workers turned their boats over to the new more profitable cargo, Klondikers.[15] The stampede that overran the north was out of proportion to the amount of gold present in the Klondike. Three other rushes richer than the Klondike had already happened in the nineteenth century, in California, Australia, and South Africa. But none moved the world like the Klondike. The news spread faster, expectations were higher, railroads and water transportation were in place to move large masses of people, and everyone could get on board. "Hurrah for the Klondike!" was the rallying cry.[16] Of the one hundred thousand who set out for the Klondike, mostly were impetuous young men in their twenties, although one in ten was a woman.[17] Thirty to forty thousand reached the burgeoning town of Dawson at the juncture of the Yukon and Klondike Rivers. Less than half even looked for gold, and probably four thousand found some. A few hundred got rich and of those, only a handful kept their wealth. It could be argued that nearly forty thousand men wasted $1,000 each in their futile pursuit. That loss was someone

The demand for steamship transport to Alaska during the Gold Rush of 1897 gave rise to the Seattle-based Alaska Steamship Company. (Courtesy of the Alaska State Library, Skinner Foundation Collection, PCA44-03-180.)

else's bonanza: By March 1898, the gold seekers had spent $60 million purchasing rail and ocean transport and getting "outfitted" to take on the Klondike.

Dawson, a town that mushroomed at the mouth of the Yukon and Klondike rivers—the center of the Klondike bonanza—went from bleak to boom to bust in a little over three years. Five months into the gold rush, the town ran low on food and other supplies. The arctic winter was setting in, the sun had vanished, rivers were frozen solid, and trails were impassable.

After the ice thawed in the spring, supplies got through and the prospectors poured in again. By July, with a population close to forty thousand, only slightly smaller than Seattle, Dawson was being hailed as the San Francisco of the North. For twelve months Dawson was a metropolis "with almost every amenity available to civilized cities the world over. In the shadow of the arctic circle, more than 4000 miles from any city of comparable size, the town had telephones, running water,

FOR THE WEALTHY UPPER CLASSES of the United States, the last years of the nineteenth century were celebrated as the Gay Nineties. The rapid expansion of East Coast industries created vast wealth for a newly emergent "society set." While these people reveled in the indulgent zeitgeist, they generally disregarded the misery that existed for most of the workers who labored to produce the wealth. "To aspire to great fortune in the nineties was as respectable and honorable an emotion as was patriotism in wartime."[18] The era showcased the yachts and mansions of the Vanderbilts and Rockefellers but turned a blind eye to the sweatshops and tenement houses, while banks foreclosed on mortgages and people died of hunger on the street. The labor reform movement was just gaining ground to challenge the inequities. Millionaires and hoboes alike fixated on the perennial hope of striking it rich.

Gold was a preoccupation of the nineties. The scarcity of it brought on the Panic of 1893, which precipitated a depression. The worst economic crisis to hit the nation in its history pushed unemployment to almost 20 percent. People hoarded gold dollars because their value remained steady while the value of paper dollars declined. Plus, throughout history, gold was the most valuable metal, being stable, not perishable, corrosive, or consumable. When rumors spread of the discovery of rivers full of gold in an obscure region in the far north of the Yukon, the populace grabbed onto the news as the miracle they had hoped for, the promise the depression was at an end and prosperity was at hand.

steam heat, electricity, hospitals, fine hotels and restaurants, motion picture theatres, men in tailcoats and women in Paris gowns attending symphonies."[19]

But the bust came as suddenly as the boom. The Klondike had been oversold and the supply of gold could in no way meet the demand of the hordes swarming that frozen outpost. Many in Dawson desperately searched and hoped for another miraculous bonanza, and once again, in midsummer 1899, an incredible discovery fired their resolve. A fortune in fine gold dust was found in the sands of the remote beaches along an area called Cape Nome. These riches had been lying hidden at the ocean outlet of an obscure little river just across the Bering Strait from Siberia.

For Dawson entrepreneurs lusting after the next bonanza, the glitter of gold uncovered in Nome set them off again. "Here was the stuff of legend—gold from the sea."[20]

In a single week in August 1901, over half the remaining population deserted Dawson, jumping on boats and heading out to Nome. The great Klondike stampede ended as quickly as it had begun.[21] In the summer of 1898 there had been tens of thousands of people in Dawson. By 1901, there were fewer than one thousand.[22]

While the Klondike's fortunes rose and fell, Treadwell's population and profit continued climbing steadily. For those willing to stay put, the Treadwell mines plodded along as usual, pulverizing, producing, profiting, and paying its "wage slaves." Many in Treadwell worked through the winters, saved up their wages, took the summer off, went farther north to try their hands at prospecting, and then came back to the underground drudgery to accumulate earnings for the next summer's expedition.

Treadwell management, always on the lookout for discovery of that mother lode of hard-rock gold that could be mined like Treadwell, offered free ore assays to all prospectors. The Treadwell store found another kind of mother lode: outfitting prospectors on their way to the Klondike. Touting itself as the best, cheapest, and closest source for doing this, the Treadwell Company staged a campaign to compete with the aggressive and wildly successful outfitters marketing in the port of Seattle.

Other Gastineau Channel entrepreneurs knew the money was not in finding gold but in supplying miners' needs. Some found the gold in rubber boots. Climbers staggering with overweight loads up the Chilkoot Trail toward the Yukon would lighten their packs at every opportunity, discarding their heavy rubber boots after getting downriver to Dawson. Two young lads retrieved the mountain of footwear to take back to Juneau for resale to newer arrivals. As a result, hundreds of pairs of the same boots went up over the passes time after time.[23]

More than a decade before the Klondike discoveries, the presence of the Treadwell mines had helped launch a lucrative Alaska shipping industry, bringing in materials and shipping out gold bullion. The gold rush accelerated development of the marine highway because the Inside Passage offered a major route to the overland staging areas for the goldfields. The glut of prospectors joined tourists seeking adventure,

At the 1904 Lewis and Clark Centennial Exposition in Portland, Treadwell Superintendent Joseph MacDonald (left) and Assistant Superintendent Robert Kinzie compare the $7.2 million paid for Alaska to the $22 million value of the gold mined at Treadwell to date. When the mines shut down in 1922, they had repaid the Alaska purchase price nine times over. (Courtesy of the Alaska State Library, Winter and Pond Collection, P87-385.)

missionaries setting up schools, and corporate employers building mines and canneries, along with the steady stream of job seekers and settlers. And for more than two decades after the Klondike ballyhoo faded, the mines of the Juneau gold belt, led by Treadwell, expanded the stream of commerce flowing into Alaska. By 1899, Treadwell's 880 one-ton stamps had pulverized over 664,000 tons of ore and produced close to $1.7 million worth of gold, with gold valued at $20.67 an ounce.[24]

The Treadwell gold display was the centerpiece at the 1904 Lewis and Clark Centennial Exposition in Portland, Oregon. The exhibit showed a gold foil-covered cube representing the $7.2 million price paid for Alaska in 1867. Next to it a stack of fabricated "gold" slabs showed the 1904 value of the Alaska Treadwell Gold Mining Company: $21,817,296. In its first twenty-two years of production, the Treadwell mines had repaid the Alaska Purchase three times over.

Treadwell citizens prided themselves on being at the frontier but not in the wilderness. They aspired to a level of material well-being that late-nineteenth-century Americans were growing to expect. They looked to the company to keep them sheltered and well fed, providing cottages, bunkhouses, dining halls, medical care, and entertainment. Staying connected to the modern world was important; ferries and steamships provided daily transport across the channel or down to Seattle. True, the gold seekers got a lot of attention, but most immigrants to Alaska sought jobs. The Treadwell enterprise was the first developmental surge in Alaska's history to provide appreciable numbers of jobs that promised to be long term.[25] The town boasted that the extraordinary mother lode of gold-bearing quartz, dependable stream of money from investors around the world, and ever-advancing technology made Treadwell immune to the boom-and-bust cycle of placer bonanzas.

For decades, the tourists came in droves to see the glaciers, the Native villages, and the salmon canneries capturing the Alaskan silver treasure and to witness the alchemy of turning rock into gold. But halfway between the Gay Nineties and the Roaring Twenties, steamship brochures no longer noted Treadwell among the stops. Something happened on the shores of the Gastineau Channel, something once as unimaginable as the sinking of the unsinkable *Titanic*.

TWO

Treadwell Mines: The Story in Brief

The ore bodies are practically inexhaustible. . . .
No such body of gold bearing quartz is known to
be in existence elsewhere. . . . A hundred years
from now these mines will continue to be in
successful operation.

—*ALASKA MONTHLY MAGAZINE*, OCTOBER 1907

T HIS GREAT ALASKA STORY BEGAN in the 1880s, on Douglas
Island across Gastineau Channel from the settlement that became
known as Juneau. Here, a unique company town flourished and
over two thousand workers toiled day and night turning chunks of rock
into bricks of gold. This was Treadwell, another kind of gold rush that
preceded, succeeded, and surpassed the short-lived and much-ballyhooed
Klondike Gold Rush.

One of the early prospectors drawn to the promise of Alaska gold was
John Treadwell. The man who became the founder and first superintendent of the mines that bear his name was born in 1842, in St. Andrews,
New Brunswick, Canada. Treadwell became a carpenter like his father. In
the 1870s, he moved to California, where he gained experience as a placer

John Treadwell (front row, second from right) was an unassuming man of moderate temperament. He did not drink or smoke, and he rejected violence as means to settle frontier disputes. He made a fortune and died a pauper. (Courtesy of the Alaska State Library, Stein Collection, p172-16a.)

and lode miner. In the summer of 1881 he was in San Francisco, overseeing home construction for banker John D. Fry, when news came of a rich gold strike in Silver Bow Basin behind the town that became Juneau. Fry, along with his friend James Freeborn and other investors, grubstaked Treadwell and sent him to Alaska to look over mining prospects.[1]

By the time he got to the area, Treadwell found that most of the rich ore had been dug and claims staked. Disappointed, he decided to look around at sites across the channel on Douglas Island before returning to San Francisco. Along the way, he met a French Canadian prospector, Pierre Joseph Erussard (French Pete), who shared a similar lament. Erussard, a local entrepreneur, had heard rumors of a large gold-bearing quartz outcrop across on Douglas Island. He had staked two adjacent claims there, but assays showed only a low-grade ore. Erussard needed money, because he had opened a store in Juneau and the next boat was bringing his merchandise. Doubtful of the prospects, but not wanting to return to his San Francisco backers empty-handed, Treadwell bought Erussard's "Paris" claim (sometimes spelled Parris), on Paris Creek, September 13, 1881, for $400. Treadwell collected twenty-two sample bags of rock from the site and took them back to California.

In San Francisco, the assay showed promise. The lode of low-grade ore could be profitable if worked on a large scale. The venture would require a stamp mill, which used multiple giant iron hammers pounding large chunks of ore to release the tiny particles of gold embedded in the quartz. To fund the enterprise, Freeborn, Fry, and Treadwell formed the Alaska Mill and Mining Company. Treadwell returned to Douglas Island in May

In 1882, John Treadwell's first mill had five stamps. By 1914, five mammoth mills housed a total of 960 stamps. (Courtesy of the Alaska State Library, Norton Collection, P226-306.)

1882 with a five-stamp mill, the workhorse of lode mining, and a new era of Alaska gold mining and territorial development began.

John Treadwell's experiment with a five-stamp mill proved successful in processing ore profitably, and in 1883 he replaced the pilot mill with a 120-stamp mill. The first year, production from placer miners working the area had reached $45,000, while lode production using five stamps was only around $11,000. However, after Treadwell ramped up his mill from five stamps to 120, production jumped exponentially to $280,000 by 1885.[2]

During the 1880s, Treadwell got his namesake mine up and running and expanded his mill to 240 stamps. The 240 Mill, as it was known, was the world's largest mill under one roof. By 1885, he was able to process three hundred tons of ore a day, while consistently making a profit.

Treadwell in 1899, showing the hoist, an expanded 240 mill, the superintendent's residence, and the machine shop on the wharf. (Courtesy of the Alaska State Library, Winter and Pond Collection, P87-0333.)

The successful enterprise attracted capitalists. In 1889, a group of investors that included the Rothschild brothers incorporated as the Alaska Treadwell Gold Mining Company and purchased the mines for $4 million; John Treadwell sold them his interest for $1.4 million and returned to California. Treadwell did not flaunt his new wealth. Those around him "would scarcely take Mr. T for a millionaire. He looked no better than the miners."[3]

The new company put ATGMCo stock on the Paris and London stock exchanges, successfully raised capital for significant expansion, and brought in Frederick Worthen Bradley as consulting engineer. During the 1890s, four huge new mills with an additional 640 stamps came on line, and in the early 1900s, mill expansion added eighty more stamps.

The lode that Erussard tapped into, and John Treadwell purchased, proved to be mammoth. Over the next four decades a four-mine complex

ON PARIS CREEK, Treadwell's experimental mill operation came up against a group of placer miners who were working the accessible quartz on top of the lode. The placer and the lode operations were in competition for the water, and the squatters almost drove the lode miners away. Treadwell's San Francisco associates were ready to send two hundred armed men to Douglas Island to clear out what they saw as claim jumpers.

John Treadwell did not support extreme measures. He wanted an orderly way to access the water. The Alaska frontier district had no established government authority to step in at that time, so Treadwell appealed to the U.S. Navy stationed in Sitka under command of Captain E. C. Merriman. Merriman sailed the USS *Adams* up the Gastineau Channel and helped draw up an official agreement between Treadwell and the placer miners. It read: "John Treadwell is to have the use of the water in the Creek or ditch known as Paris or Hayes Creek during the night, or twelve hours, and [the placer miners] the other twelve hours or during the day, the placer mining companies . . . agree not to blast the lode but only to wash the surface ground."[4]

developed on the site. Four mines under three corporate owners were mining one lode of gold. In the early 1890s, two additional mining companies started up, initially financed by the Treadwell Company. The Alaska Mexican Gold Mining Company (AMGMCo) (1891) developed a mine on property seven hundred feet south of the community of Treadwell, and the Alaska United Gold Mining Company (AUGMCo) owned two separate properties: One was a claim on a seven-hundred-foot strip of land separating the Treadwell mine from the Mexican mine. This became known as the 700 Foot mine. The other property was adjacent to the Mexican mine's south side and was known as the Ready Bullion mine. Each of the three companies was financially separate, conducted its own milling and mining operations, and ran its own crews. Treadwell Company was overall manager and banker and also financed the support facilities. Together the four mines were known as the Treadwell complex.

ALWAYS ESCHEWING VIOLENCE, Treadwell was recognized as a man of vigilance, patience, and extraordinary character.[5] A polite and unassuming bachelor, he did not drink or smoke, which was unusual in Alaska at that time. He demonstrated his character in a volatile situation involving much-maligned Chinese laborers who at that time were being persecuted throughout North America, Congress had passed the Chinese Exclusion Act in 1882, which prohibited immigration from China. In 1886, Treadwell brought in Chinese men to work year-round in the mines, because during the summers white miners went off prospecting and the Alaska Natives went to fishing camps. The Chinese men worked hard and for lower wages, and when white miners demanded that all Chinese be fired, Treadwell stressed that he had unfilled jobs in the mill and needed all the workers he could find. The local marshal said the town was stirred up against the Chinese and, if a mob formed, not a handful of men would come to Treadwell's aid. Someone advised fortifying the mills with armed guards, but once again Treadwell rejected the idea because of the potential for violence. The agitators bombed the Chinese lodgings, dragged the men out, packed them on two small ships, and set them adrift down Gastineau Channel with only the clothes on their backs. Treadwell sent a boat after them with fifteen sacks of rice, the only food they would have. The boats later returned to Juneau; the eighty-seven refugees were never heard of again. Only one Chinese man remained in the area, Chew Chung Thui, better known as China Joe, a baker. He was protected by locals because he had shared his flour with prospectors in a harsh winter when they were all working the Cassiar region of British Columbia.[6]

The gambler's luck and miner's intuition of French Pete Erusssard and John Treadwell launched the Treadwell mines, but other factors contributed to their phenomenal success.

First and foremost, nature supplied a huge ore body and an abundant supply of available mountain water that, coupled with gravity, could be harnessed for hydropower and for use in the milling process. The site's waterfront location on Gastineau Channel expedited transportation, since everything could come and go by steamer. Because of the Japanese current, the climate was relatively mild, allowing year-round operation.

Second, the mines benefited from a steady supply of labor. Experienced miners from around the world flocked to the town, drawn by the promise of good wages and comfortable living conditions.

Third, the composition of the Treadwell lode was such that large pillars of the ore could be carved out and left in place to support the mined-out stopes (cavities) rather than constructing underground timber supports, which took more time and money.

However, without the guts and genius of a University of California School of Mines dropout, Frederick Worthen ("F. W.") Bradley, these advantages would not have resulted in such profitable innovation.

The Treadwell complex was a capitalist venture dedicated to producing the maximum amount of gold at the least possible cost in order to deliver profits to stockholders, and Bradley was the man to do that. Starting as Treadwell's consulting engineer in 1900 and then as president in 1911, Bradley brought together the world-class financial investment and ongoing technical innovations that made the mines world famous, setting records for making high-level profits from low-grade ore.

At Treadwell, Bradley inaugurated practices and technologies to constantly refine the mining and milling process for greater efficiency. He had the largest hoist in the world shipped in to centralize the lifting of ore from three of the mines. He introduced a central coarse crushing plant to reduce ore from each mine to a mill-feed size and send it on to the appropriate mills for the fine crushing. The coarse crushing step resulted in increased tonnage moving through the mills.

For extracting the gold from what was left after the milling process (the concentrates), the company under John Treadwell had first used a chlorination process with a plant on site. Then Bradley arranged for the Treadwell Mining Company and Bunker Hill and Sullivan Mining Company in Idaho (where he was also president) to buy a smelter in Tacoma, Washington, to process ores from both companies. For this "Bradley congratulated himself on solving the problems for both [mines] while making a substantial profit."[7] In 1910, Bradley switched the Treadwell mines to a newer cyanidation process that was more economical and could

The machine shop kept the parts of the mills in running order, the stamp rods straightened, the drills sharpened, and the ore cars repaired. (Courtesy of the Alaska State Library, Case and Draper Collection, P39-0913.)

Treadwell's foundry was the most advanced of its time and operated until 1944. Molds were used to cast replacement parts for all mining operations and for other industries of the region. (Courtesy of the Alaska State Library, Case and Draper Collection, P39-0919.)

be carried out in a new plant built in the mining town, thus eliminating shipping costs.

Bradley understood that the Alaska operation had to be self-sufficient and could not be dependent on the Outside, a thousand miles by sea to the south. To reduce time spent on construction and repair, the company maintained a machine shop, carpenter shop, electrical shop, sawmill, and foundry. F. W. enlarged the central steam electric power plant for use in winter months because hydropower was seasonal. A large, modern assay office kept a prospect file on all mines in Alaska—especially those that might offer a potential claim for Treadwell.

Bradley made Treadwell profitable by controlling costs. The price of stoping or breaking the ore in the mine depended on the ore itself. However, the expense of loading cars, moving to bins at the shaft, hoisting, crushing, and tramming the rock to the mills could be shaved through close attention by management.

Rail cars were stacked with bags of concentrates from the mills and winched up to the plant. Once at the plant, more precious metal was extracted through cyanidation. The gold was moved on to the refinery to be made into bullion. (Courtesy of the Alaska State Library, Winter and Pond Collection P087-0346.)

BORN IN 1863, Frederick Worthen ("F. W.") Bradley was a poor boy who attained fame and wealth at a young age as a mining engineer with no college degree. By the time he was twenty, he had left the University of California School of Mines and gone to work in the field. As a young man, he borrowed $5,000 from his mother to save the bankrupt Spanish mine in Nevada County, California, where, in 1887, he first established a record for low-cost gold mining. He was barely thirty years old when he became president of the Bunker Hill and Sullivan Mining Company in the Coeur d'Alene district of Idaho. With other mining interests in Mexico, Nevada, and Alaska, he was a rich man by 1900, when he became consulting engineer at Treadwell mines.

Bradley knew mining and he knew finance. He talked the talk of engineers and bankers. He liked the gambling aspect of mining and was drawn to projects that other financiers and engineers considered too risky. His response to many mining ventures was, "No, I am not interested. . . . There are no problems in that." To him, the only intriguing part of the Yukon Gold Rush was speculation about the source, the mother lode. Placer miners thought they were the risk takers. But Bradley disagreed: "Placer mining is like operating a factory. You dig in the ground. You know exactly what is there and then proceed to take it out." To interest Bradley, there had to be a surprise, a prospect with a possibility that deep in the earth a rich ore deposit might unexpectedly be found.

Bradley worked hard. The picture of tenacity, with piercing eyes, an aquiline nose, and firm-set lips, he had a scholarly countenance, a thoughtful approach, and a mind like a steel trap. "If he said this was the way things were, that's the way you did them. You didn't argue with F. W." A great correspondent, he wrote concise letters with nothing extraneous, always in a beautiful flowing handwriting.[8]

With his astute knowledge of mining and finance, Frederick Worthen Bradley made record-breaking profits working the huge Treadwell lode of low-grade ore. (Courtesy of the Alaska Electric Light and Power Company.)

As the enterprise forged ahead to keep up with its own reputation, more ore was mined at a faster pace while minimizing costs. Management had determined early on that the Treadwell lode could be mined without the expensive and time-consuming step of constructing underground timber supports in the working spaces. Instead, twenty-five-foot-wide pillars were left in the body of ore as it was being mined, and the remaining cavities were left open rather than back-filled with waste rock. By 1909, the four mines were a patchwork of hundreds of cavities reaching a half mile down in the earth. The farthest-south mine, the Ready Bullion, reached out under Gastineau Channel. The underground space was like an empty honeycomb, and the configuration was unstable. Cave-ins were inevitable.

In 1909, slabs from the walls of the open pit known as Glory Hole sloughed, but little attention was paid because it did not affect the underground workings. Then, in 1911, huge masses of rock fell in stopes of the Treadwell, Ready Bullion, and 700 Foot mines. A significant cave in the Mexican mine came in May 1913; subsiding was noted on the surface displacing the tram track; and a severe shock was felt at the surface when the dividing line between 700 Foot and Treadwell mines gave way. This extensive cave was seen later as the "beginning of the end." A 1914 cave at the 1,210 foot level of the Mexican mine created a blast of air that blew an ore train backward for fifty feet.[9]

Men working below the surface were continually listening for the sounds of disturbance and the rumblings of "working" rock. Townspeople who lived on the surface noticed the structures of the town listing as the ground shifted beneath them. However, the need to increase production and profits delayed any management action despite the obvious risk.

The corporate structure of the mining complex compounded the complications of the situation underground: a single body of ore and three competing ownerships. The Treadwell Company owned the surface facilities and had managed the enterprise from the beginning. The Treadwell mine historically had produced the most ore, but by 1916, the drilling showed that the Treadwell stopes were getting leaner. The richer portion of the ore body was found in the 700 Foot and the Mexican mines, owned by the other two corporate partners. The Treadwell management began proceedings to consolidate the three companies; they called for increased production to improve the bottom line. This required going back through the mine, finding—and robbing—pillars that still held high-value ore, precipitating more cave-ins.[10]

In October 1916, acknowledging the escalating rate of collapses, the management formulated a forty-month plan to stabilize all the mines and prevent flooding by building bulkheads and dams in the tunnels and using tailings both to fill empty stopes and to raise a barrier on the beach to "prevent any possible flood of sea water."[11]

Then on April 21, 1917, six months into implementing the plan, an extraordinarily high tide cut through the beach, pushing a stream that seeped, then flowed, then poured into a crack in the surface near the

UNDERSTANDING THE STORY of Treadwell requires some comprehension of the steps involved in turning rock into gold. The deposit of gold in Treadwell's multiple mine complex was huge, but because it was low-grade ore, it took eight and a half tons of ore to produce an ounce of gold. The process involved many steps and each had its own location, workers, and technology. In the early years, the ore was blasted out of surrounding rock in the open pit known as the Glory Hole. Then shafts were sunk and at intervals of 110 to 140 feet deep, the miners would drill and blast to push out from the shaft and carve a string of big rooms (stopes), all connected by tunnels. After the ore was blasted from the face of the lode, it was broken into chunks (mucked), loaded into small train cars (skips), and pulled (trammed) by hand, mule, horse, rope haulage, or locomotive to the shafts and brought up by hoists. At the surface, ore was dumped into crushers, where it was reduced to a mill-friendly two-and-a-half-inch size (mill feed) that was loaded into rail cars and moved along the narrow-gauge railway to the mills, where it was fed to the stamps.

The center of the operation and the beating heart of Treadwell was the stamp mill, made up of two parts: the battery floor and the vanner room. The battery floor housed the stamps, twelve-foot-long steel rods with hundred-pound hammer heads that ninety-eight times a minute fell seven inches onto a mortar, crushing chunks of ore. After being pulverized, the wet sandy pulp ran across amalgamation tables where free gold, released by crushing, collected on copper plates where it amalgam-

natatorium, gouging out a gaping hole that sucked the channel waters down into the fragile underground chambers. The weakened pillars supporting the mines could not hold. In a few hours, three mines—the Treadwell, the 700 Foot, and the Mexican—caved in and flooded with seawater. The Ready Bullion mine was saved from the disaster because a bulkhead had just been completed in the tunnel connecting it to the other three mines.

The population of Treadwell plummeted after the disaster. The miners who stayed on found employment with the Alaska Juneau Gold Mining company across the channel, or continued working the Ready Bullion

---

ated with mercury. This "free milling" part of the process released 55 percent of the gold in the ore. The amalgam was heated (retorted) to separate out the molten free gold, which was poured into molds to produce eighty-pound bricks.

The 45 percent of the recoverable gold that was still embedded in the ore required further processing. Ore washed to the foot of the amalgamation table went to another room onto rows of slowly revolving inclined rubber belts (vanners). The lateral shaking of the belt agitated the mixture while small jets of water played on it. Heavier ore with remaining metal (concentrates) washed off into a trough while the water and the remaining waste sand (tailings) flowed out into Gastineau Channel.

To extract the remaining gold from the concentrates required complicated methods. Over the years, management experimented with three different processes of recovery:

1. A chlorination plant that roasted the concentrates, "impregnating the ore with chlorine gas and afterwards leaching with water." The plant killed all the vegetation on the town's hillsides.
2. Smeltering, which required shipping the concentrates to Tacoma, Washington.
3. Cyanidation, in which gold, dissolved in a solution of sodium cyanide, was captured and separated through heating: In 1910, Treadwell settled on this more cost-effective process, building a cyanide plant and refinery on the south edge of town.[12]

"Turning Rock into Gold"

The rock is blasted with giant powder,
    And broken with hammers, deep in the hills;
Whence, hoisted by buckets to the surface,
    'Tis trammed in cars to the various mills.

The rock then crushed to three-inch size,
    Is passed to the stamps to pulverize;
These stamps, one thousand pounds in weight,
    Splash out the rock to the amalgam plate.

From the plate to the vanner,
    The sands then drop;
Which separates the values,
    With its vibrating top.

Then the sands of small value
    Are taken in haste,
To the big filter presses,
    To be run to waste.

Up the long track
    The concentrates go;
Then, weighed, they are fed
    To the tubes below.

To two hundred mesh,
    Are the concentrates ground,
As the tube filled with pebbles,
    Goes round and round.

Taken from the dance program of the 1910 Cyanide Ball, which celebrated the start up of the new cyanidation plant. (Courtesy of Willette Janes.)

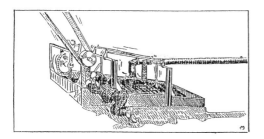

To the classifier then,
This fine product goes,
Where the coarse is raked back,
And the fine overflows.

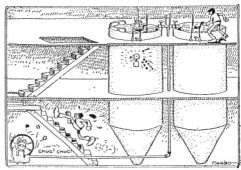

This overflow goes into the Pachucas,
To a cyanide solution protected with lime;
Thrice agitated by air, and decanted as well,
The gold is dissolved in two days' time.

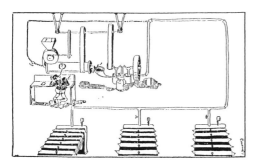

Into the gold solution
Comes a replacing zinc,
Which throws down gold precipitate
Black as ink.

The precipitate, fluxed
With litharge, is fed
To the blast furnace, where
The gold melts with the lead.

The lead bullion then
Into the reverberatory is cast,
Where, the lead cupelled off,
Leaves gold bullion at last.

So by boat to the mint
Goes the gold bullion then;
Whence, stamped into coin,
It comes back to the men.

Stamp Mill Statistics

The principle behind the stamp mill was an ancient technology—the Egyptians had used iron pestles, stone mortars, and slave labor to do it.

The ever-pounding stamp mills were the key to Treadwell's success in making a profit processing low-grade ore: eight and a half tons of ore to produce one troy ounce of gold.*

Over three decades, the number of stamps at Treadwell increased from 5 to 960.

1882	5-stamp test mill set up
1883	120-stamp mill replaces original mill
1887	240 stamps at the 240 Mill (Treadwell mine)
1891	60-stamp mill set up at Mexican mine
1897	120 stamps at the Mexican mine
1899	300 stamps at the 300 Mill (Treadwell mine)
	120 stamps mill at Ready Bullion mine
	100 stamp mill at the 700-Foot mine
Total	880 stamps in five mills for five mines

Later additions:

1911	20 stamps added to 700 Mill
1913	30 more stamps added to 700 Mill

mine until that site could no longer produce profitably. The week before Christmas, 1922, the Ready Bullion shut down. Now all four of the great Treadwell mines were abandoned.

At their peak in 1915, the Treadwell mines boasted the world's largest stamp mill and hoist, and a total of 960 stamps pulverizing a world-record five thousand tons a day.[13] From 1882 to 1922, when the last mine closed down, the Treadwell complex of mines and mills processed

1914   30 stamps added to Ready Bullion mine
Total   960 stamps

By 1914 at peak production, the four mines were feeding five thousand tons of ore a day to 960 stamps in five mills:

- The ore from the Treadwell mine went to two mills with a total of 540 stamps:
  - 240 Mill (240 stamps)
  - 300 Mill (300 stamps)
- The Mexican mine had one mill with 120 stamps:
  - Mexican Mill (120 stamps)
- The 700 Foot mine had one mill with 150 stamps:
  - 700 Foot Mill (150 stamps)
- The Ready Bullion mine had one mill with 150 stamps:
  - Ready Bullion Mill (150 stamps)

* Gold is measured in troy ounces; twelve troy ounces makes a troy pound, whereas sixteen ounces makes a common pound. The Treadwell mines' total production of 3.3 million troy ounces of gold equaled 226,286 avoirdupois pounds.

twenty-eight million tons of ore and produced 3.3 million troy ounces of gold. The weight of the gold tells the story better than quoting the 1922 dollar value, because at that time the price of gold was capped federally at $20.67 an ounce. Even at that value, Treadwell's output repaid nine times over the 1867 purchase price of Alaska.[14] (In 2009, the value of gold reached $1,000 per ounce, which would make the Treadwell output worth $3.3 billion.

THREE

An Unusual Company Town

Nothing quite like Treadwell had existed before.

T HE TOWN OF TREADWELL FASCINATED tourists because it brought together two contemporary phenomena: gold fever and the company town. Most people's image of the gold rush came from the chaotic camps of Klondike prospectors. And company towns in the industrialized eastern United States were best known as compounds of wage slaves laboring as cogs in the great capitalist machine. Treadwell would not describe itself either way. The largest hard-rock gold-mining operation in the world never considered itself a camp, and the proud townspeople were disdainful of tourists who expected to find locals living in shacks, tents, or even igloos. The big gold rushes of California and Alaska/Yukon had produced no notable company towns. Nothing quite like Treadwell had existed before.

In the same era and region, the infamous gold-mining towns of the Far North—like Dawson and Skagway—had mushroomed from camp to city due to the energies of rugged individualists and fiercely competitive prospectors in search of personal fortunes. The people who created Dawson and Skagway operated as entrepreneurs, setting up stores, boardinghouses, laundries, bars, and brothels. The people of Dawson were self-reliant. "Everyone knew how to build his own boat or cabin, handle a dog team, treat scurvy with spruce bark tea and how to navigate fast water."[1] Those gold-mining towns were random accumulations of people and businesses; a sense of community rose up in this sparring jumble despite the strong individualist streak.

By contrast, the company town that flourished around the burgeoning Treadwell enterprise was an intentional support system for the mines. To succeed on the northern frontier, the company management set up the necessary services: sawmill, cyanide plant, foundry, and machine shop. The workers and their families lived in a community alongside a maze of gritty mines and mills, but also had access to an indoor swimming pool, a library, a ballroom, bowling alleys, basketball and tennis courts, a finely appointed barber shop, and Turkish baths.

The company store and meat market were better stocked than any along the West Coast. The workers lived in steam-heated bunkhouses and ate in two boardinghouses that could feed five hundred at a sitting. Among its other wonders, the town had Alaska's first hydroelectric plant and the largest hoist in the world. There were cozy cottages, a school, an elegant mansion for the superintendent, and a clubhouse for all to use. A narrow-gauge railroad and boardwalks linked the town together. A company hospital was just next door in Douglas.

Wages were better than those at Ford Motor Company, and the record of two hundred deaths over forty years was better than the national norm. Constant hazards of falling rock, toxic fumes, dynamite explosions, and mine fires caused gruesome accidents, but the company hospital saved lives. Worker benefits included compensation for injuries and funeral expenses.

The town was completely privatized, with all services provided by the company. Everything from the pool towels to the giant flag in the plaza was marked with the company logo, a "T" centered in a diamond. Every job served the company, and Treadwell's clocks ran on California time, an hour earlier than Alaska, since corporate headquarters were in San Francisco.

The culture and tenor of the town varied with the personality of the superintendents. John Treadwell, a modest, unassuming bachelor who did not drink or smoke, was acknowledged as a man of patience and character. A decade later Joseph MacDonald, "a brash, despotic and violent man,"[2] who was toughened in the bloody mining wars at Idaho's Bunker Hill and

The company operated a department store where food, clothing, and other goods could be bought on time. Townspeople also shopped in Douglas and Juneau. (Courtesy of the Kelly Family Collection.)

Sullivan mines and was always armed, ruled with an iron hand. Robert Kinzie and his socialite wife oversaw Treadwell's golden era of prosperity in spite of strikes by the Western Federation of Miners. Later, after Kinzie was forced to resign, company president F. W. Bradley installed his brother, Philip Bradley, a jovial man who played pool with miners, knew them by name, and worked hard at boosting morale during the town's demise.

Children considered living in Treadwell a lark, an exciting place to grow up and they were lucky to be there. In fact, the town came about as an intentional economic institution and part of the corporate scheme. As an industry in the remote Alaskan frontier, the gold-mining company needed to provide housing and other necessities for employees. The goal was to attract workers and minimize turnover by offering good working

TREADWELL HAD A TWIN in Kennecott, a copper industry-based town that also helped open the Alaskan frontier. In 1900, deep in the Wrangell Mountains, up on the edge of the Kennecott glacier, two prospectors heading for the goldfields stumbled onto what was to become one of the richest deposits of copper ore ever to be found. With money from the Guggenheim brothers and J. P. Morgan, the Kennecott Mines Company formed in 1906, and later became the Kennecott Copper Corporation. Demand increased with the industrial age and World War I; copper was like green gold.

Kennecott referred to itself as a camp and a mine. The camp held the central industrial zone made up of a fourteen-story concentration mill and associated structures, a hospital, a sawmill, a store dairy, a school, and a three-story bunkhouse for single men (not miners). Like at Treadwell, all buildings were painted red because red paint could be made cheaply from the roasted concentrates leftover from the mills. Kennecott buildings had white trim. For entertainment, there was a softball field and a tennis court that also served as an ice rink. The mill camp served as home to managers and professional men with families. At the height of operations, the town numbered six hundred, and 50 percent of the workforce was employed in the mill. Unlike Treadwell, the Kennecott miners lived not in the camp but two miles away up the mountain at the mines. The two areas were connected

and living conditions.[3] Early company towns were known to be paternalistic, announcing their intent to create a better life for employees, with decent housing, schools, and a morally uplifting society. But the bottom line was always about efficiency because industrial workers were considered parts of the machine. Decades of management experience had demonstrated that efficient production required control over labor. In a company town, steady wages and good living conditions were provided, and "in return bosses expected stable hard working employees who would eschew the evils of drink and most important, not fall prey to the siren call of union organizers."[4]

These towns were built to maximize profits. One way to generate profits and recoup wages was to require workers to shop in the company

by aerial tramways. According to one historian, "the makeup of the workforce at camp, which was predominately professional men and the well-educated company managers, precluded the labor unrest that characterized most company towns. The proletariat workforce lived at the mine and was not allowed in camp." Growing up in the camp, some Kennecott Kids, as they called themselves, noticed quite a difference between staff people and nonstaff people and even "a little bit of discrimination whether you're Danish or Norwegian or Swedish." There were no documented cases of labor problems at camp, but oral history accounts noted that management "put troublemakers of any ilk on the next train out."[5]

The nearest town "where Kennecott did its sinning" was McCarthy, five miles down the railroad tracks. In contrast, workers in Treadwell could walk half a mile to Douglas City to have access to the saloons and brothels, as well as churches and fraternal organizations.

In addition to the absence of labor troubles, Kennecott boasted that its kids never had chicken pox or measles or other childhood afflictions so common in less isolated towns. Neither Treadwell nor Kennecott used child labor. Families loved their lives in the remote location, 190 miles inland from the coastal town of Cordova, where the "tranquility of seclusion translated into little crime, disease, or disruption."

store, live in the company housing, and pay fees for the recreational clubs and the hospital. At the same time, these medical, housing, and education benefits were an advantage to the company, because healthy and contented workers would be more productive and less prone to strike. In Michigan, the Hecla Copper Mining Company, which set up the nation's first industrial hospital in the 1870s, was criticized by other mining companies for "pampering their employees." But the company asserted that well-doctored employees directly improved production figures.[6]

Like many company towns of the American West, Treadwell was located in an area of dazzling natural splendor, surrounded by snow-capped mountains, lush forests, glaciers and ice fields, rushing rivers and waterfalls. But the source of the most awe-inspiring appreciation

THE INDEPENDENCE MINE was another Alaska hard-rock gold-mining site. Gold was discovered in 1886, southeast of Anchorage at the three-thousand-foot level of the Talkeetna Mountains. Robert Lee Hatcher staked the first claim in Willow Creek Valley in September 1906, and a hundred other claims followed. Lode mining was expensive and required pooling resources to raise money and reduce expenses. The Alaska-Pacific Consolidated Mining Company (APC) was formed in 1938 and at its peak in 1941, it employed 204 men on a 1,350-acre site with twenty-seven structures. Freight that came from Seattle to Anchorage had to be hauled up to the mine on wagons. Twenty-two families lived in nearby Boomtown, and eight children attended the territorial school in the bunkhouse. The mess hall served five meals a day, with tea, coffee, and fresh pastries available around the clock. The mine produced 34,416 ounces of gold; and the miners later claimed that the years at Independence were the best times of their lives.[7]

was under the ground, and the tributes and the poetry celebrated their Aladdin's cave of riches.

Unlike many company towns, Treadwell's design did not stress aesthetics. The settlement had sprouted up along a strip of the Gastineau Channel shoreline and spread half a mile up a stumpy hillside that had been stripped of coastal forest. The town was built right on top of the four mines. The two hundred buildings were all mixed together: mine hoists and mills, residences, bunkhouses, dining halls, clubhouse, and foundry. The only unifying aesthetic was the red and green color scheme. The townspeople's daily lives unfolded in the midst of the ongoing mining and milling operations.

Treadwell did not have the ever-present smoke of a copper smelter town, the sawdust burners of a timber town, or the slag heaps of a coal mining town. However, the two ubiquitous by-products of the gold mining and milling process were sand and sound. At Treadwell's five mills, piles of waste rock grew alongside mills that spewed out millions of tons of sand tailings, silting up the bay and creating a broad expanse of sandy beach. The incessant noise could be considered another kind of pollu-

The cars carrying ore from the mines to the mills sped along trestles through town day and night. (Courtesy of the Anderson Family.)

Residents stroll the plaza, not bothered by the incessant noise. (Left, assistant Superintendent house; center, Treadwell store; right assay office.) (Courtesy of the Anderson Family.)

ONE OF AMERICA'S MOST famous company towns was built in 1880 in Illinois by George Pullman for his railroad-car company. In a time when workers usually lived in tenements, this was a radical concept. The carefully laid-out town, on the far edge of the industrial city of Chicago, had finely designed houses, stores, a library, churches, and places for recreation and entertainment. Twelve thousand employees and their dependents lived there. Pullman's vision combined altruism and economic rationality, uplift and efficiency, social concern and self-interest in equal parts.[8] A London newspaper called Pullman's creation "the most perfect city in the world."[9] Employees were required to live in Pullman, even though cheaper rentals could be found in nearby communities. One employee noted, "We are born in a Pullman house, fed from the Pullman shops, taught in the Pullman school, catechized in the Pullman church, and when we die we shall go to the Pullman Hell."[10]

Tourists bringing home photos taken 1250 feet underground helped spread the fame of the Treadwell mines. (Courtesy of the Michael and Carolyn Nore Collection.)

tion. Visitors to the town described the sound as deafening, whereas the people who lived there found silence disorienting on the two days of the year the mills were still.

Although miners everywhere considered it bad luck to have women around the working sites, women did go into the Treadwell mines. Superintendent Kinzie made a practice of bringing his wife, Veronica, down to view the opening up of a newly exposed face of the gold-bearing quartz. The world was eager for details about these caves of gold, so female writers and excursionists were allowed down in the mines to see the cathedral sized rooms with the glittering gold held fast in the quartz. In some camps women worked as waitresses in the boardinghouses, but Treadwell filled those positions with Japanese men. Treadwell hired its first woman in the office in 1915, shortly before the cave-in.

The familiar lament "I owe my soul to the company store" rose when wages were paid in scrip rather than money. Infrequent pay days plus readily available credit produced chronic indebtedness for workers forced to shop at the poorly stocked company store. In Treadwell, scrip was used during the mines' early days; later on, workers were paid in gold coins and townspeople could choose where to shop. The company store and butcher shop were the best stocked in Alaska, carrying basic food and clothing, plus luxury goods. If it wasn't in the store, people did not have to resort to the Sears or Montgomery Ward catalogs, as in many company towns. Instead, they could ask the Treadwell store manager to order special items that were brought up from San Francisco or Seattle by steamship. Still, some Treadwell families chose to trade at the stores in Douglas, and peddlers were seen about town. The Tlingit offered their carved and woven artifacts. Workers had alternatives that provided leverage against company limitations and demands. People had gardens, dozens of kinds of wild berries free for the picking, and an abundance of game, fish, and shellfish. Treadwell bordered on the city of Douglas, and Juneau was a fifteen-minute ferry ride across Gastineau Channel; both towns offered lodging and shopping.

Many company towns that mined minerals high in the mountains or cut timber deep in the woods could control workers' movements because the only way in or out of town was the company-owned railroad. Treadwell owned no such transportation link, and the town had major

The company store provided every kind of food, practical and elegant clothing, prospector supplies, and Christmas toys and gifts. (Courtesy of the Douglas Island News.*)*

steamship lines calling at its pier several times a week; workers took frequent trips south or Outside for health, shopping, or a holiday. The corporate miner who still harbored dreams of striking it rich could work in Treadwell during the winters, save his wages, and hop a boat to go north in the summer and prospect for his own claim.

By all appearances, company towns that melded working and living domains made employees vulnerable to their employers' control. But "workers rarely were passive. In company towns across the country, they actively participated in struggles to define their living and working conditions. Labor strife in company towns dramatized the continuing conflicts between capital and labor, ethnicity and Americanization, and discipline and democracy that marked industrializing America."[11]

According to the 1900 census, Treadwell's population was largely made up of single young men, most of them transients and foreign-born aliens. (Courtesy of the Alaska State Library, Dexter Collection, P40-26.)

Unions regularly targeted company towns to organize workers. Any labor moves to strike for higher wages, better living conditions, or job safety were countered by management calling in federal troops or threatening to shut down or flood the mines. Treadwell followed the same pattern. Superintendent Kinzie and the Western Federation of Miners faced off in 1907 and 1908. Kinzie called in federal troops and swore he would close the mine before recognizing the union. However, the union succeeded in pushing for a fifty-cent increase in wages from $3 to $3.50 a day.

Company towns were acknowledged as fiefdoms of white upper-class industrial barons. Still, increasing waves of immigrant workers came from southern and eastern European countries. Cultural barriers plus the lack of English language skills increased the gulf between employers and workers. Treadwell management encouraged workers to learn English, and also to take citizenship classes and become naturalized.

The staff at the Mexican boarding house. (Courtesy of the Kelly Family Collection.)

Many companies deliberately hired people from a wide variety of ethnic and racial groups, hoping that the cultural differences would keep workers from assimilating enough to organize against management. In 1907, this practice backfired in Treadwell when fighting broke out between Japanese and Montenegrin workers living in the same company bunkhouse. The Western Federation of Miners seized the opportunity to organize the workers, form a union, and demand that the company allow workers to live where they chose. The striking miners successfully negotiated the lifting of the requirement for employees to live in the Treadwell bunkhouse. The company agreed to give each employee a $30 monthly allotment for room and board wherever he chose.

Nothing unified a company town—or any other town of the early 1900s—like baseball.[12] Prowess on the baseball diamond was often a guarantee of employment. Treadwell was well known for recruiting summer workers from the ranks of the athletic teams at the state universities of California and Washington. Interest was so high that the company purchase of new uniforms for the Treadwell baseball team rated a feature

The Treadwell baseball team's Southeast Alaska champions, 1913, with Kelly's Uncle Bobby Coughlin (lower row, second from the right). (Courtesy of the Michael and Carolyn Nore Collection.)

article in the *Douglas Island News*. Tons of sandy waste tailings from the mills became the baseball field for a formidable team that successfully challenged Douglas, Juneau, Skagway, and all other comers in the annual Fourth of July tournament. The company built grandstands to house fans and the twenty-seven piece Treadwell Band. They even installed a drinking fountain.

Alaska was barely a territory, and still forty years from becoming a state, when World War I broke out, and, in the tradition of company towns, a fierce patriotism swept Treadwell. Then the town's own great calamity contributed to increasing the fervor. One week after the United States entered the war, a devastating cave-in closed three of the Treadwell mines, and hundreds of jobs disappeared overnight. Droves of men left to join the military in the United States or in their homelands of Serbia and Montenegro. Those who remained in the stunned mining community sought new purpose in the war effort.

Treadwell had champion basketball and football teams, swimmers and skeet shooters. (Courtesy of the Alaska State Library, Barquist Collection, P164-29.)

The miners and skilled workmen who stayed on in Treadwell worked in the Ready Bullion mine or across the channel at the Alaska Juneau mine.

Contrary to oft-repeated proclamations from management and the local papers that Treadwell would rise again to its former greatness, no effort was made to pump out the three flooded mines. The cost of restoring the complex would overwhelm any profit from resuming operation.[13] The threads of the town's fabric were unraveling.

MANY COMPANY TOWNS no longer exist in any form. Some aren't even dots on the map.

The Pullman company and town were hit hard by the Panic of 1893 and the depression that followed. A falling demand for Pullman cars led to layoffs and a widespread strike when management refused to negotiate on rent for the houses in town. The strike marked the beginning of a new era for labor by demonstrating "the growing power of workers to disrupt production."[14] The town was eventually annexed to the city of Chicago.

A few towns sustained a presence and mystique down through the years. Port Gamble, Washington, a logging and milling site, is the longest-lived company town in the country. With its white-steepled nineteenth-century church and Victorian houses, it gained landmark status as a New England village transplanted to the Pacific Coast.

Several mining sites carried on as ghost towns capitalizing on ruins. Real estate developers turned others into retirement communities. In response to the depressed price of copper, the Kennecott mines closed in 1938, after twenty-seven years of operation that produced 4.625 million tons of ore. The area was designated a National Historic Landmark in 1986. The Independence mine closed in 1951, and was placed on the National Register of Historic Places in 1974. Later the site was donated to the State of Alaska Parks and Outdoor Recreation to establish the Independence Mine State Historical Park. Restoration is underway to return the camp to what it looked like in 1939. It will be used as an interpretive site for understanding how a gold-mining town worked.

At least one company town has been immortalized in fiction. Alpine, in the Cascade Mountains of Washington, was the site of a timber operation from 1910, until it was demolished in 1929 after the mill closed. Now it serves as the setting for Seattle writer Mary Daheim's mysteries featuring a newspaper editor turned sleuth.[15]

In its decline and fall, Treadwell was an example of the dynamics of capitalist development that "creates, alters and destroys company towns."[16] Production needs had driven the company to discount the increasing danger of cave-ins. Competition among owners for control of the company pushed management to shave down the supporting pillars underground where the rich ore remained, precipitating the shocking cave-in of 1917.

Between 1910 and 1920, the mine cave-in and World War I resulted in Treadwell's population dropping from 1,222 to 325. Douglas City went from 1,722 to 919. With the source of its wealth inaccessible, the mills dismantled and sold for scrap and its population drastically reduced, the town limped along. In 1926, a huge fire, driven by an October Taku wind, burned most of Treadwell's wooden buildings to the ground. The town was gone.

In its heyday, Treadwell pulsed with a vibrant and diverse community energy. The families of the superintendents, managers, machinists, and hoist operators, as well as the students from mining colleges who came for the summers celebrated the wonders of technology and capitalism. At the same time, the indigenous Tlingit, the Chinese laborers, the union activists, and the miners from around the world lived another story of deep-seated prejudice, treacherous conditions that killed, maimed and crippled workers, all part of an industrial system that valued them primarily for their roles in increasing production and profit. These stories wove together to create a unique town.

FOUR

<hr/>

Company Family through Boom and Bust

"We are staying."

—WILLY KELLY, APRIL 22, 1917

F ROM 1899 TO 1925, through boom and bust, the Kelly family lived it all. The everyday lives of Willy, Nell, Mayme, Raymond, Marion, and Honey wove into the dramas of underground explosions, miners' strikes, and the mounting evidence that the mine that was their livelihood—and the literal foundation on which their house stood—was about to cave in.

Around the same time as the Klondike madness, more solid, sensible adventurers like Willy Kelly heard about the money to be made at the mines on Douglas Island. He knew that the lure and lore of prospecting for gold drew thousands of people to the frozen Far North, by boat, train, horse, and mule, many slogging up the icy Chilkoot Pass trail—the meanest thirty-two miles in history—to take their shot at getting rich. But an established mine that produced real gold bricks in such quantities as to pay dividends to stockholders, as well as wages for a workforce, appealed to another kind of opportunist, men like Willy Kelly.

For Willy, it started back on March 9, 1899, in Alameda, California, when he married his sweetheart, Ellen Cecelia Coughlin, a frail, petite woman with a tiny waist, wispy hair the color of a fawn, and wide green eyes. The Oakland paper announced the marriage and noted that "Mr. and Mrs. Kelly will leave in a week or two for Alaska where Mr. Kelly will enter the employ of the Treadwell Mining Company." The front page of the same paper headlined "Much Distress at Dawson" where Klondikers were "stranded, hungry, and many destitute."[1]

At the time the young newlyweds were sailing north, another ship followed the same route, carrying more gold stampeders and two of the largest boilers ever brought to Alaska, to provide steam power for the Treadwell Mines. The Kellys arrived at Treadwell just in time to participate in the celebration of the opening of the largest stamp mill in the world. The *Douglas Island News* heralded "300 stamps added their thunderous applause to the success of practical mining on Douglas Island, and no invention known to practical miners for the handling of ore and extracting the gold is omitted. Douglas Island can boast of having the largest mining plant in the world."[2]

Willy and Nell moved into a cottage in the town of Douglas, knowing that when they had children they would move into one of the Treadwell cottages the company rented to families of skilled workers and managers. Skilled machinists like Willy were needed to build and maintain parts for the stamps and ore cars. Cost and efficiency demanded that the mine make everything from ore cars to wheel cogs on

Willy Kelly, right, a loyal company man, worked in the Treadwell machine shop from 1899 to 1925. (Courtesy of the Kelly Family Collection.)

Interior of machine shop. (Courtesy of the Alaska State Library, Case and Draper Collection, P39-0921.)

site, rather than relying on resources that required a five-day boat trip to Seattle. The Treadwell machine shop, a long, narrow building that dominated the pier, was full of lathes that Willy used for "truing up" or straightening the stems of the stamps.

As the mine and the town grew, so did the family. In nine months, on December 1, son Raymond was born. "Willy is happy," the *Douglas Island News* noted on December 2, 1899.

Barely a year later, in early 1901, Nell took young Raymond back to Hayward, California, to be with family for the birth of their second child, Marion. In May, Nell and the two young children returned to Alaska on the SS *Senator*, accompanied by Willy's teenage brother, Milton Kelly, and Nell's brother, Bobby Coughlin. As the ship was coming into Treadwell, the captain announced that a young steerage passenger headed for Skagway might have smallpox, so the ship must return to Port Townsend, Washington, for quarantine. Before it left Gastineau Channel, relatives of the captive travelers were allowed to get near enough to the ship for shouted conversation. As Nell held three-month-old Marion up at the rail, Willy

Willy and Nell Kelly with baby Marion, 1902. (Courtesy of the Kelly Family Collection.)

Kelly caught a first glimpse of his baby daughter. While waiting in Port Townsend for the ship to be fumigated, a passenger wrote to the anxious families that no new smallpox cases developed and "Mrs. Kelly and her babies are well."[3]

Smallpox was a concern, but reefs and rocks were the real threat to boats in southeast Alaska waters. Still, steamships were the only way people and commodities could travel between this Alaskan panhandle and the outside world. Hardy locals boasted that "going South" to visit friends, see a doctor, shop, or have a baby was part of their way of life. One local woman noted: "If the Japan current should suspend operations, the path to Puget Sound [and points south] would be kept warm by Alaskan travelers. Many a staid Eastern community would be shocked at the reckless unconcern with which the Northland regards a sea voyage of a thousand miles or so."[4]

The passages, straits, and canals that weave southeast Alaska together are dotted with reefs, rocks and icebergs. On a foggy August night two months after the SS *Senator*'s quarantine delayed the Kelly family homecoming, the SS *Islander*, flagship of the Canadian Pacific Navigation Company, traveled south along the west side of Douglas Island. One of the most luxurious passenger steamers afloat, famous for elegant dining and excellent cuisine, it boasted richly upholstered chairs, deep

UNTIL THE TURN of the century, the United States had done little chart-ing of channels and hazards of the Inside Passage; in the gold rush years between 1898 and 1900, more than three hundred ships were damaged or sank floundering on reefs or crashing into rocks. Seeing that travel to Alaska was only going to increase, the government began surveying and marking underwater hazards. In 1902, southeast Alaska's first two lighthouses were set flashing. Despite the navigational aids, an average of twenty-four ships were lost annually over the next two decades.[5]

plush carpeting, heavy brocade draperies, and several pianos. The stained-glass doors of the state rooms depicted scenes along the route of the Canadian Pacific Railway. During the Klondike rush, the *Islander*, like every other vessel in the Pacific Northwest, carried passengers, freight, even live cattle and sheep, between Skagway and Vancouver.

On this end-of-summer trip, the 181 passengers, prospectors, and dignitaries from Dawson had thousands, maybe millions, of dollars in gold in the safe in the purser's office. At two AM, traveling at full speed in the fog, the ship hit an iceberg and sank in twenty minutes. Seventy-one passengers were lost. Along with everyone available, Willy went out to help survivors who swam or floated to the southwest shore

The Kellys at the time of their mother's death in 1905. Raymond, age five, went to live with the Stubbins family in Douglas. Marion, age four, and Honorah (Honey), age two, went to Juneau to the school of the Sisters of St. Ann. (Courtesy of the Kelly Family Collection.)

of Douglas Island and then walked the beach to Treadwell. For weeks, furniture, clothing, and bedding from the ship washed ashore and showed up later in Treadwell cottages and cabins. The search continued for the gold treasure believed to be in the ship's safe.[6]

By 1903, the Treadwell complex was digging deeper mines, expanding stamp mills, paying big dividends, and attracting investors worldwide. The Kellys were thriving, too. But soon after Willy and Nell joyfully greeted a third child, daughter Honorah, the most horrible tragedy struck the young family: Nell developed breast cancer and died the following February, the day after Marion's fourth birthday. Raymond was five, and Honey one and a half. The notice in the *Douglas Island News* read:

> After many months of patient suffering, Ellen Cecelia, age 29 years, beloved wife of William H. Kelly, passed away. . . . But a few short years ago, Mrs. Kelly came to Douglas Island a bride blessed with youth and a sweet disposition. The home was set up and three beautiful children came to add the blessing of their presence and make the measure of their joy complete. But into this loving circle came a guest all unbidden, and day by day the loving husband watched its advance with the acid grip of fear at his heartstrings. Hoping, fearing, despairing . . . sad is the little home from which the mother is gone forever. The wail of the motherless children causes the tear of sympathy to course down the cheek of the friend who is powerless to give them comfort.[7]

Below the announcement was a card of thanks from Willy: "to the kind friends whose acts of loving sympathy have helped us bear the burden of our grief, and made bright the last hours of our loved one."

Marion watched out the window as the horse-drawn sled, with Raymond riding up front, slid across the frozen ground, carrying her mother's coffin to the funeral in Our Lady of the Mines Church in Douglas. Marion hugged baby Honey, who didn't understand what was going on.

Raymond and his uncle Bobby Coughlin, Nell's brother, took a sad trip on the SS *Jefferson* to accompany Nell's remains back to California to be buried alongside her parents in St. Mary's cemetery in Oakland. Afterward, Raymond stayed on in San Francisco with relatives.

The next spring, Raymond took the steamship from San Francisco to return to Treadwell with the Grundler family, who owned the laundry in Douglas. The day after they left, a massive earthquake struck San Francisco. In the great fire that followed, Mrs. Grundler's sister lost her home, and the San Francisco office of the Treadwell mines was destroyed.

As hard as Willy tried to care for his young son and two daughters, none of the housekeepers he hired worked out, although they all wanted to marry him. After he returned from San Francisco, Raymond went to live with the mayor of Douglas, Billy Stubbins and his wife, who were good friends of Willy's. The two little girls went to St. Ann's Boarding School and Orphanage in Juneau. That sad day when the girls and their father arrived at the convent, the nuns distracted Honey with candy and dolls as her dad slipped out the door. But Marion knew what was happening. She flew out the doorway after him, down the steps of the convent, and along Harris Street as the nuns ran after her, their black capes flying. Marion ran all the way to the ferry dock. The boat left with her dad.

Marion was a slight-framed four-year-old, with alert green eyes and a dimpled chin. She was precocious enough to start first grade there at the Juneau Convent, while toddler Honey sat under the teacher's desk and learned how to string buttons and keep quiet. Going to and from class, marching up and down the steps, all the girls sang "Dear Angel Ever at My Side." Each night, up in the dormitories, Marion brushed her little sister's feathery hair. Anyone who made baby Honey cry could expect a punch from tiny Marion.

Every Saturday night Willy took the ferry from Treadwell to Juneau to visit the girls. He always brought candy. Once he brought a handmade kid-leather doll he had won by guessing the number of beans in a jar. The doll had a bisque head and a beautiful dress made by Mrs. Kinzie, wife of the mine superintendent.

On one Saturday visit, Willy asked the girls if they would like to have a new stepmother. Marion said no.

On Christmas Eve, 1906, Willy brought Honey and Marion over from Juneau for midnight Mass at Our Lady of the Mines Church and a family dinner at the Stubbins'. He brought another guest, a Miss Margaret Sullivan from Grand Rapids, Michigan, who had recently moved to the

*Willy Kelly married Margaret "Mayme" Sullivan in
1907 and brought the family back together in Treadwell.
(Courtesy of the Kelly Family Collection.)*

island and opened the Palace of
Sweets, a fruit and candy store
next to the ballfield in Douglas.

Just six months later, on June
26, 1907, Willy and Mayme, as
he called her, went to Seattle to
be married, and the local paper
noted "their friends on Douglas
Island wish them joy without
measure." They traveled on the
SS *Jefferson*, the same boat that
two years earlier had carried
Nell Kelly's remains to California. Then the new Mr. and Mrs.
William Kelly came back to
Treadwell to rebuild a family.

So it was that on a bright
July morning in 1907, Willy took
the little ferry *Lone Fisherman*
from the Treadwell wharf fifteen minutes across the channel
to Juneau, where he walked up
Harris Street to St. Ann's Con-
vent. There he gathered up six-year-old Marion and five-year-old Honey
and thanked the Sisters. The Kelly trio hurried back to the ferry dock,
loaded down with suitcases and dolls. The sun sparkled on Gastineau
Channel and bounced off Mount Jumbo over on Douglas Island. Finally,
the Kellys were together again. The ferry chugged back across the channel
carrying the sisters and their dad to a new life in a company house in the
company town of the famous Treadwell mines.

For the little girls, the fame of the mine meant nothing. They even
put aside their anxieties about a new stepmother. They were going to be
reunited with their beloved big brother, seven-year-old Raymond. The
Stubbins family had wanted to adopt him, but Willy would not hear of
it. He was determined to keep his family together.

Going from the ferry down the long Treadwell pier, the family passed the barnlike machine shop where Willy was a master mechanic. The buzz of the shop sang in their ears, and the stamp mills drummed their welcome. The great roar that rose up and poured out from the town, shaking the wooden walkway under their feet, moved inside them as familiar as their own heartbeats, that incessant rhythm that enlivened their play and lulled them to sleep.

As the dainty beribboned girls, petite like the mother they had lost, bounced up the boardwalks toward their new home, the mills were pounding out their daily quota of crushed ore. And underground, right under their feet, three hundred miners were at work, blasting and drilling.

The bright-eyed girls hardly noticed the harsh industrial look of Treadwell, the treeless slope from shoreline to foothills, the growing expanse of tailings along the beach that silted the nearshore waters to a muddy milk. After two years in the convent, Treadwell's maze of wooden sidewalks, boardwalks, train tracks, and belching smokestack sentinels looked as welcome as a playground. The gaping Glory Hole was no longer popping with explosions because mining operations had recently moved underground, following the ore deposit deeper and deeper and even under the Gastineau Channel.

Yes, this town was built to extract wealth from deep within the earth, but the Kellys hoped that on the surface a family could take root and thrive on the ragged hillside. The newly configured family now included a step-mother, Mayme—the children called her Mama—her mother, Granny Sullivan, and Granny's

The Kellys, 1912, counterclockwise from the right, back row: Willy, Mayme, Granny Sullivan (Mayme's mother), Marion (whose special-made dress covers her body cast), Raymond, and Honey. (Courtesy of the Kelly Family Collection.)

parrot, Polly. The family moved into one of the large company cottages in Treadwell in an area called Treadwell Heights, a row of houses directly above the superintendent's mansion. They were sandwiched between the two largest and loudest mills, with 300 stamps on one side and 240 on the other. Neighbors in nearby cottages included the pattern maker, the die maker, the head of the mills, and the head of the foundry.

The houses had long porches across the back and flower boxes in the front that caught the morning sun. The Kelly house had seven rooms, including four cozy bedrooms. Dependable electricity and steam heat provided comfort, convenience, and plenty of hot water. Mayme made the home warm and attractive. She had a red plush Victorian button-back couch shipped in for the parlor. Marion's assigned chore was to clean around the buttons with a brush. Curtains woven with wooden beads and silken tassels hung between the dining room and the double parlors. The window coverings were heavy net with draped cornices. The wreath pattern in the green floral carpet made a circle that worked nicely for marble games.

The Kelly house sat back fifteen feet from a double set of tracks. On the lower tracks bordering the front yards of the cottages, a miniature engine clattered back and forth all day hauling equipment to and from the mines. On a second set of elevated tracks, self-propelled trains screamed by fifty times a day taking the ore from the mines to the mills.

Margaret Sullivan Kelly was a big-framed woman, as tall as her husband, with thick hair piled on top of her head, a ruddy complexion, large, strong hands, and a stern, square jaw. Overwhelmed by the responsibility of three young children, Mayme put the family on a firm schedule: school lessons, music lessons, and church. But Granny livened up the household. A great cook and avid whist player, she taught the children card games at an early age. And she loved Irish music, hiking up her skirts to dance a jig.

Instead of going down the boardwalk to the company school, the children walked the mile to St. Ann's Catholic School in Douglas. Unless there was snow or a Taku wind, they came home every day for lunch, and Willy walked five minutes up from the machine shop to join them. Their social life revolved around the church, fund-raising bazaars, and card-playing nights. Mayme was active in the Altar Society, which cared for the church.

Young Raymond, the dutiful son and devoted big brother, had his mother's slight build and gray-green eyes and his father's dark curly hair. Serious and thoughtful, Raymond excelled in his schoolwork and faithfully practiced his mandolin lessons. He even enjoyed doing his chores. With his beloved female Saint Bernard named Rover harnessed to a wagon or a sled, he collected kindling and hauled coal up from the dock. Maintaining a big boisterous dog required daily trips to the boardinghouse where the Japanese cooks saved buckets of meat scraps for him. Because Mama would not allow pets in the house, Rover stayed at the back door or slept in the cozy steam-heated basement. Once, Rover's fat, furry pup

First Communion photo on the steps of Our Lady of the Mines Catholic Church in Douglas, 1909. Honey and Marion (center) with Raymond (top of stairs on left). (Courtesy of the Kelly Family Collection.)

named Bud scrambled out on the train track and was killed by an ore car. Rover howled when the church bells rang and barked when the Alaska Natives came to the house to sell their crafts.

In winter, Raymond added two seats to the sled and gave his sisters a wild snowy ride home from school, while he ran alongside to make Rover "mush."

With the girls delivered home to start their homework, he unhooked the sled, put on his skates, and grabbed the harness. Hanging on to Rover, featherweight Raymond on his silver blades flew up and down the flooded, frozen, and lighted Treadwell plaza. Rover got caught in the crossfire of a simmering feud between Mayme and her neighbor Mrs. Murphy over who was going to head the Altar Society. Mayme was lace-curtain Irish. Mrs. Murphy was the brick-throwing kind. The Kelly

Raymond Kelly introduces Rover, while Granny Sullivan looks on from the door of the Kelly cottage in the Treadwell Heights neighborhood. (Courtesy of the Kelly Family Collection.)

children, with Rover in tow, regularly cut through the Murphys' yard in order to stay far away from the railroad tracks. One day Mrs. Murphy came out with a .22 rifle and shot Rover in the foot. Then she put up a wire fence all around her yard. Rover recovered and the children continued to sneak through the fence. Mayme became president of the Altar Society and set new records for the Christmas bazaar fund-raising.

The Kelly cottage looked out over the grand residence on Treadwell's central plaza. The scale fit this frontier town carved out of the side of a mountain but the style was more California than Alaska. The superintendent's house, four times the size of the Kelly cottage, had three sets of two-story bay windows that faced out on Gastineau Channel. South-facing dormers gave a view far down the channel. An enclosed, windowed room, a solarium, crowned the structure.

Mayme was strict about who the children played with, but she encouraged their friendship with Superintendent Kinzie's children, Robert, Eugenia, and Hunter. The Kinzies attended the Catholic church but they went to the Treadwell company school. The superintendent's family was the only one in town that had their own lawn, a cook, and a cow. In summer the Kelly children played on the lawn; the cook, Tommy, would bring out a picnic of biscuits and cakes. When Tommy made butter, he brought a quart of buttermilk up to Granny.

Mrs. Kinzie was an elegant Irish belle, from a prominent San Francisco family. She let the young Kelly girls play dress-up even with her fine jewelry, but they had to leave when she announced she had to dress for dinner. At the mansion, there were always company officials from San Francisco to entertain. A flurry of intense dinner meetings was called for when the Western Federation of Miners (WFM) was trying to form a union in Treadwell.

At the beach, Mrs. Kinzie and Honey splash with baby Eugenia Kinzie. Raymond Kelly (rear) and Hunter and Robert Kinzie (right) look on. (Courtesy of the Kelly Family Collection.)

During that time, on their way home from school for lunch, the Kellys were surprised to encounter a column of uniformed military men lined up in front of the Treadwell Club. The talk about miners going on strike did not affect the children, who stopped to play spelling games with the soldiers. The soldiers commented on how smart the children were and, in turn, Marion admired the soldiers' red, white, and blue enamel collar pins that said "U.S." One soldier said, "Would you like one?" Marion replied, "Oh, yes! And can I have the other one for my brother?"

The Kellys did not pay much attention the day the local chapter of the WFM called a general strike to gain recognition for the union. Willy was a company man and not inclined to join those "belligerent Slavonians," as the management called the striking miners. And more important things were going on in Willy's life. On the day the strike was called, Mayme gave birth to a stillborn daughter. The devastated mother, whose ruddy complexion was not from vigor but a sign of heart and kidney problems, was in "a very precarious condition."

Mayme began taking regular boat trips to Seattle, often on the SS *Humboldt*, to recover her health. Then, in March 1910, back only hours from a trip south to the doctor, she fell into bed exhausted. At 11:25 PM,

About 1913

The Treadwell Club Band, of Treadwell, Alaska, who use and recommend the C.G. Conn Instruments of Elkhart, Indiana, as the best instruments in the world.

The Treadwell Club Band played for parades, dances, baseball games and in miners' funeral processions. Willy Kelly's brother Milton was a drummer. (Courtesy of the Kelly Family Collection.)

the mine whistle pierced the night. She listened for the signal. Three long blasts—the surgeon's whistle. An accident.

A huge explosion had rocked the Mexican mine. People rushed to the scene to pull out the wounded and pile them into trains of ore cars, which rushed them to the hospital in Douglas. From their window the Kelly children watched the trains career by, so close they could see the wounded miners' arms and legs sticking out of the cars. Thirty-nine miners died in the disaster. Willy spent several days retrieving belongings of the victims who were fellow members of the Redmen, the fraternal society that had just elected him as chief of records. For days, the children's uncle, Milton Kelly, drummer in the Treadwell Club Band, played in the never-ending processions that escorted dozens of miners' bodies to the cemetery. By tradition, the band played a somber tune on the way out to the burial and a bouncier one on the way back.

A bright spot that spring was the opening of the company's new indoor heated swimming pool, the "tank." The ladies and children were permitted to swim two days a week.

The following summer, the pool closed down after many children became ill, including ten-year-old Marion. One afternoon she went into her bedroom, reached up to pull the light string, and her legs gave way. Mayme called from the other room where she was resting on the couch: "Marion, quit horsing around and get up off that floor."

Marion said, "Mama, I can't."

Bedridden for weeks, Marion felt a weakness moving through her body. The doctor could not help; he inexplicably had advised her to "Keep your fingernails clean because the disease is going to come out that way." For a while, Marion couldn't walk, and Honey and Raymond wheeled her around in a baby buggy. Willy massaged her legs every night and made her a cane from a pool cue. She regained some strength and the doctor made a brace for her shoe.

When Mayme noticed that Marion's spine had begun to curve, she bundled her onto the SS *Curacao* and took her down to Children's Orthopedic Hospital in Seattle. The dreaded diagnosis was polio. Mayme would not leave Marion there for in-patient care because the hospital was not Catholic.

The doctors' prescription: Marion's frail little body was wrapped in a body cast, from under her arms to her hips, a suit of armor to be worn for eight years.

Every six months Marion and Mayme took the boat to Seattle for treatment and to have the cast changed. Sometimes the trip south was scheduled for the Fourth of July so that Marion did not have to be on the sidelines at the Treadwell plaza and watch the footraces that she always had won in years before.

Christmas was a big occasion on Douglas Island, almost as big as Fourth of July, the only other day in the year when the Treadwell mines closed down and the stamp mills were silent. By November, the snow had fallen, covering the town's grime and stumps with a batten of white. The great mound of waste rock from the 300 Mill became a prime sledding slope. The frozen plaza was the ice-skating stage, as kids, couples, and families glided, twirled, and frolicked into the evenings. Upstairs at the Treadwell store, the whole floor was turned into a glittering toy department, with all the latest playthings shipped from San Francisco.

The Christmas bazaar at the Catholic church was a major event for Treadwell, and a seasonal focus for the Kelly family. Planning started in early fall, and as head of the Altar Society, Mayme helped organize it. The parish ladies sewed satin and lace dresses for the beautiful porcelain dolls to be raffled. When polio kept Marion from skating, sledding, and running about during the year, she trained her fingers to fly, doing fine needlework, producing exquisite embroidered pillows and complicated tatting pieces to sell at the bazaar. She also perfected songs on the piano. Christmas 1913, the Kelly children were the featured performers at the parish concert. The diminutive trio performed "O Sanctissima" with Raymond on mandolin, and Marion and Honey on the piano. Marion did a recitation of "Santa Claus on the Train," Honey recited "Kris Kringle," and Raymond took part in a debate titled "Shall Our Mothers Vote?"

The bazaar was held in the basement of Douglas Town Hall, and booths were spread around the same floor that hosted roller-skating parties and dances that the Kelly children heard about but were not allowed to attend. But everyone who was Catholic turned out for the bazaar, which was the parish money maker. A sumptuous buffet featured delicacies brought up from San Francisco and the bounty of Alaska foods, including an array of berries, fish, and game; the children sang Christmas carols; and the raffles had great prizes.

One year, the raffle prize was a rare treasure: the Christ Child figure that had once been part of the Nativity scene in the chapel of St. Ann's Hospital. The fifteen-inch doll was made in Germany: all wax, blush pink, with delicately crafted limbs, carved features, limpid blue glass eyes, and curly blond hair.

Marion hated raffles and refused to sell even one ticket. Raymond was good at it. He ran through the crowd, and with the same charm and precociousness that could sell fool's gold to tourists off the boat or conduct guided tours to the Glory Hole, he sold those raffle tickets to miners and mill managers. In no time, his name was up on the blackboard list as top ticket salesman. And when the drawing came, Raymond was sitting next to the winning ticket holder, a smiling dark-eyed Slovenian miner, who turned to twelve-year-old Raymond, gave him the ticket, and said, "For you, you have it." Raymond protested. The miner, perhaps reminded of a moment with his own children back in the old country, insisted. Raymond bounded up to the stage and claimed the prize, which became part of the family Christmas celebration.

The week before Christmas, Raymond put bells on Rover's sled and delivered presents to friends. Even the stern stepmother took special effort to make the time magical for the family. On Christmas Eve, Mayme and Willy trimmed their tree and put everything out, then closed the curtains to the parlor. To keep the proper religious focus, the children could not go in until after church services. After midnight Mass the children scrambled onto the sled behind a panting and jingle-belled Rover, and raced home to find each of their rocking chairs filled with gifts.

Mayme always invited Mr. and Mrs. Brie for Christmas dinner. True, they were the only Jewish family on the island and they owned a saloon. But Mayme overlooked that because the Bries were devoted to their Irish Catholic neighbor children whose mother was very delicate and whose father was preoccupied practicing his violin. One Christmas when Marion was sick, Mrs. Brie recommended that Mayme administer a dose of castor oil. Marion turned to Honey and in a stage whisper said, "I wish she hadn't come." Mayme promptly sent Marion to bed, over Mrs. Brie's protests, "Oh, don't do that, don't do that to the child, it's Christmas." But off Marion went, without a whimper; no harsh stepmother was going to make her cry. She never cried.[8]

Like everyone in Alaska, the Kellys depended on boats for transportation. Alaskans used boats just like those down south used the train. As Marion got older, she took the boat by herself to doctors' appointments in Seattle and enjoyed the independent adventure. Sometimes she was on the boat that carried the Treadwell gold bullion being shipped south to the San Francisco mint. Once, on the trip back north, she had an intriguing roommate with a large diamond set in her front tooth and a wide-brimmed hat flaunting long chiffon streamers—the latest style for riding in the new motor cars. On arriving in Juneau, Marion brought her

THE SISTERS OF ST. ANN were important contributors to the growth and de-velopment along Gastineau Channel. As early as 1887, they started a school in Juneau, taking in orphans, boarders, and destitute children. In 1858, traveling from their Mother House in Quebec, they had opened schools in Victoria, British Columbia, before moving to Alaska.

In his 1887 report to the Secretary of the Interior, Alaska Territorial Governor Swineford wrote: "At Juneau the Catholics have a school of their own . . . with an attendance [200] . . . larger than both the Public Schools combined. . . . I have every reason to believe that it is destined to become a very important factor in promoting the educational welfare of the Territory."

The Sisters saw that the twin settlements of Treadwell and Douglas lacked local medical care and educational opportunities. They started a school in the aban-doned Bears' Nest Mine boardinghouse. In 1896, a new church and school were built. Fifty children enrolled. The sisters contracted for construction of a hospital to be operated with the Treadwell mining company, so injured miners did not have to be transported to Juneau. St. Ann's hospital, two and a half stories with fifty beds, averaged twenty-five patients a day cared for by two sisters and a male nurse. After 1913, a few rooms in an annex were set aside for female patients. (Most women stayed home for the births of their children, and took care of their own and their children's medical needs. Doctors paid home visits.)

The hospital and school were both called St. Ann's. The church was Our Lady of the Mines. A sister in Quebec painted a large canvas of St. Ann holding the standing figure of her child, Mary, extending a small hand toward a kneeling miner dressed in his work clothes with a carbide lamp (Davey) on his cap. The background shows faces of the miner's family. The painting was the feature of the hospital chapel in Douglas.

In 1916, the new wing added to the hospital was acclaimed as the best facility on the West Coast. The following year, the mine caved in and unemployment forced miners and their families to move away. The Sisters feared they would have to close the hospital. However, the next year, the Spanish influenza struck and the hospital rooms were full of Native and non-Native victims.

After the epidemic the Sisters proposed turning the hospital into a rest home for aging Alaskans, but that failed. In August 1920, six months after Mayme Kelly's death, the Douglas Island Sisters, accompanied by eight children, left for the provincial house in Victoria, British Columbia. In September 1926, the hospital was sold for $1,000, and the following month a great fire swept the island and destroyed the hospital, school, church, and rectory. (The portrait of Our Lady of the Mines had been transferred to Juneau where it now hangs in the church hall of the Cathedral of the Nativity of the Blessed Virgin Mary.)[9]

Portrait of Our Lady of the Mines shows St. Ann holding the Child Mary, who extends her hand to a kneeling miner. The painting hung in the chapel at St. Ann's Hospital, Douglas. (Photo by Andy Mills. Courtesy of Paulette Simpson.)

parents to meet the woman. As Willy and Mayme suspected, the kind, proper roommate was in fact Diamond Lil, infamous lady of the night.

Boat trips were more frequent and more fun when the children went out to Catholic high schools in Washington State. Raymond's voyage to his freshman year at Seattle College High School prompted the Stubbins family to give him his first suit with long pants. Raymond wore his usual knickers on the boat, so his parents and hometown buddies wouldn't tease him. As soon as the boat pulled away, he went to his room and changed, ready for this voyage and his new life Outside. On the boat the children were technically under the care of the captain, but in fact, the captain saw them only at meals, and the young people had the full run of the ship.

Mayme sent the children Outside to attend Catholic high schools. Raymond excelled in debate at Seattle College High School while Marion excelled in mischief at Visitation Academy in Tacoma. Honey went to Holy Names Academy in Spokane and decided she wanted to become a teacher.

The children came back to Treadwell during school holidays and the summers. On the long-awaited day of their arrival, Willy would watch out the machine-shop window for the smoke from the steamers as the ships nosed out of Stephens Passage and entered Gastineau Channel.

The Kelly family life kept a steady Treadwell rhythm even through the loss of a mother and a baby, a bout with polio and other major illness, through the Takus, fires, and ground-shaking caving. That reliable lode of gold had already given Willy eighteen years of secure employment in the machine shop. He would soon learn that the legendary caves of gold underfoot did not provide job security. Rather his own skills as a machinist were the key to his continued prosperity in Treadwell.

FIVE

The Big Hoistman's Boisterous Family

You got a lot of kids up there. How about getting them to pick some blueberries so we can make some pies for the boardinghouse?

—TONY TUBBS TO GUS ANDERSON

AUGUST (GUS) ANDERSON RAN the central hoist in the Treadwell mines. His family, a big, boisterous Swedish bunch, had eight stair-step children, four boys and four girls. Marion and Honey Kelly looked up to the older Anderson girls, Kari and Lydia, who were free spirits, bolder and more daring than the constrained Kelly girls. Gangly Irving Anderson was a few years younger and a head taller than Raymond Kelly, but still he looked up to Raymond, and was fond of Raymond's father, too.

Irving liked to brag about his own dad. Gus Anderson ran the biggest hoist in the world in the largest gold-mining operation in the world. For all the young boys of Treadwell, the central hoist was a magnificent machine to look at and a thing of beauty in motion. The one-thousand-horsepower Allis-Chalmers machine could raise two four-ton loaded ore skips at a rate of twenty-three hundred feet per minute.[1] Gus sat high up

Gus Anderson operated the Treadwell mine's big hoist, one of the awe-inspiring machines that impressed tourists and town boys alike. (Courtesy of the Alaska State Library, Case and Draper Collection, P39-0912.)

on a platform at the hoist gears, always attentive to the ringing of bells indicating when a cage full of miners was lowered or a skip full of ore had to be lifted. He could not leave his post up there at the controls; often Irving climbed up the ladder and took him lunch.

An adventurer at heart, Gus ran away to sea from his home in Sweden at age fourteen and changed his name from Frugendhal to Anderson. Working as a high rigger, he honed skills that he later put to use to build the big Ferris wheel at the Chicago World's Fair. Gus first came to work for the Treadwell Mining Company in 1898. But the lure of Klondike gold drew him into the rush going over the Chilkoot Trail to Dawson. There he made money, not by digging gold, but through his knowledge of steam engines. He ran a "donkey engine" that thawed the ground for placer miners. In Dawson, he contracted typhoid fever and ended up in the hospital in Seattle. His friends came down to urge him to go back to Treadwell, where wages were good, some miners were striking, and they

During that age of industrial romance, Treadwell machines were admired as sculptures. (Courtesy of the Juneau-Douglas City Museum, 2009.07.005.)

needed a man to run the hoists. He returned and took over running the famed machine.

A big man with a bushy moustache, he sported a trademark brown hat like the Royal Canadian Mounties. For formal occasions, he changed to a plug hat, a derby, that he wore for funerals, jury duty, and his Knights of Pythias meetings. Family and coworkers respected him as a fearless and fiercely independent man. He crossed the picket line during the 1908 strike because he thought it was important that the machinery be kept running to keep water out of the mines.

His wife, Frederika, was a strong and competent woman, whom he met on a trip back to Sweden. When he returned to Alaska, Gus sent for her and they were married in Seattle. The family grew quickly, with a child born about every two years. Like the Kellys, the Andersons were woven into the fabric of Treadwell life. Frederika, a devout Lutheran, taught Sunday school at the church where they read their Bible and sang hymns in Swedish. The Sunday sermon was in Swedish, too, but Frederika had the children tell her what the sermon was about—in English. She insisted

Gus and Frederika were engaged in Sweden. She traveled to Seattle to marry him. (Courtesy of the Anderson Family.)

the children speak English, saying, "You are Americans." She looked down on immigrants.

Mrs. Anderson was also the family doctor. When Irving was three months old and got whooping cough, his mother slept holding him on her chest so she could slap him on the back when he coughed. When the doctor finally came by he said she had done a good job. Then her son Frank got blood poisoning from cutting his leg on a piece of glass in the snow. This time, the doctor said he would "have to amputate, or you're going to lose that boy." The townspeople advised Frederika to take his advice, but she said no. Gus backed up his wife: "You just let her take charge of it." She took Frank home and applied her old-country method of curing infections. She filled large onion shells with fels naphtha soap and cloves, set them in the oven till the soap melted, then laid the poultice on the wound, changing it day and night. After twelve hours, the red streak up Frank's leg disappeared. Once again, the doctor grudgingly admitted she had "done a good job."[2]

For preventive medicine, the Anderson children wore little cheesecloth bags full of asafetida around their necks. This foul-smelling gum resin from plants of the parsley family was supposed to keep germs away. Irving knew it kept people away, so maybe that's how it worked.

Gus stockpiled supplies and foodstuffs, prompted by the appetites of a growing family plus vivid memories of nearly starving up in the Yukon. When he added bedrooms to his cottage, he built a big pantry outside on the back porch where he hung hams; bags of rutabagas, onions, and parsnips; and twenty-eight-pound sacks of flour. The Anderson yard was a cultivated plot; they raised potatoes, and took the biggest down to the Douglas store to brag. Gus planted cottonwood trees around the house because he liked the smell of them in spring when the leaves came out.

Monday was the family's day for cooking and laundry. Irving brought in wood and coal and Frederika got a hot fire going in the stove. She baked bread, beans, and stew, and heated the water for the laundry. She hung the sheets, stockings, and underwear out, even in winter when clothes froze on the line. She ironed the children's dresses and shirts that she had made herself. Special care was required for her husband's dress

Gus and Frederika Anderson, a hardworking Treadwell couple. Six of their eight children were born on Douglas Island. (Courtesy of the Anderson Family.)

shirt for church and his Knights of Pythias meetings. The collar and cuffs each had to be hand dipped in starch.

In the evenings, setting the big round cylinders on the Edison phonograph, the family played their favorite song over and over—"Put on your old gray bonnet with the blue ribbons on it and we'll hitch old Dobbin to the sleigh"—while the girls danced and the boys jumped around. One afternoon a week Frederika had a group of Treadwell ladies over for tea, and she told fortunes from tea leaves—always good fortunes. "You

Lydia Anderson (front) and her sister Kari (behind her in cap) enjoyed many boating parties with Treadwell's young people. (Courtesy of the Anderson Family.)

are going to get a letter, and you are going to be happy about it." There was no liquor in the house, and no cards. That was the making of the devil, she said.

Gus felt that with his family responsibilities it made sense for him to work in a steady-paying corporate job. But he always harbored hopes of a gold strike up in the Klondike. When he grubstaked some prospector friends, his wife cried for a week, telling him, "I am working hard and you give these men money and they just bring back rocks."

Frequently, Frederika took the boat to Seattle for health reasons, and even the local paper noted that she was "rundown and overworked."[3] The older girls, Lydia and Kari, were a handful. The adventuresome young people of Treadwell staged dances and skating parties, picnics on nearby islands, and hikes up Mount Jumbo.

Even with strict parents, the girls had active social lives, with lots of boyfriends. When they knew they would be out later than their curfew, they arranged for younger brother Karl to leave a string, attached to the end of his big toe, hanging out the window. When the girls got home, they tugged on the string. Karl came down and sneaked them in. One of Lydia's boyfriends, a Frenchman whom they called "the Count," proclaimed his love and vowed to give up his French citizenship to marry her. She declined that offer, and instead the Count taught her and Irving to play tennis at the new court the company built near the mansion.

The vigilant mother tried to keep track of the girls' activities. Moving pictures, a brand-new invention, were a novelty at the Treadwell Club. Charlie Chaplin and *Perils of Pauline* seemed to be acceptable; but she wouldn't let the children see Theda Bara, that "wicked woman who wore rouge." When it came to rouge, both parents were in agreement. The girls started wearing it and their father hit the ceiling. "You have to be part of the red light district to have rouge on your face." The girls cried, but to no avail.

Frederika opposed the children going swimming in the tank, the company swimming pool. Lydia and Kari begged and pleaded until she relented, and they all joined the weekly swims, the water carnivals, and races. The big boys put on a diving contest and showed off. Karl could already swim the length of the pool. When the girls were learning to swim, Gus said, "I don't know how you can ever learn to swim. I'd think you'd drown in all those swimming clothes, stockings, and bloomers." He thought bloomers without the coat were modest enough. But his wife insisted her daughters wear the full swimming costume. One summer day, Lydia and Kari set out to swim in a small lake up behind town in the meadows along the Ditch, and took their dog Murphy with them. Every time the girls plunged into the icy pond and swam out, Murphy paddled after them, grabbed their bloomers, and pulled them ashore. Only later did the girls learn that submerged in the middle of the lake was a huge pipe that sucked water down into the stamp mill. Murphy, their ever-present Swedish family dog with an Irish name, had saved their lives.

Like all the Anderson children, Irving had chores at home and jobs in the town. One assigned task was to keep the kindling box full. Harnessing Murphy, to a wagon, they headed to the Treadwell store for broken-up crates from the canned peaches and tomatoes that came in on the boats. Irving was even grateful for one Taku wind that lifted the roof off the Treadwell Club, crashed splintered wood down in their front yard, and brought the kindling right to his front door. From the wharf, he and Murphy hauled bags of coal off-loaded (along with rats) from Norway.

Irving delivered the Alaska Daily Empire *to Treadwell residents. (Courtesy of the Anderson Family.)*

Irving also had a paper route. Every day at five PM, the ferry *Alma* brought the *Alaska Daily Empire* papers to the float alongside the Treadwell wharf. On the way down to pick up the papers, he'd stop midway to see his friend in the machine shop, Mr. Kelly, who worked with the big lathe. Always curious, Irving liked to poke around, and then wipe his greasy hands on the *ADE* newspaper bag he carried over his shoulder. When Irving had an extra paper he gave it to Mr. Kelly, who, in turn, made him read it out loud. Irving stuttered, but he could manage the headlines.

Irving had many friends in the machine shop. Mr. Mugford made runners for his sled and taught him how to sharpen his skates, Mr. Samuelson played mandolin at all the dances and wanted Irving to take lessons, like Ray Kelly, but Irving just couldn't sit still long enough. A German machinist regaled Irving with unconvincing stories of the glories of war.

The paper route paid $1 month. Irving inherited the job from his brother when Karl took on a new summer responsibility herding Superintendent Kinzie's four cows down past the boardinghouse to the green grass of the baseball field. When there was a ball game, Karl shoveled cow pies off the field.

When the first telephone line was strung between Juneau and Douglas, Kari got a job as telephone operator on the night shift. The man who owned the line repeatedly tried to call Treadwell, and never got an answer because Kari was asleep, so he fired her. She cried. Her dad said, "When you go to work, you have to do what they want you to do, just like I do what they want me to do." During the Christmas season Kari worked at the Treadwell store, when the whole top floor turned magically into a child's holiday dreamland full of dolls, sleds, and toys of every sort brought from San Francisco.

Irving's restless energy often got him in trouble. One day, roaring down the hill from the assay office in his rattling wagon, he crashed through the porch of the butcher shop, running into the delivery dog, and almost knocking out a post. In the winter, flying down the snow-covered hill by the 300 Mill on his newly sharpened sled runners, he would wear out his shoes because he had to drag his toe to steer. When the central plaza was frozen over, Irving was always excited to join people skating all hours of the day and night and repeatedly pulled off the soles of his shoes when he clamped on his skates. He was late starting first grade at the company school because on the day before school started he jumped into a pile of hay, hit a hard steel frame, and broke his arm.

Walking to the Treadwell school down by the 700 Foot Mill, the Anderson children had to cross an elevated tramway, climb steep steps, and walk a narrow boardwalk parallel with the railroad tracks. On occasion they had to stop and step back as a shrieking locomotive flashed by pulling a flat car bearing a cot shrouded in a blanket.

Irving started school in one classroom, with one teacher, and two outhouses. Irving's only classmates in the morning session were Jimmy and Elsie Manning.

The Swedish family inherited a dog named Murphy from a miner who left town. The dog saved Lydia's and Kari's lives. (Courtesy of the Anderson Family.)

A Treadwell sledding outing, 1913, with Irving Anderson, George Benson, Frank Anderson, Eleanor Murphy, Mark Smith, and Charlotte Price. (Courtesy of the Juneau-Douglas City Museum, Mahaffy Collection 92.22.005.)

The spring 1916 class of the new Treadwell school. Back row, left to right: Willie Price, Mark Smith, Dayton Depew, Mark Daniels, Una Crowe, Christine Campbell, Charlotte Price, Miss Chasteen, Elroy Ninnis, Frank Anderson, Alex Morgan, Jimmy Manning, unknown, Ray Carol, Clifford Anderson, Mrs. Tascher, unknown, Philip Bradley, Irving Anderson, John Pugh.

Their father, Jake, was the foreman in charge of the Ditch, and their mother was a Tlingit. To teach the alphabet, the teacher drew a big letter on the students' desks and gave them split peas to outline the letter over and over. Irving was self-conscious in class, and he stuttered and mixed up Swedish words he learned at home, Slovenian words he learned from the miners, and Tlingit words Jimmy taught him. With a short attention span, the bored boys instead played tricks, shoveling snow down the chimney and into the outhouses. By 1915 the school-age population had increased, so a new schoolhouse was built near the new office building.

One payday, Irving watched the Treadwell paymaster as he handed out the gold coins to the miners. Irving noticed that the oilcloth on the table where the paymaster sat had a hole in it, so he slid his hand under, and pulled out a $20 gold piece. He took it to Gabriel Paul the storekeeper, and asked, "How much candy can I get for this?"

"Where'd you get it?"

"Found it. I'll show you where."

"Does your dad know?"

Front row, left to right: four unknown, David Ramsey, Dorothy Anderson, two unknown, Dorothy Metzger, unknown, Legget, Peggy Legget, Helene Smith, Virginia Metzger, Dagmar Youngsbrown, John Pugh, Elsie Edmonton, Douglas Price, unknown, Hugh Chilean. (Courtesy of the Juneau-Douglas City Museum, Mahaffy Collection, 92.22.004.)

Mr. Paul took it and gave Irving a bag of chocolates. Irving said, "I'd rather have doughnuts."

The Treadwell baker was famous for his breads and sweets. Irving seldom had gold coins, but sometimes he had a newspaper left over from his route and he traded it with the baker for a sugar-coated doughnut.

Gus Anderson once got into a conversation with Tony Tubbs, the boardinghouse manager, who made a proposal: "You got a lot of kids up there. How about getting them to pick some blueberries so we can make some pies for the boardinghouse?"

Five of the Andersons set off with lard buckets, up the trail at the back of their house to a thick patch of luscious blueberries they knew grew near the Glory Hole. (Usually, they had strict instructions to stay away from the steep-sided crumbling pit.) They came home with all their buckets full.

"I don't know what to do with them all," Frederika complained.

Gus said, "Put 'em in the bathtub. In fact, let's *fill* the bathtub!" They went out the next day and filled their little buckets again and again, until the bathtub was brimming with blueberries. The proud father went down to the boardinghouse and told Tony, "We have a whole bathtub full. How am I going to get them to you?"

Tony sent the Japanese house boys up with water buckets and carried them all down—enough pies for three hundred miners, compliments of the Anderson kids. Gus got an extra $20 for the effort; the kids got nothing; and Frederika was left with a permanently blue bathtub that embarrassed her when people came to the house.[4]

One Christmas Irving received a new BB gun. To try it out he hid in his basement and shot at the windows of his neighbor, Mrs. Chelaine. The ping-pinging terrified her. For months, her husband, who worked underground in the mine, had been telling her that drilling was "coming awful close to where they shouldn't be." She thought the sound meant that the mine was collapsing and the house was cracking right under her feet. When they found out that the Anderson boy had pelted the house with BBs, the assistant superintendent was furious and told Gus to get that boy under control.

Irving's dad was disturbed too. But for a different reason. From up on his hoist operator's platform, he was seeing signs that the mine was in trouble. The foundation of the hoist house cracked and tilted a couple inches off to the side. He was bringing up more and more water from the mine, which had reached twenty-three hundred feet below the surface. Gus told Frederika, "It's time to get out of here. These mines are going to get

Newlyweds Kari Anderson Preston and Charles Preston. (Courtesy of the Anderson Family.)

flooded. I've been hoisting saltwater night and day." He began making plans to leave Treadwell and move back to Seattle, where he had found a good job in the Bremerton shipyards.

They were ready to go in spring of 1916, when Kari Anderson—having undergone a metamorphosis from Treadwell tomboy to young woman—announced her surprise engagement to Charles Preston, the boy next door, the mine's chief electrician and one of Treadwell's most handsome bachelors. Their summer wedding was held in the Anderson living room. The clergyman was the same man who, twenty years earlier, had married Gus and Frederika in Seattle, after Frieda's long journey from Sweden. The newlywed Prestons left on the SS *Spokane* to honeymoon in California, where they bought an automobile and then motored to Seattle. They took the steamship back to Treadwell in August 1916 and moved into the newly remodeled and refurbished Preston cottage next door to the Andersons' former home.

After refusing the proposal of marriage from "the Count," Lydia considered what to do with her life. She knew she did not want to become a maid to other people; she wanted to do something she could be proud of. After Kari's surprise wedding, Lydia took a Canadian Pacific steamship to Victoria, British Columbia, and enrolled in the Royal Jubilee Hospital School of Nursing to become a military nurse.

That autumn, the remaining Andersons—children and parents—left on the SS *Alki* to move to Seattle. Kari carried on the Anderson presence in Treadwell. Now expecting a baby, she looked forward to an exciting life as wife of a rising star in the Gastineau Channel mining community. The happy newlyweds could never have foreseen the tragedy the next two years would bring, first to the town and then to their own family.

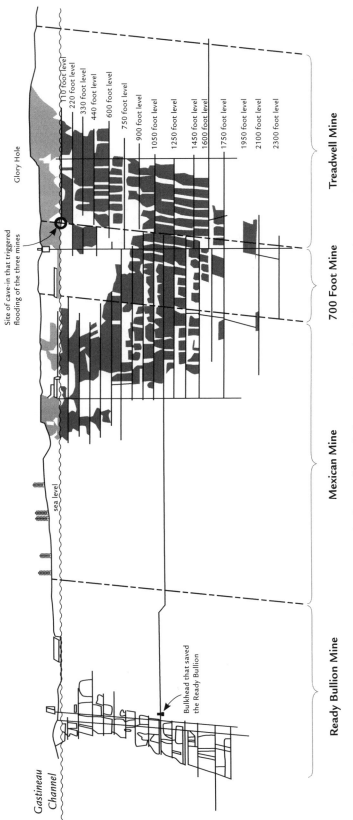

Longitudinal section showing the underground honeycomb of stopes beneath the town of Treadwell (from Wernecke 1916; redrawn by Dixon Jones).

SIX

———◆———

Tough Grind of the Hard-Rock Miner

*The man who is not afraid of work can
accumulate money faster at Treadwell than at any
other place in the country.* —ALASKA MONTHLY, 1907

UNDERNEATH THE TOWN OF TREADWELL'S cozy cottages and
tennis courts, swimming pool and clubhouse, another life was going on. The four mines—the Treadwell, the Mexican, the 700 Foot,
and the Ready Bullion—were like four giant underground hotels with
hallways and vast rooms, called stopes, carved out of that great lode of
gold-bearing ore. On an average day 350 men moved about in the tunnels
and stopes that made up the underground workings.

If the pounding stamps were the heartbeat of Treadwell, the lifeblood
was the steady stream of ore blasted from deep in the earth, hauled up
and fed nonstop into the stamp mills. The underground work of the
hard-rock miner was dangerous, requiring a special breed of man with
inner strength and courage. He worked as deep as a half mile below the
surface in cramped, hot conditions, often with just the glow from candles,
always on lookout for falling rock or moving equipment.

Hard-rock mining was a growing industry in the United States in
the late 1800s. To attract experienced miners, Treadwell promised good
wages. By 1908, a driller made $3.50 a day, the company kept the cost of

Every day, 350 to 400 men were at work in the stopes and drifts of the four mines. (Courtesy of the Alaska State Library, Dexter Collection, P40-19.)

living low in the town, and room and board was $1 per month. The European markets provided both capital and labor, and Treadwell recruited workers from London, Paris, and Zurich. The mine employed people of over a dozen nationalities, mostly from northern, central, and southern Europe.

Miners worked around the clock in eleven-hour shifts, with a one-hour break to come up to the boardinghouse for a midday or midnight meal. Morning and evening, they went into the mines at seven and back out at six. As one shift finished, they set off blasts to bring down walls of ore for the next shift to break up and hoist to the surface. The hour between shifts allowed nitroglycerin fumes from dynamite to clear the mines before the next shift went in.

One August night in 1915, Earl Pilgrim, who was sound asleep in bunkhouse no. 4, awoke with a start to find his middle-aged Swedish roommate

The 1903 Treadwell workforce included 220 Americans (not including Alaska Natives), 200 Austrians/Slavonians, 32 Japanese, 24 Germans, 11 Scots, 8 Russians, 1 Turk, 205 Scandinavians, 40 Finns, 29 Irish, 23 Italians, 9 Indians, and 2 French. (From Redman 1988, p. 28. Courtesy of the Alaska State Library, Case and Draper Collection, P39-0976.)

standing above him crying, "Oh, my God, my God, Earl you are killed! I dreamed your body was lying there at the bottom of the shaft."[1]

Earl, son of a Colorado miner, was on break from the University of Washington College of Mines. The Treadwell management recruited college students from Washington and California to come work for the summer. The ranks of miners thinned out seasonally when many die-hard prospectors went off to the Yukon to work their own claims while the ground was not frozen. The Alaska Native workers, who traditionally lived off the land, went out to their fishing camps to gather and prepare food for the coming winter.

Earl did not go right back to sleep. He wondered whether this was a warning not to go back down in the Mexican mine. But he had taken this job knowing it had risks. In the morning, he left the steam-heated bunkhouse and went to the boardinghouse for his hearty breakfast of oatmeal, beef steak, sausage, potatoes, hot cakes, corn bread, and coffee. This company fed its miners well!

At the shaft house of the Mexican mine, Earl picked up the quarter-sized brass ID tag with his assigned number printed on it. Tags were hung on a board with corresponding numbers. At the end of the shift, workers dropped their tags into a box and the shift boss hung them back up on the board with corresponding numbers. When any tag was missing, the search began, for fear a miner had suffered an accident. Usually the problem was less serious. Miners fell asleep, or new hands lost their way, or just forgot and walked off with their tags. They were tracked down at the bunkhouse or boardinghouse. A man twice guilty of this blunder was fired.[2]

Earl put on his miner's cap with a carbide lamp and picked up a can of carbide for refills. (Before carbide, the miners had depended on candles, a dim and undependable light source.) Four miners, including the cageman, a chute puncher, and a mucker who broke up rock, climbed into a double-deck steel cage, on a thick steel cable that wrapped around a great drum controlled by the hoist engine. The cageman pulled the bell signal "1-2—3-2" that told the hoist operator "twelfth level, men on, lower." One bell meant to hoist up, two bells meant lower the bucket, three bells meant there were men in the bucket.[3] According to strict rules, there was to be no horseplay, no smoking, no playing with the bells, no carrying tools or explosives in the cage.[4] The cage plunged into the darkness, at a regulated speed of "no greater than 800 feet per minute," past descending levels, occasional flashes of lights, the hum of voices, and clash of machinery, to stop at the level twelve station. The cage stopped to take on or let off workmen at the station, and took on cars loaded with ore going up, or empty cars going down. The floor of the station had boxes of candles, coils of fuse, and a cask of water with a tin dipper hanging on a nail. At the station the men who had a few minutes' break stopped by to hear the news from the surface. There was more chat and sociability here than in any other part of the mine.[5]

From the station, miners walked out the tunnel along tram tracks. They stepped aside for cars of ore on their way to the dumping places. Cars were loaded with ore by the chute puncher and a mucker, who moved the ore around. Each car held one ton of ore, and when four cars

In the early years, the only source of light in the stopes was from candles the miners carried to stick in their hats or on the walls. (Courtesy of the Alaska State Library, Dexter Collection, P40-31.)

were loaded they formed a train pulled by a horse or mule attended by a driver and a brakeman. The ore was dumped back at the station and the horse pulled the empty cars back up to the stope. "As the men passed a familiar horse they gave him an affectionate pat that was returned by a low pathetic whinny of recognition and pleasure."[6] The mules and horses were lowered down into the mines in slings under the skips and cages. The animals lived and worked underground until they became ill or died. Old Tom, the big white horse adopted by the Kinzies, had spent many years underground.

These hard-rock miners had soft hearts, too. Earl told the story about one old fellow who always carried down armfuls of green grass, apples, and sugar, and the horses nickered at the sight of him. If they passed him in a drift, and he didn't have any treats for them, they gave long, low whinnies and kept turning their heads to look after him.[7] Another story told of a miner on shift in the mine who found a cold, hungry pigeon. The

1250 LEVEL, TREADWELL MINE.   SWIHART

The miners brought apples for the horses, which spent all their lives working underground. (Courtesy of the Michael and Carolyn Nore Collection.)

miner wrapped it in his handkerchief with the greatest care and tenderness, placed it in a sheltered spot until he came off shift, and then brought it to the surface and set it free. The local paper that usually referred to miners with ridicule and prejudice, noted: "we hope there are many other miners on Douglas Island who would have done the same thing. For that kind of men make good neighbors."[8]

Earl first started out as a chute puncher, putting in several shifts until the boss came by and asked: "You ever operate a rock drill? Show me!" Earl skillfully set up the Ingersoll-Sergeant drill and demonstrated fifteen minutes of ear-splitting rat-a-tat-tatting into solid quartz. He stopped, and in the silence so sudden and intense that it hurt almost as much as the noise, the boss proclaimed, "OK, you're on your own. Your stope boss, a Polack named Starrie, will be by soon."

As a machine man, the pay was better, but risk and responsibility were greater, too. Earl went to work cutting out a new stope, created in the ore body by drilling holes, tamping dynamite into them, spitting the fuses, and getting out for the blasting and caving of the ore, which would be "mucked out" in the next shift.

LANGUAGE DIFFICULTIES CONTRIBUTED to accidents, although the mine's posted "Rules and Regulations" stressed that "carelessness is more dangerous than ignorance." The rules contained 110 admonitions in nine categories, covering from "Shafts and Cages" to "Sanitation," all in small print, in English. A sampling of the directives included:

- No smoking or horseplay on cages.
- Keep ladders and platforms in the manways clear of loose rock.
- Do not go into a stope or bulldoze chamber until the same is reasonable clear of smoke.
- In blasting holes no fuse must be used of a length shorter than five feet. Do not smoke while handling explosives.
- After spitting [lighting] fuses, always stay within hearing distance, count the number of shots and carefully note the number of missed holes. When coming off shift, always report missed holes.
- Scraps and refuse from lunch buckets must not be thrown at random in the mine.
- You must use sanitary appliances which are provided.
- When rounding a curve or running through a foggy drift, move your train slowly and sound your gong.
- Before spitting fuses, the blasting signal must be given to the [hoist] engineer and no fuse must be lighted until he replies by hoisting the bucket or skip a few inches, and lowering it again.
- Never attempt to go to work when you have been drinking, however little, for then you are in no condition to go underground, [as] the heat or lack of fresh air increases the effect of liquor.
- When a boss tells you that you are doing something dangerous, stop doing it. He is responsible for your safety and knows what he is talking about, that's why he is a boss.

One of the first things that had been pounded into his head about machine drilling was to touch the surrounding rock faces to feel for vibrations. Solid rock gave faint vibrations, but loose rock, even if it appeared firm, transmitted the machine's blows quite noticeably. He was always

careful. Some men whom he worked with were not. One day, a few feet
from him a mucker was swinging a heavy hammer on a big slab of rock.
These muckers broke up the big chunks or set them up with dynamite
"bulldozes" that were blasted between shifts. The stope boss came along,
touched the young mucker's shoulder, and pointed to the edge of the slab.
"See what ya got here?" Barely visible was a short length of fuse. The boss
carefully dug around and pulled out the fuse, a primer, and four sticks of
dynamite. This unnoticed, unexploded charge could have been acciden-
tally set off as ore was moved along the path to the car. Explosions like
that had caused many deaths, maimings, and loss of limbs.

Five years before Earl arrived, the Mexican mine had been the site of
the town's most deadly disaster. Around 11:25 PM on March 3, 1910, the
shift was ready to go to the surface for their midnight meal break. At the
1,100-foot level, forty-eight miners gathered at the station, chatting, while
they waited for the hoist to take them up. Suddenly, a horrific explosion
blasted out from behind them. A total of sixty men had been at work
on the 1,100-foot level that night. Several had gone up earlier, and some
were late getting to the hoist because their watches were slow, but most
were standing at the station.

Three long blasts on the Mexican whistle—the "surgeon's call"—
pierced the night. The wounded and dying were hoisted up, loaded into
ore trams on the surface. The cars sped along the rails and trestles to
the town of Douglas. People peered from cottages along the way and saw
the little train stop at the street below St. Ann's Hospital. They heard the
tread of booted feet going up the incline and saw miners' lamps gleaming
in the darkness, carrying lines of stretchers. Some stretchers stopped at
the dead house; others went on to the hospital. Men stood with bared
heads while their buddies were carried in.

Thirty-nine miners died from the force of the blast, falling rock, and
noxious gases. The explosion was so violent a man farther up the shaft
at the 900 level hoist station was killed. The mine closed for twenty-four
hours for funeral services. The dead miners had belonged to every church
in Douglas: nine Catholic, seventeen Serbian Orthodox, four Congre-

gational, and seven Lutheran. Over several days, the solemn corteges paraded to the cemetery.

The source of the explosion was traced to eight cases of dynamite stored in a magazine located near the hoist station. The area had been designed so that in any accidental explosion, the blast would be directed toward the shaft, to force the fumes up the opening, so miners working in the area would not be suffocated. Unfortunately, the miners were in the direct path of the blast. Two horses were in a stable near the station. One was "blown to atoms," and the other was unhurt.[9] Some miners' bodies had landed in the bottom of the shaft, just like the horrible nightmare of Earl's roommate five years later. The explosion was the worst tragedy in Alaska mining history.

TREADWELL MANAGEMENT COURTED the educated, athletic elite of West Coast universities. The immigrant miners' experience was different. Like the Alaska Native population, foreign workers were often targets of prejudice. The management, the townspeople, and the local papers often characterized Slovenians (which could include Syrians, Montenegrins, Herzegovinans, Hungarians, and Poles) as ignorant, lazy, and troublesome. The ranks of the miners, machinists, mill workers, and boardinghouse staff included French, Swiss, Finns, Norwegians, English, Irish, Japanese, Australians, Turks, Austrians, Russians, Italians, Belgians, Germans, Swedes, Danes, Scottish, Welsh, Canadians, Greeks, Indians, and Americans. Most shifts underground had half English-speaking workers and the rest divided between Scandinavians and Slovenians. Many of the foreign workers were convinced that management did not want the miners to be able to talk to each other, as a way to discourage unions. On the other hand, management encouraged foreign speakers to bunk with English speakers, learn the language, and get promoted. In 1914, when war was raging in the miners' Balkan homelands, many Serbian, Montenegrin, and Greek miners quit their jobs in Treadwell to defend their native countries on the other side of the world. The *Douglas Island News* took notice: "We call them ignorant foreigners [but they show] a high degree of personal patriotism that puts the U.S. to shame."[10]

For Earl, the nightmare images were less of a threat than the real-time sounds he listened for in the silence between drilling and blasting. Taking broken ore out of a stope left it wide open and removed the support from the side walls. This created pressure within the wall and the rock began to "work," announced by cracking timbers, flaking rock faces, and deep-seated rumbling noises from within the rock itself. There had long been dire predictions that "someday" there would be a cave-in and the Gastineau Channel would pour into the mines. The Ready Bullion was the only one of the four mines where the drilling followed the lode out under the channel.

One day, Earl thought the prediction, rather than the dream, was coming true. His shift, working at the 1,220 level, received a warning that

THE REPORT OF THE TERRITORIAL MINE Inspector for the year 1913 included the following schedule of benefits for injured employees or their heirs, effective November 4, 1912.

1. Fatal, no dependents	funeral expenses only
2. Fatal, married, living with wife, no children	$1,000
3. Fatal, married, living with family with children	1,000
4. Additional allowance made for each child under 14 years of age	500
5. Fatal, not married, with sole dependents in the United States	500
6. Fatal, with or without children living in a foreign country, married	500
7. Fatal, unmarried, with widowed mother sole dependent in foreign country	500
8. Total blindness	2,000
9. Loss of one eye	300
10. Loss of two limbs	1,500
11. Loss of one hand	500
12. Loss of one foot	300
13. Loss of either leg above knee	650
14. Loss of either leg below knee	500
15. Loss of both legs above knee	2,000
16. Loss of both legs below knee	2,000
17. Loss of either arm above elbow	650

upper levels were collapsing. The chute puncher looked down the tunnel, then ran to the shaft and rang for the cage to go up so he could get orders about what to do. Back at the drift, an earthquake jolt followed by a loud hissing sent air rushing down the drift toward the shaft. As the powerful blast pushed Earl and his partner toward the shaft, they grabbed a loaded ore car and held on. With the rush of air came clouds of rock dust. A flood of water poured down the shaft. At the station they were met by the mucker, the brakeman, the mule skinner, and a mule. The skinner, a usually unexcitable Dutchman, was breathless: "The wind blow me along and brakeman come flying over my head!"

He had been picked up bodily by the rush of air that blew the empty four-car train off the track. The mucker stepped back into a niche and was

18.	Loss of both arms above elbow	2,000
19.	Loss of either arm below elbow	500
20.	Loss of both arms below elbow	2,000
21.	Loss of either thumb	200
22.	Loss of either index finger	150
23.	Loss of either middle, ring, or little finger	150
24.	Loss of an ear	100
25.	Loss of the nose	150
26.	Loss of a great toe	150

27. In all cases of fatal accidents funeral expenses not exceeding $125 will be allowed by the company.
28. In case of temporary disability, injured party, if unmarried and living with no dependents, will receive no compensation other than he is entitled to, such as surgical attendance and hospital facilities.
29. If married and living with family at time of accident, he will receive no compensation for first seven days, and thereafter for a period not exceeding three months, $1.50 for every day lost.
30. No relief under this schedule unless release is signed.
31. Amputation made against the advice of company surgeon will not be compensated for.

There were 1,700 employees in and about the mines and mills.
Inspection was made May 22 and 27, 1913.[11]

not bothered. The mule stood still. The water roared down the hoisting compartment of the shaft. The five miners sat down to wait, guessing at how long it would take the water to fill up the great labyrinth of workings below them. There was no escape.

But, like the nightmare, their fears did not come true. The cascading torrent lessened, and through the water stream a cage arrived, carrying the shift boss. He explained that the cave-in extended clear to the surface, but not out under the channel. The water came from a broken dam in a reservoir that had been constructed at the 770-foot level to hold excess water pumped from the mine. The shift boss told the shaken crew they could go home if they wanted, or they could continue to work the shift. Earl was the only one who stayed. The boss took him up to the broken dam, gave him a hammer, and told him to break up the concrete and clean it out so a new dam could be built. In three days a dam was ready.

Earl proved himself tireless and versatile. He tackled any assignment underground, and proved to be a fierce competitor in the all-important Fourth of July games.

Life in Treadwell was good for Earl. He considered staying on through the winter, until his classmate Clark "Brick" Will, who was also working in one of the mines, came into his room and announced: "I'm going to Seattle on the SS *Jefferson* in the morning. Better pack up and come along; we're already nearly a month late for school." Earl left with him.[12]

SEVEN

———◆———

View from the Mansion

On the maps it was called the Superintendent's Residence, but it really was a mansion, grander than the governor's mansion across the channel in Juneau, the newly designated capital of the District of Alaska. —MARION KELLY

Like Willy and Nell Kelly, Robert and Veronica Kinzie came to Treadwell from San Francisco as newlyweds. Veronica Kennedy was a San Francisco debutante; Robert was an 1894 graduate of the University of California School of Mines. Kinzie had worked for F. W. Bradley in the Esperanza mine in Mexico. Impressed by the young man's grasp of hard-rock mining, F. W. brought him on as assistant superintendent of the Treadwell complex in 1901.

In a few short years, Robert unexpectedly rose to the top position at the age of thirty-one, after a strange twist of events when Superintendent Joseph MacDonald was forced to resign after shooting a miner.

MacDonald, superintendent since 1901, had a reputation as a despotic and violent man. Always armed, he was famous as a great pistol marksman, and could shoot the spots out of a playing card at fifty paces.[1]

The superintendent's residence dominated the center of town. Those who lived there called it "The Big House." The assistant superintendent's home ("The Little House") was just across the plaza. (Courtesy of the Alaska State Library, Case and Draper Collection, P39-0893.)

Treadwell Mines Superintendents

1881–1889	John Treadwell
1889–1890	Thomas Mien
1890–1898	Robert Duncan
1898–1901	John P. Corbus
1901–1904	Joseph MacDonald
1904–1914	Robert Kinzie
1914–1917	Philip R. Bradley
1917–1918	Russell Wayland
1918–1922	Lou Metzgar

Sarah Corbus (right), wife of Superintendent John Corbus (and sister-in-law of previous superintendent Robert Duncan), shares tea in the mansion, 1900. (Courtesy of the Alaska Electric Light and Power Company.)

On the morning of May 14, 1902, the superintendent came out of the mansion to the plaza to confront a miner, N. C. "Yakima" Jones, an ex–deputy marshal, known as a gentle man and a devout Quaker. Several months earlier, MacDonald had had a verbal altercation with Jones and threatened him in public. Jones had repeatedly petitioned the superintendent to close down the mines on Sunday so workers could attend church. MacDonald would not hear of it. After a heated exchange of words MacDonald fired the contents of his revolver—four bullets—into Jones, who died an hour later. MacDonald was indicted for the murder, but he pleaded self-defense. The trial brought claims of bribes and threats to eyewitnesses. MacDonald presented some character witnesses, and he went free.[2]

The pastor of Our Lady of the Mines church lamented, "The case was evident and public sentiment sided with the innocent murdered man, there was no one to say a word and denounce MacDonald. Judges, press, jury dared not to speak out . . . and MacDonald came out of the whole proceedings the hero of the country. Poor country, venal press,

The Corbus cousins and dog in the garden of the mansion, 1900. (Courtesy of the Alaska Electric Light and Power Company.)

weak justice, low grade of humanity!" Another incredulous local minister wondered "how a violent man of such low moral and intellectual instincts who never walks about unarmed, can be put at the head of 1,200 men." He further opined, "[Think of] what good could be done if a better man were in his place."[3] Within a year, MacDonald was moved out of his job, and the "better man" put in his place was Assistant Superintendent Robert A. Kinzie.

In 1904, the Kinzies moved from the assistant superintendent's spacious residence, called "The Little House," into what management called "The Big House" (and the townspeople called "The Mansion"). The Kinzies had two young boys, Hunter and Robert, soon joined by a sister, Veronica. Life in the mansion was a blend of the ambitious mining moguls and glamorous San Francisco socialites. Even in this frontier mining camp, Veronica Kennedy Kinzie maintained the role of gracious hostess. The five bedrooms and two living rooms of the Big House served as a hotel for visiting notables. Financiers, politicians, and mining engineers from all over the world came to this northern outpost to explore the Treadwell mine complex and its town.

When dignitaries were expected, Mrs. Kinzie ran up to the glass-enclosed turret that topped the mansion, and looked out the south-facing windows. When she spotted the passenger steamer turning into Gastineau Channel, she knew she had three quarters of an hour to get ready for the guests. To help in her demanding role, she had a Japanese cook, a Japanese houseboy, and a Mexican governess for the children.

In the Mansion's formal dining room, with its cream patterned wallpaper, mulberry carpet, and California-style bay window facing the channel, guests sat around a huge oak table, which had a bell hidden underneath to call the servants. They ate salmon, halibut, venison, and sometimes bear, drank fine liquors, smoked their pipes and cigars, and discussed the technological miracle happening literally under their feet.

The steady production, profitability, and large workforce of this corporate enterprise made it a target for union organizers, so another hot topic around the dinner table was how to keep the Western Federation of Miners from forming a union at Treadwell.

Robert Allan Kinzie, graduate of the University of California School of Mines, came from a military family. His father fought in the Civil War. (Courtesy of the Alaska State Library, Robert Allen Kinzie Photograph Collection, P13-001.)

Usually, the Kinzie children were not invited to VIP dinners, but when dessert was served Robert and Hunter crept down the grand staircase to look through the balustrade, hoping to catch the eye of a sympathetic guest or be offered one of the delicacies from the chef. Upstairs, the boys entertained themselves shinnying high up pipes to the soaring ceilings in the playroom. (The builders had come from the tropics, where high ceilings made sense to keep the rooms cool.) While matters of profit and politics were being discussed on the main floor, the boys jumped up and down on the leather couch at the end of the upstairs hallway. Once, they bounced through the window and ended up on the ground under the dining-room window, disrupting dinner.[4]

Soon after he took charge of the Treadwell complex, young Superintendent Kinzie planned a grand reception for Wilford B. Hoggatt, a former mine superintendent in the Berner's Bay district north of Juneau. President Theodore Roosevelt had just appointed him Governor of the District of Alaska. The Kinzie boys were included for this special occasion. Mrs. Kinzie's practice was to send her children a formal invitation through the mail, to put them on their best behavior. That dinner and reception scheduled for April 18, 1906, was abruptly canceled when an earthquake of historic magnitude struck San Francisco. On Douglas Island, business came to a halt as most Treadwell residents had friends or relatives in San Francisco. (Among the thousand people who perished in the quake was the sister of the Treadwell company treasurer, who was killed when her chimney collapsed.) As the Treadwell company headquarters on Powell Street succumbed to the conflagration, rescuers dragged out the vault containing Treadwell's business records and mining maps. Officials waited two days for the vault to cool down before opening it, but as soon as the door was cracked, the contents spontaneously burst into flame. Everything was lost. Among the structures that survived the quake and fire was the United States Mint, the repository of Treadwell gold bullion. Before the ashes were cool, authorities laid blame on San Francisco's "era of irresponsible pell-mell development that built in unstable areas and blindly pursued profit while ignoring principles of sound engineering." The phrase had some relevance in those heady days of Treadwell, when pursuit of profit trumped sound engineering in the mines' support systems too.[5]

Gastineau Channel residents took up a collection for earthquake relief. Contributions included $99 from Douglas, $1,822 from Juneau, and $3,600 from Treadwell.[6]

<hr />

Mrs. Kinzie entertained as her husband's position required, but she did not accept many invitations to tea or cards. She wanted to be available if her husband called and invited her to view a new face, or take a trek to the Ditch. "Seeing a new face" meant going down into the mine with him when a promising new vein of gold-bearing white quartz was uncovered. Underground, she greeted the miners and asked about their children.

Her husband's invitation to a winter trip along the Ditch meant strapping on skis or snowshoes for an uphill climb behind the town, following along an eighteen-mile web of creeks, ditches, and flumes that collected water and channeled it down to drive the water wheels powering the mills. Up there Superintendent Kinzie checked in with Jake Manning, the longtime Ditch tender, to see how things were running: Could water be drawn from the pond high up in the muskeg? Were there ice chunks blocking passage?

Veronica Kennedy, former socialite, tried to adapt to the life of the mining town her husband ran. She had been smitten with Robert Kinzie from the time she laid eyes on him in high school. She even fished and hunted with him. At their cabin on nearby Admiralty Island she killed her first and last deer, whose great brown eyes haunted her for months. She never ate venison again.[7]

Mrs. Kinzie was proud of her husband's success in Treadwell. When they first arrived, the camp was in a deplorable state. Superintendent Kinzie rebuilt the rooming and boarding houses, and built the Treadwell Club with services and activities to keep the miners happy. For any workers getting married, he offered an allowance to build the house they wanted (as long as they painted it the company colors) in the belief that family men were more stable employees.

Mrs. Kinzie didn't understand the complaints and threats of the miners who wanted to strike to form a union. They frightened her. In

Treadwell town leaders and army troop members pose on the mansion steps during the labor strikes of 1907–1908. Superintendent Kinzie is in the middle on the left, in the light-colored hat. (Courtesy of the Alaska State Library, Case and Draper Collection, P39-972.)

San Francisco, someone had thrown a bomb on to the porch of the mine's president, F. W. Bradley. His wife, Mary, looked out her window to see him crawling away on his hands and knees.[8]

Mrs. Kinzie knew that her husband had received a letter saying "if you don't stop fighting the union we'll get every one of your children from the first to the last." He hired two Pinkerton detectives from Seattle to be with the children at all times. The men took Robert and Hunter to school and back, and even watched them while they played in the yard. Finally, Kinzie appealed to his friend the governor, who shared his anti-union sentiments. The superintendent knew that government power was on the company's side and he could count on every lawman and judge to back the owners over the workers. He requested soldiers from Fort Seward in Haines.

One misty spring morning in 1907, Mrs. Kinzie looked out the bay window of her second-story bedroom and saw a troop of uniformed men coming up from the pier. Before the morning shift of miners went to work, a city of tents rose like mushrooms in the plaza. The officers moved into the comfortable Little House next to the Mansion.

The army was there to intimidate union organizers. But for the children they were a source of entertainment. The soldiers staged a show at the Treadwell Club and taught the Kinzie boys a new song that became young Robert's favorite: "I went to the animals' fair, the birds and the beasts were there, the old baboon by the light of the moon was combing his auburn hair. . . ." These thespians were the same troops that Marion Kelly later charmed out of their "U.S." lapel pins, one for herself and "one for my brother."

Kinzie had another use for the Pinkerton men. Keeping close tabs on gold production, he noticed the assay office showed a higher value of ore going into the stamp mill than the gold recovered in the process. Some was missing. Finding a leak was difficult because the milling and gold-recovery systems were so complex. Kinzie hired a detective, who tracked a local woman making regular trips to a Seattle assay office where she deposited gold. The detective had her arrested, and she confessed that her husband stole "small portions" of the gold-mercury amalgam and took it home to extract the gold. They had retrieved 164 ounces.

Surprisingly, there had been only one other theft of gold in Treadwell, in 1894. In the chlorination plant someone had sneaked in and "cleaned out" the tanks of collected precipitates that were 90 percent pure gold. Three hundred sixty ounces of gold were missing. The local marshal tracked down and arrested two men and recovered all the gold, the final cache hidden on Killisnoo Island sixty miles away.[9]

People took risks like this because the United States was in the grips of gold fever, which was still evident at the 1909 Alaska-Yukon-Pacific Exposition in Seattle. Treadwellians boasted that the most conspicuous feature of that international exposition was the gold exhibit: an elaborate booth, beautifully ornamented and brilliantly lit. The center held a six-foot glass cube and in this, on a stand of black velvet, sat five of the largest

A picnic at the beach. Left to right: Honey Kelly, Mrs. Robert Kinzie, baby Eugenia, Marion Kelly, unidentified man and two women in rear, Mr. and Mrs. David Kinzie with son David, Hunter and Robert Kinzie in foreground, Merle Thomas behind them. (Courtesy of the Kelly Family Collection.)

nuggets found in the Territory of Alaska, along with towers of 125-pound gold bricks and a sprinkling of nuggets and dust.

Visitors to the exhibit saw a panorama of the great Treadwell mine with its famous Glory Hole and they also received a twenty-five-page illustrated booklet rhapsodizing on "Treadwell: An Alaskan Fulfillment." The paean asserted that "the great mine can afford to leave the veil of the Future undisturbed, pointing merely to the Past and Present as justification of her right to the title."[10]

Back up north in Treadwell, this booklet and vials of fool's gold remained the top souvenirs that steamship tourists wanted. Raymond Kelly and Robert Kinzie were the entrepreneurs. Raymond saved the glass vials from chemicals used in his photography hobby. Then he and Robert Kinzie scouted the vanner room at the 300 Mill and scavenged pyrite chunks to fill the vials. When Robert's father learned about the eager young prospectors, he sternly scolded Robert for getting in the way. Raymond continued his venture alone.

Treadwell was full of adventures for young boys like Hunter and Robert Kinzie, even if they were the boss's sons. Some days, they ventured early in the morning to the blacksmith shop near the pier, and if they built up the charcoal in a proper form for the blacksmiths on the forges, they were allowed to heat a piece of iron and hammer it out. On the way back, the boys stopped in at the butcher shop, where great slabs of meat hung on hooks and green pickles and black and green olives filled big barrels. If the boys delivered meat to the townspeople, the butcher paid them with a handful of briny olives. Some evenings, the brothers rounded up the four company cows and brought them back to the barn to be milked. The boys' reward was having fresh milk squirted right into their mouths.

From the glass cupola atop the mansion the boys watched dancing green waves of the aurora borealis flittering behind snow-covered Mount Roberts, which seemed to float above the Juneau ice fields. One morning in 1912, the sun rose red in an ash-filled sky after Mount Katmai erupted on the Alaska Peninsula 750 miles away. Powdered ash coated the glass panes. If the boys went outside, the dust stung their skin, like being attacked by insects.[11]

The Kinzies had a menagerie. They rode Old Tom, the big white horse, now retired after working for years down in the mines. Four or five kids got on Old Tom's back as he wandered around the flat area between the assay office and the store. When Tom got tired of his passengers, he walked under a pipe that went over the road and pushed everybody off. The boys hitched their goat to a red cart built by the company carpenter, a man from Belgium. He also crafted a fine little oak barge for Robert, who lost it in a stream that swooshed out into the channel. The boys had pet rabbits, a deer, a bear cub, and two poor porcupines that the miners taunted by tossing their hats at the quills, breaking them off.

The Kinzies attended the Catholic church and sat in front of the Kellys. The boys' mother often put her arm around them, and Marion Kelly envied the affectionate gesture until she learned that the boys were being told to keep quiet and hold still.

Treadwell sat in a basin of treasures. Above the tree stumps and haze that hung from the smokestacks, a glacier-studded, mountain-rimmed pocket held the town. From the ground, gold came up out of the noise and grit of the camp. A few miles down the channel, icebergs, "making a noise like some huge animal in mortal pain," separated from the Taku glacier. When the walls of ice broke into pieces and splashed down, water shot up fifteen feet and made the sea look like soapsuds. The Kinzies could watch from their wraparound porch as the icebergs floated past Treadwell.

The superintendent often sent men out to lasso a piece and put it in sawdust in the icehouse behind the Mansion so the family had ice all summer long. Big chunks of ice hauled ashore cooled the mines' compressors and saved energy. Fishermen regularly corralled the bergs and sold them to the company for a penny a pound for use in cooling machinery. A five-degree reduction in temperature brought a 1 percent savings in efficiency[12]—and efficiency was an F. W. Bradley imperative. Nature could be appreciated, but Treadwell's story of success came from putting nature to work.

Icebergs were both useful and dangerous. In February 1910, the channel filled with floating ice, and several eight-hundred-to-one-thousand-ton bergs lodged against a beachside train trestle, grinding a scow to bits and endangering the wharf. Kinzie ordered them blown up, and the blast sounded like the old days of surface mining at the Glory Hole.[13]

That same month, the company completed construction of an eagerly anticipated swimming pool. Mrs. Kinzie's brother, Assistant Superintendent Eugene Kennedy, a former star swimmer at University of California, announced plans for swimming lessons, competitions, water polo teams, and carnivals.

The next month brought another bleak reminder that daily life in Treadwell was dangerous. On March 9, as Superintendent Kinzie worked late into the night over some mine plans at his office in the Mansion, a powerful explosion rocked the 1,100-foot level of the Mexican mine. At midnight, responding to the shrill call of the company whistle, Kinzie ran to the mine and for the next forty hours worked to rescue or account for miners. Thirty-nine men were killed.

Tragedy in the mine was mirrored in a Kinzie family tragedy. At the time of the explosion, the superintendent's wife and children were in San

Every winter the company flooded the plaza for ice skating. Superintendent Kinzie with Assistant Superintendent Kennedy and their wives joined in the ritual. (Courtesy of the Kinzie family.)

Francisco, where three-year-old Veronica died from an intestinal blockage in spite of the best care available. This devastating blow left young Robert, who had a special bond with his baby sister, heartbroken. To distract him, his ninety-year-old grandfather took him out to witness an historical event, the arrival of Halley's Comet, streaking with its brilliant long tail across the California sky. "Look at that, Robert! It's the closest the comet has ever come to the earth and the first time ever photographed! You'll see it fly by again in seventy-five years, when you're eighty-five!" Ten-year-old Robert couldn't imagine being eighty-five; he wondered if Raymond Kelly in Treadwell got a picture of the comet with his Kodak.

Robert was reminded of the comet a few years later when he saw a fire in the Treadwell head frame. He and Hunter and their mother stood at the Mansion window, their new baby sister, Eugenia, asleep in the nursery. Big burning timbers and boards flamed into the air, from the huge chimney created by the shaft and head frame, then came down and shattered sparks all over. Once again, their father and uncle, the superintendent and assistant superintendent, rushed to the site to get the miners out of the way of the treacherous updraft.

One brutally cold winter, Superintendent Kinzie rushed to a fire at the coal bunker near the Ready Bullion mine a mile down the beach. When the fire was under control, he started back in the driving rain and howling Taku wind. He crawled home along the railroad, clinging to the ties between the tracks. His distraught wife met him at the door with a hot drink and then struggled to cut the frozen buttons off his ice-encrusted coat.[14]

Fires were a regular hazard in an industrial mining town, and the management knew how to train and prepare for them. However, a more worrisome predicament for the management was evidence of ongoing caving in the mine and land slumping on the surface. Tracks and trestles dropped several feet, making them useless for carrying the materials and ore throughout the town.

Near midnight, on October 28, 1913, a violent shaking roused the whole town. Underground caverns collapsed like dominoes along the line between the Treadwell and 700 Foot mines. The sleeping townspeople awoke abruptly as dishes rolled from shelves and crashed onto cottage floors.[15] And the next day everyone went back to work as usual.

In his decade as superintendent, Kinzie had dealt with fires, explosions, strikes, cave-ins, fatal accidents, and personal threats. And yet the Treadwell complex maintained its position as a mining phenomenon of unlimited promise.

Kinzie focused on that promise of the future. He knew that increased production meant a need for more power, and acquiring water rights was as important as mining claims. Kinzie and a partner staked the water rights on the Speel River south of Juneau, planning to profit from the water power that could be developed there. President F. W. Bradley felt betrayed: He thought Kinzie went outside his authority to take a personal interest and should have signed the rights over to the Treadwell Company. This created a bitter rift between Kinzie and Bradley. In 1914, Kinzie and his brother-in-law, Assistant Superintendent Eugene Kennedy, were forced to resign.[16] They moved back to California.

The Kinzie family departure left the town shocked, saddened, and puzzled. No official explanation was given for the abrupt move after Kinzie's thirteen years leading the golden age of Treadwell. The company employees gave an elaborate farewell dinner dance where the outgoing superintendent was presented with a gold ring with the trademark Treadwell "T" outlined in diamonds. This was the logo on the Treadwell flag that a proud and patriotic Kinzie erected years before in the plaza next to the largest, tallest American flag flying in Alaska.

To replace Kinzie, Bradley turned to family. He brought in his younger brother, Philip R. Bradley, as the new superintendent. Phil was a mining engineer who had graduated from the University of California and had worked in Canada, South America, and British Guiana. He and his wife, Mabel, a jovial and amiable couple, moved into the Mansion with two boys, rambunctious ten-year-old Philip Jr., and easygoing eight-year-old Hank. Within a year they prepared to welcome a new family

The Bradleys gathered on the steps of the mansion. F. W. with his brother Philip; Philip's wife, Mabel; their sons Hank and Philip Jr.; and twin daughters Ruth Frances and Frances Ruth. (Courtesy of the Alaska Electric Light and Power Company.)

member, and were surprised when Mrs. Bradley gave birth to twin girls, Ruth Frances and Frances Ruth. They had to wire relatives in San Francisco to send duplicates of everything.

The Bradleys put their mark on the Mansion, adding bedrooms, an expanded nursery, and a classroom where the governess schooled the boys. The playroom housed a big train set that attracted all the kids in town. The room was also the setting for ballroom-dancing classes and boxing lessons from Jack Wilson for the Bradley boys.

Bradley was well liked by the men who worked for him. Even the miners called him Phil. He knew their names and treated them as friends, regularly joining them for a game of pool. He had a good sense of humor and a spirit of adventure. As a hobby, he experimented with hydroponic gardening, raising tomatoes in the mansion's glassed-in turret and pollinating them with a camel's-hair brush. Young Philip's chore was to carry water up to the top floor each day.

Irving Anderson, the hoist man's son, and Hank Bradley, the superintendent's son, became pals. They played every day and went to motion pictures at the club and swim days at the natatorium. Once, a bunch of miners thought it would be funny to take the boss's son down to the red-light district in Douglas; Irving went along. The ladies just waved to them and called out, "You be good boys, now!"

Irving developed a boyhood crush on the Bradleys' governess, Mrs. Chastain. He offered to take her on a hike to see the spring flowers up along the Ditch, in the fields behind town. The Bradleys' cook packed them a lunch with sandwiches of liverwurst pâté, an exotic food to Irving. Mrs. Chastain was thrilled when they reached the high field filled with violets, Johnny-jump-ups, and butter yellow lilies floating on a pond. She said she wasn't invited out often and this was the most beautiful walk she had ever taken. She told Irving about her country, Mexico. When they got back to the Big House, the Bradley boys joined them and the Japanese houseboy brought out soda pop, another luxury not available at the Anderson home.[17]

When the Anderson family moved to Seattle in 1916, Phil Jr. took over Irving's *Alaska Daily Empire* paper route. He met the boat each day at five PM, and continued Irving's tradition and stopped by the machine shop, where Willy Kelly helped him fill up the tires of his bike.

With the other boys of Treadwell, Phil Jr. joined right in to sell fool's gold and photos to the excursionists coming by steamship from the Outside. Unlike Raymond Kelly, who sold homemade postcards, Phil Jr. struck a deal with well-known local photographer Ed Andrews, and got a percentage selling Andrews's professionally done local scenes and portraits.[18]

⁂

Fooling the tourists was great fun, and Philip Bradley Sr. joined in. A mountain ash tree grew next to the picket fence in front of the mansion. Hank and his father strung fresh lemons on wires and hung them on the branches, so it looked like they were growing there. Tourists stopped and took photos and marveled at one more wonder of Treadwell. The mining camp had touches of California: a mansion with bay windows with flower boxes and a wraparound porch, raspberry bushes, tennis courts, a swimming pool with carnivals and water polo teams, a skeet-shooting range, a grand waterside social club—and even a lemon tree.

However, Bradley and the management had more serious matters to deal with. In 1917, Philip Bradley became Treadwell's general manager and consulting engineer, the powerful position formerly held by his brother, F. W. Bradley. Russell Wayland was named superintendent. (The Bradleys continued to live in the Mansion.) Underground cave-ins had been increasing in the mines and the surface facilities were being affected, too. Another threat had come from across the channel. Bart Thane, the aggressive manager of the Alaska-Gastineau Gold Mine, had determined that the three-way fragmented ownership of Treadwell made the operation vulnerable; he had designs for a takeover and set about buying up stock. The shrewd and well-connected F. W. Bradley rallied his financial partners to thwart that takeover. F. W. then put things in motion to consolidate the four mines into a single organization.

A decade earlier, Superintendent Kinzie had faced down the threat of the Western Federation of Miners, saving himself and F. W. Bradley from what would have been for them a loathsome and intolerable situation: a powerful union operating in the Treadwell mines. Then F. W. had squelched the challenges to his authority coming from both Robert Kinzie and Barth Thane. But the Bradley brothers were learning that other powers could threaten their control and their profits. Forces were at work that would make the Western Federation of Miners struggle just a footnote to the story.

EIGHT

❖

Labor Troubles and the Western Federation of Miners

The workers are more powerful with their hands in their pockets than all the property of the capitalists. —JOSEPH ETTOR

WHEN THE TWENTIETH CENTURY OPENED, investors in Douglas Island's Treadwell mines rhapsodized about their endless supply of gold.[1] Boasting close to two thousand employees and twenty years of record-setting production, the mine owners congratulated themselves. High wages and good working conditions had kept the mines and the town humming, and most important, management felt, their approach had kept unions out.

Working thousands of feet underground, hard-rock miners were well aware of Treadwell's central truth: Without their labor, mine owners couldn't make a dime. And the owners knew it. Despite the company's ability to call on the forces of state power—the national guard, the army, and local lawmen—the owning class feared the one thing that could halt the flow of money into their pockets, a strike by an industrial union.

The organized labor movement had been growing across the United States. Mining was one of many large industries—like auto, steel, rubber, meat packing, and railroads—that were making America the world's undisputed powerhouse. In the late 1800s, unions in America were growing too, to promote and protect workers' rights, better pay, shorter working hours, and safety in the workplace. As the country touted the explosion of wealth, union organizers were intent on linking corporate profits to the exploitation of workers. As the captains of industry waged a bitter war against workers who tried to organize into a union, the leaders of the working class strove to empower their compatriots to believe that, in the words of organizer Joseph Ettor, "all they have to do is recognize their own solidarity. They have nothing to do but fold their arms and the world will stop. The workers are more powerful with their hands in their pockets than all the property of the capitalists."[2]

———◦◦◦———

Union mergers of the copper, silver, and gold miners of Montana, Idaho, Colorado, South Dakota, and Utah mirrored the conglomeration by industry. Miners resolved to form an industrial union for all mines across the United States into Canada and Alaska. The Western Federation of Miners (WFM) was formed in 1893 by the merger of several miners' unions. Spreading across the West, WFM represented copper miners from Butte, Montana; silver and lead miners from Coeur d'Alene, Idaho; gold miners from Colorado; and hard-rock miners from South Dakota and Utah. The movement gained momentum at the Bunker Hill and Sullivan Company silver mines in Idaho, where F. W. Bradley was president.

At Bunker Hill and Sullivan Company, Bradley used all the powers at his disposal to oppose unions and organizers. His initial refusal to raise miners' daily wages from $3 to $3.50 escalated conflict, resulting in the bloody union strikes of 1899, declaration of martial law, and the incarceration of seven hundred men. At Bunker Hill, Bradley could take credit for surviving a decade-long attack from the WFM, defeating the union, and destroying its power in the Coeur d'Alenes. "Not surprisingly, the Western Federation of Miners directed an intense hatred toward Bunker Hill and Sullivan and its leadership, while the management of mines throughout the West hoped to emulate Bradley."[3]

Mine management frequently requested the assistance of state militia and federal troops to keep order during strikes. When Bunker Hill company guards shot and killed five strikers, the workers from the mine disarmed the guards and marched a hundred scabs (strikebreakers) out of town. Idaho Governor Frank Steunenberg declared martial law and asked President William McKinley to send federal troops, who rounded up strikers and supporters and threw them into the bull pens. Governmental authorities often supported management and opposed not only the unions but also all social legislation that might interfere with businesses' right to run its affairs in any way it deemed necessary.

To galvanize new recruits, WFM organizers told stories of the bull pens and other company attempts to crush unions. They told about twelve hundred miners held in the Coeur d'Alene mining district for six months. Many died while their families starved, and only twelve were ever charged with a crime. Stories of the Bunker Hill and Sullivan Company strikes in Idaho spread through union newspapers across the country. Stories were also told about Telluride and Cripple Creek, Colorado, where thousands were herded from their homes at the point of the bayonet, loaded into freight cars as if they were cattle, and deported by the military without trial or charge except that they were union men.[4]

Repression of union activity was answered by violent strikes and militant action, which came to be seen as trademarks of the Western Federation of Miners. Cripple Creek strikers protesting long hours and low

---

IN IDAHO, Governor Frank Steunenberg had worked steadfastly to break the miners' union. Even after his retirement in 1905, he remained a force. He was killed by a bomb that exploded on his front gate. The killer was not a union protestor, but an agent provocateur named Harry Orchard, who was hired by mining-company interests. Orchard first claimed he had been paid by WFM officials to murder the governor, but later confessed to the truth. Renowned lawyer Clarence Darrow won an acquittal for officers of the WFM, including William "Big Bill" Haywood, who had been charged with the murder.[5]

pay had dynamited mine buildings and equipment. Management there finally made concessions and agreed to an eight-hour day and miner's pay of $3 day, which became the union standard.

By 1905 the WFM boasted forty thousand members. That same year miners, loggers, field hands, cooks, and all wage earners who wanted "one big union" joined the newly formed Industrial Workers of the World (IWW, also called the Wobblies). Labor was on the move. Organizers for the Wobblies criss-crossed North America, riding the rails to spread the word of One Big Union. Many Western Federation miners did not embrace the more revolutionary class warfare of the Wobblies.

As new frontiers opened, WFM looked to Alaska, where it saw a "rich lode of unorganized miners"[6] to bolster its membership. In 1905, the WFM had not one member in Alaska; by 1908 there were six thousand in at least three Alaska goldfields: Nome, which had "stolen the thunder (and most of the miners) from the Klondike,"[7] Ellamar, and Treadwell.

In spring 1907, WFM organizers came to southeast Alaska, and on March 29 called a meeting in Douglas. This was the third organizing attempt in ten years and organizers correctly read a new ripeness there. Treadwell employed nine hundred underground miners and an eager crowd of seven hundred attended the meeting. Organizers capitalized on ongoing gripes about company rules that required single employees to live together in company housing even when there was deeply held animosity between various cultural groups. "The boardinghouses were on the verge of explosion," wrote one historian, when a Montenegrin shot a Japanese cook. The WFM organizers deftly channeled the hostility to focus on Treadwell management, and "instead of a riot, the town was faced with a union."[8]

Single miners complained that company housing was expensive, $1 a day, and dangerous. To recruit the married employees to the union, organizers urged opposition to a mandatory deduction of inflated fees for the Treadwell Club and hospital services. By the end of the rousing evening of March 29, the crowd came together to form Douglas Island Miners' Local No. 1, designated as WFM Local 109, led by Yanco Terzich, a Montenegrin.

The freshly minted union presented its grievances to Superintendent Kinzie, who in the hidebound tradition of mine managers vowed that

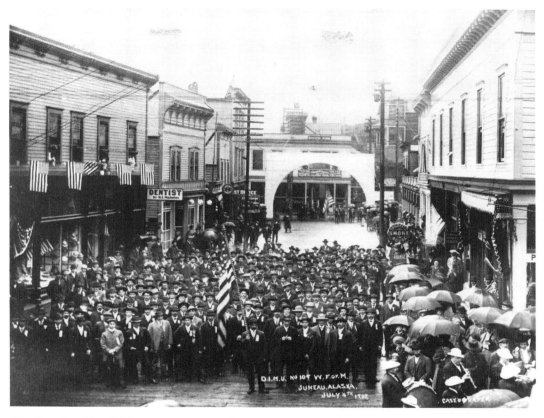

The Douglas Island Miners' Union Number 109, Western Federation of Miners members marching in the Fourth of July parade, 1907, Juneau. (Courtesy of the Alaska AFL-CIO records, Archives and Special Collections, Consortium Library, University of Alaska Anchorage.)

he would "close the mines before he would deal with the Douglas Island upstarts." Known as "an anti-union martinet of the first order" Kinzie promptly fired all union miners.[9]

An expanded crowd of eight hundred miners met on March 30, and in a show of newfound solidarity voted to strike until the company agreed to two demands: Pay miners $30 a month to cover room and board wherever they wanted to live, including Douglas and Juneau, not just the company facilities in Treadwell, and rehire all fired employees.

Predictably, Kinzie refused the demands. Fearing violence and possible destruction of mine property, he called for federal troops from Fort Seward in Haines "to keep the union anarchists from Treadwell's powder

*Soldiers from the Tenth Infantry at Fort Seward in front of the Treadwell Club.
They came at Superintendent Kinzie's request. Little Marion Kelly admired
a soldier's collar pins, and he gave them to her. (Courtesy of the Kelly Family
Collection.)*

magazine." Kinzie received support from Governor Wilford B. Hoggatt,
Marshal James M. Shoup, and Judge James Wickersham. Governor Hoggatt was "extremely concerned about the ability of 75 soldiers from Fort
Seward to hold off the 700 to 800 strikers," whose actions were "growing
more dangerous" by the day.[10]

An article in the *New York Times* on that day reported the event as
much less threatening:

March 29. Company F, Tenth Infantry, arrived at Treadwell early
to-day on the army steamer Peterson with orders from Gen. Bush
of Vancouver Barracks to aid the local Marshals. The arrival of
the troops was unexpected.

There is no disorder here. A number of arrests of miners for carrying concealed weapons have been made, but a peace committee of the union is keeping a strict patrol of the town, and there is little if any drunkenness.

Supt. Kinzie says that ten cases of powder were stolen from the Treadwell mine. This is denied by the union leaders.

The vision of marauding miners and an unguarded powder magazine caused trepidation among mine managers everywhere. But their real terror found root in corporations' primal fear of a loss of power and loss of profits. Adding to the threat, the unions were not the only agitators against the capitalist system. Public opinion was weighing in through an editorial in Wrangell's *Alaska Sentinel*. V. P. Snyder, a U.S. Commissioner, blamed the strike on the Treadwell companies. Snyder made the owning class nervous when he called for government ownership of all enterprises "employing more than 50 men."[11] He shared the conviction of the miners, who pointed to their low wages and dangerous working conditions and proclaimed it unjust that the mine owners "do not find the gold, mine the gold, or mill the gold, but by some weird alchemy all the gold belongs to them." Snyder was removed from his government job after publishing another radical editorial proclaiming socialism as a great creed that promised practical solutions to such evils as strikes.[12]

This socialist sentiment was tucked into Wobbly songs and the literature passed from worker to worker in reading rooms and bunkhouses wherever men toiled in the industrial empires. Union newspapers and pamphlets raised issues of class struggle, race, free speech, the treatment of women, and foment in the European countries. Management might be surprised to know that miners read the classics, history and political works by Marx and Engels. Somewhere on Douglas Island striking miners were singing the rousing lyrics of "The International," the workers' anthem in the Wobbly songbook:

Arise, ye prisoners of starvation!
    Arise, ye wretched of the earth,
For justice thunders condemnation,
    A better world's in birth.

No more tradition's chains shall bind us
  Arise, ye slaves; no more in thrall!
The earth shall rise on new foundations,
  We have been naught, we shall be all

Chorus:

'Tis the final conflict,
  Let each stand in his place,
The International Union
  Shall be the human race![13]

Up against a solid force of strikers, Kinzie tried to get some miners to side with him and settle with the company. He leaked a rumor to the *Alaska Daily Dispatch* that the Treadwell mines had been sold to the notoriously antiunion Guggenheims. "This tactic which was supposed to stampede the union into settling with the existing management was apparently too subtle for the Treadwell employees . . . and had no effect on the strike."[14] Strikers' morale was boosted by a report from Ellamar that importing strikebreakers there had failed miserably and the scabs had all joined the WFM. Fights broke out in Douglas and Treadwell saloons as brawlers on the side of strikers battled pro-company supporters. The superintendent took note of the seven hundred workers who backed the strike, and he was getting pressure from his own superiors in San Francisco for a settlement of the shutdown. On April 19, 1907, Kinzie announced that Treadwell would bow to the union demand for $1 a day payment to miners in lieu of board at the company housing. Strikers who had been fired could come back to their jobs without discrimination. But Treadwell would remain an open shop where union membership was not a precondition of employment, and union members and nonunion members would work side by side. Furthermore, the union was to be a protective organization. It could not collectively bargain for wages and conditions. The union agreed, mindful that if things got bad they would strike again.

Only a month after the settlement, miners' discontent again arose. Kinzie had brought in lower-paid immigrant labor to split the union into a two-tier system. Most of the Treadwell miners were foreign-born Finns, Serbians, and Montenegrins, but the company did employ a large number

of "white" native-born Americans. The superintendent encouraged forma-
tion of a "white-man's union" made up of English-speaking employees,
mostly surface workers. This group would break away from WFM Local
109. He hoped this would weaken the WFM and stir anti-immigrant
feelings. He was helped by the fact that local newspapers were filled with
heated antiunion rhetoric and anti-foreign ridicule.[15]

Kinzie got his way with the help of local officials. On February 12,
1908, Mayor M. S. "Mike" Hudson of Douglas announced that a new
miners' union would be formed that would be open to English-speaking
whites only. At a miners' meeting held on Valentine's Day speakers condemned the WFM, saying that the union "encouraged foreign leadership."
After anti-immigrant speakers rose to denigrate non-native, non-English-
speaking miners, a vote was taken to create the Alaska Miners' Union
(AMU) with a membership of one hundred.

A second union formed with encouragement from the Treadwell management.
The Alaska Labor Union No. 1 was for white English-speaking members.
(Courtesy of the Alaska AFL-CIO records, Archives and Special Collections,
Consortium Library, University of Alaska Anchorage.)

The AMU was a company union, made up of workers who were aligned politically and socially with the owning class. To the WFM miners, the new union was known as "Kinzie's scab hatchery." WFM Secretary Sewald Torkelson wrote in *Miner's Magazine* warning all miners not even to consider finding work in Treadwell as members of this "sweetheart" union.

Then Torkelson made a mistake that split the union and bolstered the company's position. To neutralize company criticism that the WFM "encouraged only foreign leadership," Torkelson pressed members to vote for a "white man's" ticket in the election of officers. However, the most popular possible contender for president of Local 109 was Yanco Terzich, a Serbian; Torkelson considered his origins a liability. As a protest, most WFM members refused to vote. Only sixty-four members cast ballots and those were for the "white" candidate.

Terzich petitioned WFM headquarters in Denver for permission to take Local 109 out on strike to prove that he was the legitimate leader of the majority. His supporters wanted to push for the eight-hour day and other demands that had been left out of the 1907 settlement with Kinzie. They called for a minimum wage of $3.50 per day, an end to club and hospital fees, and abolition of the foreman's control over assigning jobs. On March 20, Local 109 voted to strike for the second time in two years.

True to its anti-WFM underpinnings, the Alaska Miners' Union crossed picket lines, but the WFM ranks—which included most of the underground workers—held fast. True to its penchant for supporting company values, *Alaska Monthly Magazine* wrote: "The class of men who have been successful in the mines keep themselves aloof from unions. Socially considered there is no town in the states that gives more attention to the amenities of civilization than Treadwell." The *Douglas Island News* also discounted workers' demands and asserted that "complaints are unheard of, unless of blueberry pie being served in lunch boxes two days in a row."

Brawls broke out between strikers and "non-strikers" or "scabs" depending on what side one took. Kinzie had three men arrested for threatening his life.[16] Federal troops arrived again. Douglas and Juneau police cracked down on strikers, arresting two unionists for displaying guns on the picket line to frighten strikebreakers. Thirty strikers were nabbed by Douglas authorities on charges of "verbal assault." Kinzie enlisted strikebreakers from the ranks of unemployed miners in Seattle and San Francisco. WFM representatives aggressively picketed the recruiting center in Seattle and tried to block the new hires from getting on the SS *Humboldt* that was headed to Treadwell. But Kinzie had acted so fast that strikebreakers were on the boat before they could be warned away.

Treadwell strikers were heartened when Charles H. Moyer, their hero and national president of the WFM, came to Treadwell, Ellamar, and other Alaska mining towns to bolster the morale of his union men. When Moyer attempted to meet with the Treadwell superintendent to work out a compromise, Kinzie refused. Moyer did get a chance to give a major address in Juneau. He had a national following as a tough union miner who had taken many blows from the butt of a soldier's or policeman's rifle, making sarcastic remarks to his captors before losing consciousness. Moyer captivated audiences with his stories. In Juneau his speech at the Elks Club drew the largest crowd that had ever assembled in the newly designated capital town.[17]

IN THE MIDST OF THE FERVOR stirred by the Western Federation of Miners, union ties were often stronger than ethnic connections. During the 1907 labor struggles, two miners were killed underground: One was union, one nonunion, but both were to be buried by the Greek Orthodox Church. After services for the union member, his comrades asked the priest not to perform a service for the nonmember. The priest refused to honor the request, so the union members locked the church door and broke off the key. The funeral procession of the nonunion victim marched from the Serbian Slavonic Harmony hall and ran into the union group in front of the church. The horses were frightened and threatened to run away with the hearse. The union members didn't want the nonunion man buried in the consecrated ground of the Serbian cemetery. Two hundred Serbians, union and nonunion, filled the streets. The U.S. marshal enlisted neutral miners and townsmen to calm the group, and the procession and burial continued.[18]

Despite all the union efforts, the company went back to full production, and by February 1910 the strike faded away. Union influence rose up again in the election for Alaska congressional delegate when a WFM-backed Socialist candidate finished a strong second to Judge James Wickersham. The union voice (and threat) could take credit for the 1908 rise in Treadwell's wages that had been unchanged since the 1890s. That raise brought drillers' pay to $3.50 a day. (Henry Ford, the heretofore capitalist standard, was paying his auto workers $2.83.)

The dream of an Alaska completely organized by the Western Federation of Miners died at Treadwell. The union maintained a minimal presence in Nome, Juneau, and Valdez through World War I.[19] In 1916, the WFM became the International Union of Mine, Mill, and Smelter Workers, or the Mine Mill.

After the last Treadwell mine shut down in 1922, all mining activity was moved to the other side of Gastineau Channel, at the Alaska-Juneau Mine. The seeds of union spirit were transplanted, too.

NINE

<hr />

The Tlingit: Ancient Culture Meets Modern Industry

*By their own definition, the Tlingit were the
People of the Place That Had Everything.*

T HE PACIFIC COAST STEAMSHIP COMPANY's "Alaska Totem
Pole Route" promised encounters found only in the wild upper reaches of the continent: a close-up view of the Taku Glacier, a walking
tour of the famous Treadwell gold mine, a real Alaska Native village at
Wrangell. Provocative descriptions focused on the looks and customs of
the Tlingit and the mystery and power of their art, portrayed as that kind
of an exotic indigenous culture that curious tourists are drawn to.

> Coming up the inside passage the ship passes many Indian vil-
> lages, all belonging to a single great tribe, the Tlingit, bound
> together by a common language. It is not often that one would
> want to call a tourist's attention to an Indian village, for the aver-
> age encampment . . . is not the most attractive sight . . . but in the
> Tlingit town . . . they are the artistic savages of the world. In front
> of each log house, are one or two tall posts called 'totem poles,'
> which are logs on end, but on the seaward face, the savage sculptor
> exhausted all the resources of his barbaric imagination cutting

in hideous faces and figures . . . the houses are carved inside and out. Every utensil they have is sculptured deep with diabolical but well executed designs, and their spoons of mountain sheep and goat horn are marvels of . . . work.[1]

Arriving at Douglas Island, tourists disembarked next to another Tlingit Native village that stretched along the narrow beach from the sawmill in the town of Douglas down to the Treadwell wharf. Railroad tracks from the sawmill to the mines ran along the beach side of a double row of cabins on pilings, a few feet above the extreme high-tide mark. The air was filled with the smell of fish and the sound of dogs barking, children playing, chanting, and singing. Most cabins had boats or ca-

The Alaska Native village bordered the beach between the towns of Douglas and Treadwell. The railway connected the lumber mill with the mine complex. (Courtesy of the Alaska State Library Photograph Collection, P01-0965.)

noes in front because the Tlingit were a seafaring people, historically traveling as far south as Puget Sound in finely built and richly decorated cedar canoes.[2]

Early prospectors came to southeast Alaska in search of gold embedded in rock. Upon arriving, they encountered an indigenous people embedded in a culture formed over centuries, even millennia. Records show that in 1794, Captain Vancouver noted the presence of an Indian village on the west shore of Douglas Island. The Tlingit lived here, one of the many Native peoples that inhabited the four hundred miles of coastal mainland from British Columbia to Yakutat. Some stories describe a Douglas Island encampment that dates back nine thousand years.[3]

Tlingit means "the people," and the Tlingit named this area along the Gastineau Channel the "Place That Had Everything." By their definition, they were the People of the Place That Had Everything. The bounty they celebrated included a forest full of game; underbrush thick with berries, plants, and roots for food and medicine; and the generous sea and streams full of salmon, cod, herring smelt, halibut, eulachon (candlefish), seals, sea lions, shellfish, clams, mussels, sea urchins, and seaweed. The mountains were home to deer, bear, mountain goats, ptarmigan, grouse, and marmot. Because of the availability of a dependable and nutritious food supply, the Tlingit were not nomadic. They had permanent villages and hunting and fishing camps across an area. They stayed in place and developed a stable and sophisticated social structure that also allowed a high level of artistic expression.[4] Long before the area became known as the Juneau Gold Belt, two groups of Tlingit lived here: the Auk, centered on Auke Bay north of Juneau, and the Taku, based on the Taku River south of Juneau.

The Tlingit did not understand the excitement and greed that gold set off in white men who were coming into the area. Hunting was the Natives' primary occupation, and they found gold a poor substitute for lead bullets. When their lead was gone, they melted down pewter pots, and when that ran out, only then would they laboriously pound gold out of the rock to make bullets. Occasionally someone found a useful nugget easily pounded out to fit the barrel of a gun. The Taku traded valuable

pelts of marten, mink, fox, bear, lynx, wolverine, ermine, beaver, and land
otter from the interior for goods such as blankets, tobacco, powder, and
flintlock muskets.

It wasn't the Alaska Purchase of 1867 that changed the lives of Tlingit, although they did express "their dislike at not having been consulted
about the transfer of the territory." The idea of whites settling in their
midst without being subject to their jurisdiction was troubling.[5] It was
the discovery of gold that forever altered the Tlingit way of life.

In August 1880, an Auk named Kaa wa.ee led prospectors Richard
Harris and Joe Juneau to a nugget-rich creek that the Tlingit had always
called the Place of the Flat Fish because it produced a massive salmon
run each year. To the newcomers, this became Gold Creek, site of the
first gold rush on the mainland along Gastineau Channel.

Beginning in 1881, prospectors and industrialists swelled the population in Juneau and across the channel on Douglas Island. Towns grew
up to support the placer miners, the underground lode mining, the giant
mills set up to process gold ore, and the fish canneries to capture the
wealth of silver salmon.

In 1880, five hundred Tlingit lived on Douglas Island. By 1900, three
hundred Natives worked in southeast Alaska canneries and the mines
of Treadwell. American mining corporations relied on the Tlingit. They
supplied wood and fresh meat, caught fish for the canneries, and cut logs
for the sawmills.

In the early days of Treadwell, blasting and hauling centered in the
Glory Hole, an open cut pit where the Natives were skilled workers. They
had a keen agility to keep steady while perched on narrow benches over-
looking the hole.[6] Sixty to eighty Native machine men worked steadily,
operating air drills, and received the regular miner's wages, up to $3.50
per day. Coming to Treadwell from considerable distances to work in
the mines, they eagerly took up these wage-paying occupations. Many
had been instructed at the mission and in the schools and spoke English
well. In 1885, Treadwell employed two hundred Natives and Chinese,
and the Alaska Natives received higher wages than the Chinese. The
Natives liked to buy things—European-style clothing (which they wore
under traditional dance regalia), household goods, and, unfortunately,
alcohol, which became a major problem. According to one storekeeper,

*The Alaska Natives were adept at mining the steep walls of the Glory Hole.
(Courtesy of the Michael and Carolyn Nore Collection.)*

"they are good traders and spend more money than the white people do, when they come in after fishing and hunting. Nothing is too good for them, they like everything small, like tiny tea kettles, and sauce pans, big enough for doll houses."[7]

This willingness to change their way of life in order to earn wages did not mean the Tlingit rejected their own culture. They used their money to contribute to traditional tribal activities, to stage potlatches, or to provide the gift to a family when taking a daughter in marriage. On Douglas Island in 1900, the bride gift ranged from $50 to $300.[8]

Managers charged with keeping the mines running twenty-four hours a day, 363 days a year complained that Natives took off in winter to attend clan celebrations and in summer to fish at traditional camps. While modern gold-mining corporations focused on quarterly stock reports of profits that made money for investors, the Natives who had been there for thousands of years focused on the land and the seasons. In June, the

This Tlingit Potlatch in Sitka called for the finest robes and regalia. (Courtesy of the Kelly Family Collection.)

sun rises at four AM and sets at ten PM In January, the hours of light are eight thirty AM to four PM Changes in temperature and daylight dictated daily life for the Tlingit. Summer was the time for fishing, food gathering, and preservation. Winter was time for social gatherings and celebrations, for making clothing, tools, and utensils. The yearly salmon runs—first king, then silver, chum, sockeye, and pink—gave the Tlingit the chance to preserve enough fish for winter.[9] Dried salmon was the basis of Native sustenance. Eulachon, or candlefish, was considered "liquid gold," an important household and trade item, because the dried oily eulachon burned like a candle.[10]

Summer fish camp was a place of intense activity. Men, women, and children worked to build traps; catch, smoke, and dry fish; and collect and preserve berries and other favorite foodstuffs, such as gray currants with salmon eggs and seal flippers in grease.[11] Women gathered spruce roots and cedar bark for weaving fine, tight baskets used for carrying water and for cooking. Natives did not go off for a summer vacation but for the essential work of survival. Winter was the time for feasts, for storytelling, carving, painting, and weaving.

Schoolteachers, too, adjusted to this primal pull on the Tlingit:

As soon as spring is in the air, the Indian gets his canoe and family ready for the out of doors. It is useless to try to teach them in a closed room, for the children are as anxious as their parents, they have the lure of the open, so their vacation starts early in March, but when the Indian summer is over, they are happy and glad to come back to the school room. The women pick berries and roots all summer until late in the fall, they come home loaded with large cans tied to their backs. "Woe to the Indian who is short of fish and berries in the winter time."[12]

When traditional food gathering and storage was disrupted by alcohol, Natives became more dependent on earning wages to buy necessities.

In keeping with the American expansionist attitude of the time, the government and military looked upon the Natives as a problem that needed to be controlled so that white settlement and capitalist development could move forward unobstructed.[13] "American laws were imposed and enforced. The traditional Tlingit laws were ignored."[14] The rationalization was that the area of Alaska was a wilderness completely owned by the United States government. If they acknowledged Tlingit law, the United States had to buy the land, and they refused to do that. The Natives had no rights as citizens. "They had been purchased from Russia with the rest of the country. If the Natives occupied land that a company wanted, their rights were ignored and the company claimed all rights."[15]

Discrimination, prejudice, and injustice were part of the white culture. Local newspapers regularly ridiculed Natives, describing them in derogatory and insulting terms.[16]

A missionary new to Alaska from the American heartland, at a loss to describe the Tlingit in terms of his own experience, described them as "not at all akin to the Montana Indians. They rather belong to the Mongolian type, . . . high-cheeked flat faces" with eyes and skin color more like Japanese and strongly built. "The fully developed shoulders, chest and arms, they owe to generations of canoe paddling ancestors. . . ." Having no comprehension of a complex language developed over millennia, what he heard were "harsh, . . . hoarse, guttural and clicking sounds, . . . wet like the climate, a wet moist language with a gurgle approaching a gargle."[17]

The well-intentioned missionaries saw Natives as "poor dusky men of the forest [who needed to be shown] the way of eternal life," unaware that from the beginning of their civilization, Tlingit had a spiritual core. They believed that in addition to the physical world, there was another world of spirits. Both realities were important, but for success it was necessary to be on good terms with the spirits. They believed in a spirit above all spirits: Dei kee aan kaawoo, or "the Far Up Chief," referring to God the Father. The people felt a close relationship to their environment and the animals they considered to be like humans. Both humans and animals both had immortal spirits. At celebrations, the most honored dancer was the one who best imitated the animal he represented.[18]

Churches in Douglas ministered to the Natives with varying degrees of flexibility and cultural sensitivity. The Russian Orthodox tradition incorporated indigenous language and culture, and adapted bilingual rituals, while the Protestants tried to supplant aboriginal culture with American English, forbidding the use of the Tlingit language.[19] Most missionaries were convinced that acculturation was the only alternative to extermination that would come about through war and disease. Protestant missionaries believed that through education they could Americanize—and thus save—the Native populations.[20]

In contrast, Quaker teachers saw the Natives as "eager to learn, quick, intelligent, shrewd, careful, though round-about reasoners [sic]. The children were eager to learn; they came before daybreak to the school where they begged for a piece of chalk to take home. The teachers saw every rock along the beach used as a chalkboard. . . . C-A-T, B-O-Y, ABC. You could tell there was a school in the village."[21]

The Native village adjacent to the town of Treadwell had a population of 346 in 1910. (Courtesy of the Alaska State Library, Dexter Collection, P40-36.)

In the first Catholic church on Douglas, the priest maintained segregation; the special Tlingit Mass and instruction took place on Fridays.[22] "The prospect of a mixed congregation would not be entertained," because the odor of fish oil and dried fish offended the whites. This smell that tourists had labeled *les Odeurs L'Alaska* was a scent the coastal Natives associated with life itself. Salmon smelled of wealth, of money. In Native language, the word for "smell of salmon" was the same as the word for "smell of copper," a valuable metal sought in trade.[23] When Natives were baptized in the Catholic church, they had a local sponsor and often took his name. Willy Kelly, a Catholic and the Treadwell machinist, was godfather to many converts, and his coworkers joked that there were "a lot of Tlingit named Kelly." Tlingit marched through the streets up to the Quaker church singing hymns heartily. Even there, half of the church was reserved for them and the other for whites.

The Natives adopted many of the styles and trappings of the white townspeople. Baby buggies replaced back cradles for the papoose, and high-heeled shoes became popular. But women still carried fish on their backs and went door to door to sell. These customs were puzzling, even frightening, to a mill worker's wife who observed:

> One day a woman passed clad in a Chilkat blanket, her face was as black as coal except for a few white lines running from her eyes down to her neck, it was the worse tattooed face I had ever seen, I would not forget it at night, I would be awake and think of that horrible face. I inquired and someone told me about the tarred face, the Tlingit woman had buried her husband; the black face was mourning she had to wear until it wears off. Sometimes they put on the same black to punish a forfeit in a different way, so they can tell which is mourning or punishment.

This woman, frightened by the tar-faced widow, was enchanted by the children:

> I used to watch the Indian children half naked in wintertime playing at low tide on the sand and nowhere in the world can they play better for you never see them fight. For a long time we heard cries coming from the water every morning around 8 o'clock. Old Indians jumped in the ice cold water dragging little children with them shouting like sea lions.[24]

When John Muir, naturalist and explorer, visited the area in 1879, he noted the gentleness and dignity of the Natives: "The Tlingit are fond and indulgent parents. In all my travels I never heard a cross, fault-finding word, or anything like scolding inflicted on an Indian child, or ever witness a single case of spanking, so common in civilized communities." Of his loyal Tlingit interpreter, killed while peacemaking between feuding tribes, Muir says:

> I saw Toyatte under all circumstances,—in rain and snow, landing at night in dark storms, making fires, building shelters, exposed

to all kinds of discomfort, but never under any circumstances did I ever see him do anything, or make a single gesture, that was not dignified, or hear him say a word that might not be uttered anywhere. He often deplored the fact that he had no son to take his name at his death, and expressed himself as very grateful when I told him that his name would not be forgotten,—that I had named one of the Stickeen glaciers for him.[25]

The Anderson family admired the painted and carved wood artwork of one elderly Native who came to their house. Mrs. Anderson bought a wooden fork and spoon, painted with bear heads and the Tlingit trademark ovoid pattern that looked like eyes. For Irving she bought a four-foot-long carved miniature war canoe, painted in red, black, and blue with eyes and whales on the high curved bow. Mrs. Anderson negotiated for it, and paid fifty cents and two loaves of homemade white bread. Frederika told the man she would like a fresh salmon. About a month later he brought one that was nearly five feet long and weighed eighty pounds. The fisherman asked for more loaves of her homemade bread. Frederika put the prize salmon in a barrel with salt to keep for winter. Irving found a place of honor in his bedroom for his treasured carved canoe.[26]

At the Kelly house, the dog Rover knew when the Indians were coming and he barked his loudest, snarled, and snapped at their feet. The children called him away. A Native woman, wearing long dress with a shawl and a blanket over her head, came to see the family. She squatted on the back porch, spreading her hand-crafted moccasins and woven baskets in front of her. This was the signal she wanted to trade.

The moccasins of hair seal were beautifully beaded and the baskets perfectly woven with designs in Native dye. Mayme Kelly regularly traded a sweater or a coat or a dollar or two for these. Once Marion offered a pair of dime-store earrings and the Native woman was going to trade a basket for them. Mayme would not allow it—the basket was so much more valuable.

In the eyes of the town youngsters, Natives were good people, with the possible exception of Bedelia, an old woman who frightened the children, shaking her stick and growling things in Tlingit. The children teased her and each other with the taunt, "Bedelia, Bedelia, Bedelia's gonna steal ya!"

Aanyaalahaash, hailed as the last chief of the Tlingit, lived in the Native village on Douglas Island from 1880 until his death in 1918. (Courtesy of the Alaska State Library, Case and Draper Collection, P39-0076.)

One Native, well known not only on the island, was Aanyaalahaash, hailed as the last chief of the Tlingit. Historically the chief of the Taku River area was important among the Tlingit because his clan claimed property rights to a major river route linking the interior and the coast. Aanyaalahaash was known worldwide because of his portrait on a favorite tourist postcard. He had an unforgettable white beard, unusual because traditionally young Tlingit men plucked their facial hair. The chief wore a gold-trimmed hat and used a cane. His wife walked behind him, acknowledging the dignity his position demanded.

The chief "understood enough about American government to court its leaders." He visited the Alaska territorial delegate James Wickersham in Juneau and presented him with a carved medicine rattle. Attesting to the chief's position, he collected "skookum" (strong powerful) papers from the territorial governor, the navy, and President Teddy Roosevelt. He sent Roosevelt an exquisitely woven Chilkat blanket.[27]

The Treadwell families, including the Kinzies and Kellys, often picnicked southeast of Douglas, on the Taku River, the traditional grounds of the Taku Tlingit. One summer day in 1912, as they played on a hillside above the beach and chased one another in the tall grass, the children discovered a Tlingit burial ground. A miniature house with a many-sided roof topped by a Russian cross stood undisturbed in the field. Next to it, a four-foot-high marker bore the name "Princess Mary, Juneau, 1900." Through a floor-length window the wide-eyed children saw a coffin and the bleak face of a skeleton. The princess was surrounded by her personal belongings, all neatly displayed: a treadle sewing machine, a small saucer filled with little colorful beads, and a beautiful red blanket trimmed with rows of shiny pearl white buttons. The children were awestruck, and respectful. They had heard stories about thoughtless rowdies who vandalized and desecrated the Tlingit miniature burial houses that dotted the region.[28]

This picnic was sponsored by a century-old fraternal order called the Redmen. The organization was patterned after the Iroquois, and its motto was "Freedom, Friendship, and Charity." Willy Kelly was Sachem (chief)

THE 1910 U.S. CENSUS stated the Tlingit population in Alaska at 4,426. Earlier estimates had put the population at 4,563 in 1890, and 6,763 in 1880. This included both the Taku and the Auk Tlingit who lived in Juneau and on Douglas Island. The decline of the populations is generally attributed to the diseases introduced by white men who came to explore and exploit the resources.

and his brother, Milton, was treasurer. This was the only local fraternal organization that Catholics were allowed to join.

While the Redmen were picnicking at Taku, the Taku Tlingit were in Juneau joining with English-speaking Indians from all over the state to form the Alaska Native Brotherhood. They drafted a constitution "to assist and encourage the Native in his advancement from his native state to his place among the cultivated races of the world, to oppose, discourage and overcome the narrow injustice of race and prejudice and to aid in the development of the Territory to be worthy of a place among the States of North America." In 1915, the Second Territorial Legislature passed an act enfranchising all Alaska Natives who could show proof of having abandoned tribal ways and adopting a "civilized" way of life.

Aanyaalahaash passed away, October 11, 1918, at age ninety, in the Douglas Native Village where he had lived since 1880. The flags on all the Native houses and boats along the channel were at half mast. The body was ferried across to Juneau where a band met the procession at the dock and escorted them to the Juneau cemetery. The front page headline of that day's *Douglas Island News* hailed him as "Last Chief of the Thlingets."

It would not be until June 6, 1924, that American Indians and Eskimos were declared citizens of the United States and entitled to vote. "Sixty years after the Emancipation Proclamation, the descendents of the very first Americans were recognized as having a right to be here. By that time, most of their lands had been taken away."[29]

TEN

❦

Fourth of July's Grand Celebration

The mines were quiet and the town made noise.

THE FOURTH OF JULY, 1908, had been memorable. The day dawned brilliant and still. By the time the molten gold sun spilled over Mount Roberts behind Juneau, the Kelly family was well into the annual ritual. It was a big day for Treadwell, and it was an extraordinary day for seven-year-old Marion Kelly.

First she had to adapt to a strangeness. It was so quiet she heard herself breathing! She heard her little sister, Honey, stirring in the bed across the room. She heard Granny Sullivan in the kitchen. The clatter and scrape of pans meant Granny was mixing up angelfood cake to be served to the baseball team after the day's game. Mama was out there too, cracking and cleaning crab for salad. Funny that the clatter could sound so musical, like a timpani. But for almost every day of the year, the ordinary sounds of the household were swallowed by the sounds of Treadwell, the stamp mills and the screeching ore trains on the elevated tracks in front of the Kelly house.

Marion took a deep breath and allowed her numbed senses to remember what quiet sounded like. Then she heard the tap-tap-snap, tap-tap-tap-tap-snap, outside her window. She looked out over the flower box that brimmed with Granny's golden nasturtiums, down the row of company houses, toward the plaza where the flag was up and a few people were bustling about.

Since no trains came along that day, her big brother, Raymond, rapped the rails with a wooden cane, popping the gunpowder caps in the tip. These were the only fireworks Mama allowed, although around the town, firecrackers exploded like rifle shots, bouncing off Mount Jumbo behind the town and Mount Juneau across the Gastineau Channel. Marion wondered why anyone wanted to blow off firecrackers when every day the miners worked with hundreds of sticks of dynamite, and there were violent explosions underground that destroyed or devastated lives.

Raymond was out early playing before he did his chores. Part of the Kelly traditional post–baseball game feast was homemade ice cream to go with the angelfood cake. As part of the ice-cream making, Raymond and his dad, Willy, went down to the water and snagged a piece of the iceberg that had floated down Gastineau Channel from the Taku Glacier.

Marion's task for this morning, like every morning and evening for the last month, was to practice running for the foot races. The prize in each age category was a $2 gold piece, and Marion had won it in years before, with Willy's coaching. He liked sports, and he was proud that Marion was feisty and determined. This dimple-chinned girl, the smallest in the fourth-grade class, could run like the wind. They walked down the hill to the plaza, where townspeople had put up the red, white, and blue bunting, fixed up wagons for the parade, cleaned, and smoothed out the baseball field, and hauled out fire hoses for the race. Willy marked off a course in the road by the raspberry bushes along the superintendent's house. Marion plucked a couple of raspberries, squatted into a sprinter's position, waited for the coach's count of three, and off she ran down the course. Over and over she ran the course. One last time, as she was taking off, her foot caught on a clod of dirt. She stumbled and fell, skidded along across sticks and pebbles. Verging on tears, she heard her dad call out, "Pick yourself up and go! Just go! Keep going!" She did, and that day, once again she took home the $2 gold piece. In years to come, that motto, and her father's loving coaching, helped her over and over as she picked herself up and kept going in her struggle with polio.[1]

Ferries brought people in from all over the region for the big day. When the SS *Georgia* came down to Treadwell from Skagway, the ball

The Fourth of July races, photographed by Raymond Kelly, 1910. (Courtesy of the Kelly Family Collection.)

teams and fans put together a band with two hundred merry-making celebrators and swarmed the wharf to meet the visitors.

At parade time, Irving Anderson's mother made certain her eight children were down at the plaza for the start, because their Swedish Lutheran family often won the prize for having the most children in the parade. True, there was another Irish Catholic family who had more children, but sometimes they didn't come out for the parade. Once, as the Andersons rushed to the plaza, Irving fell down and muddied his new suit, but Mrs. Anderson had her eye on the prize more than on the dirt.[2]

For the occasion, people dressed up in their Sunday best, girls in white dresses, with big pouf ribbons in their hair, men in suits and the plug hats they used on special occasions like funerals and club meetings. Mrs. Kinzie appreciated the Native Alaska women who came from miles around, dressed gaily with bright silk petticoats and blouses, even though many had never heard of the United States.[3] Everyone headed down to the plaza for the raising of the flag—the specially ordered American flag, the biggest in Alaska—and alongside it, the company flag with the red "T" in the middle of a diamond.

The Treadwell band led the Fourth of July parade through Douglas and Treadwell, 1908. Milton Kelly is the drummer in the back left. 1908. (Courtesy of the Alaska State Library Photograph Collection, P01-2438.)

The Treadwell band, joined by the Jones Native band from Juneau, played a few tunes on the plaza in front of the superintendent's mansion. The marshal of the day gave the order "Forward march" and with flags flying and music sounding, the procession started toward Douglas.[4]

The parade wound along the street from upper Treadwell, across the invisible boundary with the city of Douglas, then down to Front Street. As the Treadwell band led the way, the Kellys waved to their uncle Milton, who was banging the snare drum. Along the way, the band stopped at St. Ann's Hospital to play for sick and disabled patients. The featured float in the parade carried the Goddess of Liberty, a role coveted by all the young ladies of Douglas and Treadwell. One year,

GODDESS OF LIBERTY FLOAT.   DOUGLAS ALASKA JULY 4TH 1912 .

Lydia Anderson reigned as the Goddess of Liberty, with her court representing the thirteen original American colonies. (Courtesy of the Anderson Family.)

Lydia Anderson held the honored position, her float filled with thirteen girls representing the original colonies. Mayme did not allow the young Kelly girls to compete.

When the games began, the competition was fierce in all seventeen categories, from hobble-skirt races to rock drilling. Racing events featured boys and girls, Native boys, old men, married ladies, misses, miners, and mill men, plus an Indian canoe race (no more than twenty-one in a canoe), a Japanese bicycle race, and a caber (pole) toss, a tradition from the games in the Scottish Highlands, home to many men working in the mills. More chances for prizes came with the long jump, the high jump, and sack races. Prizes were generous and paid out in gold. In 1901, $1,200 was given away; and by 1916, prizes totaled $1,700.[5] For a big family like the Andersons, prizes were significant. To encourage her boys for the races, their mother bought each a new pair of athletic shoes every June. The year after Marion got polio, Mayme took her for an early July boat trip south, as sitting on the sidelines during the children's races would be too painful.

The most valued skills in town were evident in the events that awarded the largest prizes: drilling rock, handling fire hoses, and playing baseball. In a mining town, skill and strength in drilling ore and speed in fighting fire were essential. The management had good reason to motivate the miners to become competent in these areas. In a town that was 85 percent men, competition fueled motivation to hone these skills. Teams from the four mines competed fiercely in all-day competitions such as rock drilling, fire hose races, and first-aid races. Earl Pilgrim led the Mexican mine crew in the first aid team competition demonstrating speed in accident response, and won a $50 gold piece. He went right on to the foot race, where he won another $50 in gold coins. His day's winnings equaled a month's pay.

The drilling contest included single and double jacking. Jacking required holding a steel drill spike and driving it into the rock with hammer blows. In the two-man double-jacking contest, a team had fifteen minutes and an eight-pound hammer to drive a seven-eighths-inch steel spike into the rock as far as possible. In 1913, the Mexican mine double-hand team won $120 and took the record when they drilled twenty-nine and a half inches in fifteen minutes. A young Greek from the Ready Bullion mine won the single hand by drilling sixteen inches, taking home $60, more than two week's wages.

In drilling, it was men against rock. In the fire-hose race, it was men against time and water. The fire department teams competed against one another, but everyone knew the exercise was preparation for taking on the dreaded fire fiend feared by every resident—miner, manager, merchant, and housewife—in this town of wooden buildings set in a windswept canyon. The fire department had a company for each mine: the Treadwell, the Mexican, the 700 Foot, and the Ready Bullion. They competed year-round in billiards, bowling, basketball, and skeet shooting, but especially on the Fourth of July. Among the fireboys, the Fourth of July hose race was the year's crowning event.

The fire hose race offered the biggest prize ($350 in gold in 1916) because it honed skills critical to the company. (Courtesy of the Alaska State Library, Dexter Collection, P040-33.)

There were two kinds of fire-team races. For the chemical engine contest, ten firemen filled a chemical tank on a two-wheeled truck with forty gallons of fire suppressant. Then they raced the full length of the baseball field and ran a man up a twenty-foot ladder to spray a stream over the top of a building. In 1914, the Ready Bullion team did it in forty-two seconds.[6]

The hose race was over the same course. At the beginning of the race, teams of ten fireboys stepped up to the pile of five fifty-foot lengths of hose neatly coiled at the hydrant. At the starting pistol shot, a pair of team members rolled out a length of hose straight and flat on the ground and coupled it to the hydrant. A second pair ran to the end of that portion, rolled out another segment, and coupled it to the first. This was repeated for five lengths. As the first section was connected to the hydrant, the hydrant man turned on the water full force. In the meantime, the nozzle man ran the entire distance to couple the nozzle. He ran at high speed while water surged through the hose at his heels.[7] The winners were the team with the fastest legs and the nimblest hands. One year Milton Kelly had just enough time to put down his drum, change from his band uniform to his team shirt to help his team win the hose race in twenty-two seconds, collecting the $200 prize.[8]

Giving the afternoon's patriotic speech was a high honor. In 1901, Governor John Brady (who wanted to give Natives the vote) spoke. Another year, a local dignitary gave a touching tribute to the flag.[9] Raymond Kelly was always more in awe of the orators than the baseball stars.

The afternoon's climax was the baseball game, where the intra-company rivals shed their fire company uniforms and melded into one Treadwell team and took on teams from Douglas, Juneau, and Skagway. Baseball was valued, not for furthering any necessary skills of rock busting or firefighting, but for the sheer love of the game. Treadwell was a baseball town. When the team got new uniforms in 1908, the paper even noted "the dazzling zebra-stripes and awe-inspiring diamond T perched jauntily in the middle of an athletic back or just below the left floating rib."[10] Raymond Kelly and Frank Anderson both served terms as team mascot. Raymond's uncle Bobby Coughlin was catcher. After the baseball game, Mayme would invite the ballplayers up to the Kellys' house for a snack of crab salad and homemade ice cream. Granny's angelfood cake was a delicacy the men never got at the boardinghouse. Honey passed around a cut-glass bowl full of fine chocolates—a reminder of the days when Willy was courting Mayme and she was running a candy store across from the ballfield.

In 1916, the Fourth of July celebration reached a zenith. The $1,700 purse of prize money was the highest ever: $350 for the hose race, $250 for winners of the ballgame. The game was a thriller, "the best ever seen in the north." With no score up to the eleventh inning, the Treadwell team scored two runs in the last half of the eleventh. This win was hailed as the greatest success since Douglas Island was discovered by Captain Vancouver.[11]

The paper proclaimed that Fourth of July 1916 "will be remembered as a red letter page in Douglas Island history." Even as Gus Anderson was packing up his family up to move to Seattle, convinced that the mine was caving, the townspeople proclaimed confidence that next year's Fourth of July would be even grander and that Treadwell would continue to field winning baseball teams for years to come, just as they trusted that the mines would support them for decades. In less than a year, those hopes would be dashed.

ELEVEN

Double Threat of Wind and Fire

Soon the Taku will change for a Chinook and the gentle rain will come. . . . [Until then] we repeat the prayer of every householder. Watch your fires and save the water. —DOUGLAS ISLAND NEWS, 1896

MARION REMEMBERED ONE TAKU when she was eight. Even as their boat pulled out from the dock at Juneau, Marion knew. "Hold tight," she whispered to her doll, the one her dad had brought her in the orphanage and was always with her. Then she turned to her stepmother: "Mama, there's a Taku coming, and it's almost here. See the snows whirling around the top of Mount Roberts?"

A *Taku* is a fierce winter wind that spins off its namesake glacier, gathers force from the Juneau ice fields, and howls down the Gastineau Channel. This wind has blown in this place in southeast Alaska for millennia and will continue as long as there are ice fields. Then, as now, it regularly blasts through at seventy miles per hour, tears off roofs, downs power lines, and overturns sheds.

"Maybe, Marion, but we have to get home, and this is the only way we can."

Marion was right. Very soon, the hell winds of winter (as the Takus were known) churned the Gastineau Channel into a roiling cauldron of smoking whitecaps. Mayme and Marion, the only passengers aboard along with the captain and the deckhand, clung to the benches. The little ferry, the *Lone Fisherman*, pitched and sputtered its way across the channel. The ferry captain tried to approach the landing float alongside the pier in Treadwell, but the float was being pushed under with every crashing wave. The captain turned around and headed up to the Douglas landing.

Willy Kelly had been waiting and watching from inside the machine shop on the end of the Treadwell pier. When the boat could not land and pulled back out, he ran down the pier to the beach and along the waterfront, through the tide flats of mud and mine tailings, paralleling the ferry route.

Even at the Douglas dock, every wave crest knocked the boat against the landing and then dropped it back into a trough. On one surge, the deckhand grabbed Mayme's elbow and Marion's tiny hand, then jumped off onto the landing, and steered them to the gangplank as the winds whipped them. Mayme hung on to his arm and shouted into his ear, "We can't get up there, it's covered in ice." The deckhand shouted back, "You have to. I'll take you to the top and then you run to the waiting room." They inched up the icy gangplank. At the top, when the wind calmed momentarily, they ran for the shed. Midway down the pier, the Taku howled again and blew the two of them down flat on the dock. As they slid toward the edge, Mayme grabbed for Marion and Marion clutched her doll.

Mayme hollered, "Get hold of the piling! Hang on! With both hands! Just let go of that doll!" Marion's arms were too short to go around the piling. She couldn't hold on, and she couldn't let go of the doll. She screamed out, "Mother!" Her fear cracked open a closed door in her heart. She *never* called her stepmother that, only her real mother, who had died when Marion was four. Mayme moved in close and wrapped her long, strong arms around Marion and her doll, cradled them, and held on to the piling. She put her mouth against Marion's ear and reassuringly instructed: "Now we've got to be ready so when it calms down a bit, we can make it to the end of the dock." The wind paused and they dashed to the shed, where they crouched in the corner to wait until Willy reached them and helped them home.[1]

Sometimes a Taku lasted for days, whining and shrieking and "setting everything moveable in motion. It rattled the windows, found the cracks and crannies and came right into the houses."[2] In 1910, one blew down most every smokestack in Treadwell. Channel residents took it in stride. But the Takus came at low water times, when the water was frozen in snowpack up in mountains behind Treadwell. The approach of a Taku heightened fear of fire in Treadwell, a town of wooden buildings. Over the years, Taku-driven fires produced infernos that roared through Douglas and Treadwell, destroying homes, businesses, and mining facilities, which were then rebuilt—of wood.

When the Taku was blowing, Mayme Kelly laid out the children's clothes and warm boots, hats, and mittens. If the dreaded fire whistle blew, the lights went out in order to direct power to running water pumps. The combination of a fire and a Taku was terrifying, and it happened all too often. In winter, special night watchmen patrolled the town to watch for any sign of sparks or flickers of flame. Mayme lay awake listening for any alarm.

The general alarm was three long and three short blasts from the mine whistle. Then everyone listened for the next signals that told the location of the fire: one long blast for the Ready Bullion mine or mill; two for the Mexican mine complex; three for the 700 Foot, the foundry, or the clubhouse. Four blasts meant the fire was close to the Kellys' house, at the machine shop where Willy worked, or the 300 Mill (what Marion called "our mill"), or in the heart of town at the boardinghouse, store, or assay office. Five blasts meant the fire was at Treadwell mine, the 240 Mill, or the big hoist. Seven short blasts was the call for help from the fire company in the adjoining town of Douglas. Although the towns were separate, the path of a Taku or fire did not stop at any boundary.

In 1901, defective wiring started a fire in the hoist of the Mexican mine. Smoke and burning timbers fell down the shaft before warning could be sent to the miners below. Fire departments from Treadwell and Douglas took eight water hoses and seven hours to beat back the flames. Everyone feared the worst for the miners left below. But one of them, a veteran of many years underground, knew of an old shaft that led out to a pit on the surface, where the escaping miners, uninjured, were hauled up with ropes.[3]

A town of wooden buildings in a region of fierce winds required vigilance in fire preparedness. Water from the channel could be pumped through an extensive system of hoses. (Courtesy of the Alaska State Library, Case and Draper Collection, P039-0897.)

In 1904, the Taku blew for six long weeks. A fire started near the boundary between the two towns, and within five minutes flames jumped three hundred feet. The savage clang of the fire alarm and the mournful bellow of the big Treadwell whistle called frightened people from their beds. A fire started around the hospital, and the wind blew it toward the

300 Mill. Men, women, and children, white and Native, came running out with axes, shovels, and buckets. Fire companies ran their carts down the narrow track. After twelve hours, the fire was out.[4]

Because the Ready Bullion mine was a mile farther down the beach from the center of Treadwell, a towering fire in the boiler room there was first spotted from across the channel in Juneau. When one long whistle blast plus seven short blared out, the Douglas hose team sped over the planked road while Treadwell crews rushed down on the little ore trains. Fifteen minutes after the alarm was sounded, twelve hoses were pouring water on the blaze.[5]

Fires in the mine buildings usually started from the complex operations of the mammoth machinery. The Treadwell shaft house caught fire in October 1913. Young Robert Kinzie, the superintendent's son, watched the flames from the glassed-in cupola atop the mansion. Five blasts of the whistle brought six fire companies that battled the fire for an hour in the two-hundred-foot-high structure. Two ore cars (skips) positioned to be hoisted to the surface plunged through the burned floor and hurled down to the bottom of the shaft.

On the Ides of March 1911, a devastating fire started from cooking grease in the Douglas Grill, a favorite eating spot on Front Street. A cold Taku wind whipped flames that quickly engulfed the adjacent hotel and theater, spreading rapidly as the town's wooden buildings fed the fire fiend.

Irving Anderson looked out the window of his Treadwell Heights cottage and across the Gastineau Channel as towers of orange flames from Douglas reflected like the aurora borealis off Mount Roberts behind Juneau. The call went out, and one hundred Treadwell firefighters rushed over the boardwalks to their sister city. Treadwell Assistant Superintendent Kennedy climbed to the top of the Hunter Hotel to direct the firefighters.

The Juneau fire companies ferried across the channel and raced up the dock with six hundred feet of hose, which they connected to a saltwater main near the Greek church. Hydrants froze, the saltwater pumps jammed, and hoses and firemen were encased in ice. Shopkeepers carried their wares to the street. Women and children ran about shouting and crying. The firemen were forced to retreat, fearing that no power on earth

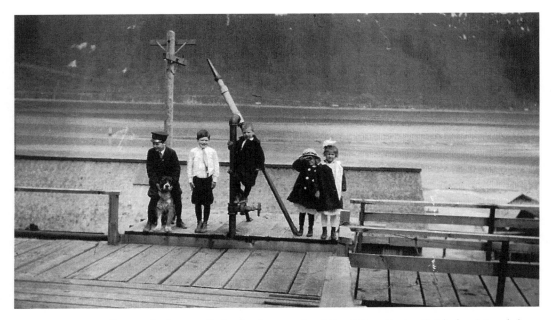

Lester Anderson climbs the fire nozzle while siblings Irving (with dog Murphy), Allen, and Dorothy pose on the boardwalk with friend Dorothy Chilean. (Courtesy of the Anderson family.)

could stop that roaring inferno. Firemen caked in ice had to be chipped out of their clothes. Mike O'Connor, who owned the grocery store where Mayme liked to shop (because he was Irish Catholic), was operating the saltwater pump out on the dock and refused to leave his post even when his own store was in flames. "Just let 'er go," he said.

The Japanese barbers lost their building, but rushed in and saved their tools and chairs. Billy Stubbins (who had taken in little Raymond after his mother died) lost his brand-new clothing emporium. Stores that were spared handed out axes, buckets, shovels, and mittens. Saloons handed out coffee and "stronger stimulants." After eighteen hours, the fire was brought under control, with no loss of life. A miracle saved the homes of Douglas from complete destruction, and a wind change let Treadwell escape major damage. The next day the business district on Front Street in Douglas was a jumble of black ruins covered with ice. A mass of wires and lines of hose froze to the pavement. The stunned townspeople combed the devastation, salvaging their clothing and household goods.

*Downtown Douglas was devoured by a Taku-driven fire in 1911. Treadwell
escaped the inferno. (Courtesy of the Alaska State Library, Andrews Collection,
P162-141.)*

In a generous gesture of community spirit, the Japanese residents of
the island searched out the weary mayor and handed him a purse with
$150 they had collected "for the firemen." Acknowledging the town's im-
portance to Treadwell and to Alaska commerce, F. W. Bradley aided the
recovery by helping set up the First Territorial Bank of Douglas.

The all-volunteer fire brigades of Douglas and Treadwell were always
heroes in the eyes of the Douglas Island residents, and the mine management understood how indispensable they were to the towns and to the
company. In 1905, a disciplined, enthusiastic (and competitive) corps of
five firefighting companies were formed, uniformed, and outfitted. It was

The Treadwell Mine Fire Brigade in dress uniforms for the annual Firemen's Ball, the premier social event on Gastineau Channel. (Courtesy of the Michael and Carolyn Nore Collection.)

no accident that the biggest prize given in the Fourth of July games was for the hose race competition between these fire departments of Treadwell. Getting that hose rolled out and coupled in the shortest time possible, and getting water surging through it, was not a frivolous exercise. The practice and the competition honed the skills that could save the town.

And it was no accident that, starting in 1905, the Treadwell Firemen's Ball was the biggest social event of the year on Gastineau Channel. Held in late summer, the ball coincided with the annual visit by company president F. W. Bradley, who came from the headquarters in San Francisco. The formal affair was as grand as the Governor's Ball. The Treadwell Club became a fairyland strung with tiny lights, the mining town ladies came out in gorgeous gowns, and a sumptuous midnight supper was served in the miners' big dining room.

Planning for the event began months in advance, and the company allocated a generous budget to properly acknowledge the value of the fire brigades. Over the years, the budget increased and the decorations became more elaborate. The *Douglas Island News* noted that "the Treadwell [firemen] are proud of their big dance and well they may be, for nothing attempted in the Northland can quite compare with it." Appropriately, they were mindful that the famous Treadwell Club, where they would be dancing, replaced a YMCA building devoured by flames years before. And the boardinghouse where they all enjoyed the midnight supper only escaped destruction in earlier years because the fireboys successfully beat back the "fire fiend."

Though hardly a tree survived on the hillsides where the town stood, a small grove of firs and alders was hauled down from higher elevations to create a bower along the boardwalk leading from the boardinghouse to the Treadwell Club. Over the club entrance the warm cheery gleam of the letters "T.F.D." in the company's red and green colors signified the hospitality and good fellowship of the occasion. One year, an eight-foot-tall gurgling fountain added a spectacular element for the elegantly dressed merrymakers to sashay past on their way into the club.

Inside, around the club's gleaming dance floor, little white lights twinkled among the boughs, berries, and bunting. Decorations featured highly polished brass fittings and nozzles from the hoses were displayed in an honored position. The music was splendid, with two full orchestras, and the newly polished oak floor was in perfect condition.[6]

The people of the Gastineau loved to dance. Women's gowns in the latest styles were shipped from San Francisco, or made by local tailors and seamstresses. The men, too, sported a variety of dress. The red shirts and leather belts of the firemen's uniforms, with bow ties added, were always considered in good taste, sporting the letters of each mine—"T," "700," "RB," "M"—enclosed in a diamond-shaped frame. The most common attire was a black suit with frock coat, though some gentlemen wore spike-tail coats.

Refreshments were served at midnight in the boardinghouse dining room. One year streamers of pink and white flowers festooned the room, suspended from the ceilings, and huge bouquets of carnations adorned the tables. Another year, red globes and Japanese lanterns cast a soft light.

TREADWELL CLUB BALL ROOM
DECORATED FOR THE FIREMAN'S ANNUAL BALL 1912.

Each year the Treadwell Club was elaborately decorated for the Firemen's Ball.
Two orchestras played for all-night dancing, and dinner was served at midnight in
the dining hall. (Courtesy of the Michael and Carolyn Nore Collection.)

The supper included cold meat, breads, salads, and all manners of pastry.
The dining room capacity of 512 could not serve the whole group at once,
so there had to be a second seating. After the meal, the crowd returned to
the hall and danced till the wee hours. One year the teenage Kelly girls,
Marion in her body cast and leg brace, sat in the balcony entranced by
the ballroom whirl. Their uncle Bobby Coughlin and his new wife, Allie,
a porcelain doll in a blue satin gown, were the most beautiful couple and
the smoothest dancers on the floor.

The twelfth annual ball, in 1916, was proclaimed the best ever—just as
the Fourth of July had been lauded the month before. "All the youth and
beauty, grace and loveliness, sturdy oaks and clinging vines of Gastineau
Channel were there. May two-stepped with December and sweet young
things fox-trotted with time-seasoned marble-topped veterans who voted
for Rutherford B. Hayes in 1876."[7] President F. W. Bradley and his lovely
wife, Mary, were hailed with delight. His genial disposition made him
popular with all, and his visit allayed mounting fears and rumors about

worker layoffs in the mine, as well as the ever-present fear of the ongoing caving in the mines and the subsidence evident around town on the surface.

Topping off the absolute perfection of the occasion, Bradley announced an upcoming increase in employees. He acknowledged and honored the firemen, reinforcing their central role in protecting the property and the people of Treadwell. He reminded all that in the great San Francisco earthquake, it was not the quake but the subsequent fire that destroyed the Treadwell headquarters and most of that city.

The Treadwell fire teams closed the year 1916 affirmed in their importance and their competence. They had performed splendidly in the Fourth of July fire-hose races, and they received accolades from the company president at the Firemen's Ball. Still, they shared a growing anxiety that their heroic dedication and honed skills that had tamed the fire fiend time after time might be irrelevant if everyone's whispered fears came true.

TWELVE

Intimations of Disaster

We are businessmen, not miners.

—SHAREHOLDERS IN TREADWELL MINES

I N THAT SUMMER OF 1916, while the town of Treadwell was savoring the best Fourth of July ever and the grandest Firemen's Ball, a team of world-class mining engineers and financiers was huddling at the mansion, deep in conversation with F. W. and P. R. Bradley. They were looking into the ticklish problem of consolidating the workings on the site and bringing them under the control of the Alaska Treadwell Gold Mining Company (ATGMCo). This was a political problem: one ore body, four mines, and three competing owners. Treadwell managed the four-mine complex, and historically the Treadwell mine itself had produced 60 percent of the gold while the other three mines combined produced 40 percent. In the Treadwell complex, each company paid a percentage of the operating expenses equal to its percentage of the total current production. ATGMCo paid 54 percent, Alaska Mexican paid 12 percent, and Alaska United, which owned both the 700 Foot and the Ready Bullion, paid 34 percent.[1] Based on the history of this division, the ATGMCo asserted its right to assume control of the company that would be formed in a consolidation.

However, contrary to the mines' reputation as the modern Cave of Aladdin with an inexhaustible vein of glittering golden rooms, the ore was becoming leaner.[2] The levels below 2,300 feet in the Treadwell mine had begun to run out of ore; the mills were partially shut down, silencing four hundred stamps. The company was conducting exploratory drilling at deeper levels. The findings at 2,800 feet were promising, which raised general optimism about the future. Time and money were required to sink shafts to access this ore, and in the meantime they had to keep shareholders happy.

The richer part of the ore body was now in the area of the 700 Foot and the Mexican mines, owned by the other companies. ATGMCo investors made it clear that, to maintain their dominant role in any consolidation, the Treadwell mine had to boost production. While consolidation debates were going on, directors stressed, "We are businessmen, not miners"[3] and instructed Treadwell management to make the bottom line look good for investors. Management had to find rich ore wherever it could. This mandate collided with the precarious condition of the mines themselves. The richest source was in the pillars left supporting the stopes in the higher level of the mine. Over the next months, ore production picked up as pillars were shaved for their high-grade ore. And the shaved pillars continued to buckle.

In the early rapacious days of stope mining in the Treadwell complex, not much thought was given to protecting the upper levels from collapse. All of the ore was taken out of an area, leaving empty rooms two hundred to four hundred feet in diameter and equally high. Over the decades, air came in contact with the exposed surfaces of the stopes and caused the surface to slake, loosening the rock.

The number and rate of underground cave-ins had increased each year, in every mine, starting in 1909 with the sloughing of the walls of the open pit Glory Hole.[4] In 1911, masses of rock fell in both the Treadwell mine and the Ready Bullion mine. With a force equal to a blast of dynamite, the events shook the pillars like an earthquake.

When the 880-foot level in the Mexican mine crashed down to the 1,100-foot level in May 1913, the tram tracks on the surface twisted and dropped down two feet, making them useless. The same year, at the line dividing the 700 Foot mine and the Treadwell mine, all levels above 1,320 feet caved, with a shock that woke the town and knocked dishes off shelves.

ON 1050 LEVEL, TREADWELL MINE

In 1915, this area was caught in the massive caving that brought pillars and debris crashing down through multiple levels of the mine. (Courtesy of the Alaska State Library, Wood Collection, p367-34.)

In June 1915, the 750-foot level in the Treadwell mine failed, bringing pillars and debris down 300 feet to the 1,050-foot level, propelling a blast of air through the mine that blew three cars into the Treadwell shaft. Cracks formed at the surface near the Treadwell shaft in some concrete foundations. Then, on July 9, caving in one part of the Mexican forced an air rush through the drifts and blew a mule-pulled ore train backward 50 feet.

Managing this challenge was daunting, especially since it coincided with the mandate to increase production. To assess the situation, in late summer of 1916, F. W. Bradley instructed the young geologist Livingston Wernecke to inspect all the mines and make recommendations. Wernecke inspected every mine level and every building. The foundation posts of aboveground structures that were out of plumb and had settled were at first thought to be a result of decaying timber foundations or soft ground. Wernecke, however, confirmed the slumping was a result of mining a large body of ore directly underneath the town. Underground, the older parts of mine had caved. The formerly open areas were now "wild looking countries."[5]

The management and the experts had differing opinions on the gravity of the situation, given the need to keep production up. The general superintendent believed "it is feasible to draw slowly and carefully so that caved or and waste will fill up spaces as they are made." The mine surveyor concurred: ". . . considerable ore can be obtained . . . [with] no dangerous increase in flow of salt water." The U.S. Geological Service geologist had a different opinion, asserting that it was "decidedly dangerous to proceed with drawing ore from any stopes above [the 1,750 foot level.]" The consensus passed on to F. W. Bradley in the July 1916 report was: "Continued drawing will cause settling and a slight increase in salt water, but if this is done cautiously no danger will result. . . ." Some movement will be felt at the surface, but "it will not be sudden or have disastrous effects . . . and no disastrous flood of salt water will follow."

Treadwell in 1915, showing the accumulation of millions of tons of sandy tailings left from the milling process. The cave-in site was at the center of the photo, just right of the oil tank on the beach. (Courtesy of the Alaska State Library, E. H. Andrews Collection, P162-05.)

Wernecke prepared a report that recommended a forty-month plan, calling for four actions: (1) build a series of bulkheads in the tunnels between the four mines, (2) fill all empty stopes with tailings to prevent further caving, (3) locate and dam the saltwater leak, and (4) build up three hundred feet of the beach with a dam made of tailings from the mine.[6]

The plan was submitted on October 17, 1916, and set for completion by December 1919, the management deadline for pushing production back up to 4000 tons a day. Work started immediately. Sandy tailings were piped into the empty stopes and in a steady stream out along the beach, building a wall of sand. Work began on a new concrete bulkhead at the 1,000-foot level in the Ready Bullion mine.

Harry Snyder, the electrician at the Ready Bullion mine, had been predicting that those big mined-out spaces, those vast empty stopes, spelled trouble. He was especially worried about cave-ins at the Ready Bullion mine. Unlike the other three mines with vertical shafts straight down into the ground under the town, the Ready Bullion shaft was an inclined slope and the blasting took place out under the Gastineau Channel.[7]

Earlier, in 1916, while helping to modernize the mine, Harry had been installing electrical lighting at the twenty-four hundred- and twenty-six hundred-foot levels. Before that, the only light down there had been provided by carbide lamps on the miners' hats; before that, miners depended on candles attached to their hats.

Working a half mile beneath the Gastineau Channel, Harry paid attention to sounds. Just as Earl Pilgrim learned down in the Mexican, the mine spoke to those who knew how to listen. All over the mine there was blasting, bulldozing the chutes, and breaking up ore at the station to get it into the bin for hoisting to the coarse crushers at the head of the shaft. If the site of a blast was distant, Harry might not hear a boom from the blasting charge. But the blast noise would be transmitted through the rock to all parts of the underground workings by a sound resembling the sharp blow of a sledgehammer on the rock. Usually, the concussion that followed the blast reached all parts of the mine and blew out carbide lamps, leaving the mine in total darkness. The exasperated miners had to strike a flint and relight the lamps.

During late 1916, when Harry was working in a drift, the blast that came through and extinguished the lamps was not accompanied by the familiar knock. Harry got a sickening feeling. Fearing that the air concussion was caused by a cave-in on the upper levels, he set out to search for it, accompanied by the head of his shift and the stope boss. His instincts were right. On one of the mined-out upper levels, newly-caved rock completely filled the empty stope.

Fear mounted that all the upper levels of the Ready Bullion were about to cave clear to the surface, letting the Gastineau Channel rush in and pour through the tunnels connecting the Ready Bullion with the three other mines.

This risk pushed the construction of the bulkhead in the Ready Bullion mine to the top of the tasks in Wernecke's forty-month plan. Like everyone else, Harry expected that in a major cave-in Ready Bullion would be the first to flood and a new bulkhead could save the other mines.

The bulkhead was built at the thousand-foot level in the connecting drift. It was another innovative design and construction feat: reinforced concrete, fifty feet in length, keyed into the side, top, and bottom of the tunnel, to make it impossible to give way.

Finished in early 1917, the bulkhead demonstrated a Treadwell hallmark: application of technology and engineering to overcome the challenges and threats of nature. A few months later, the bulkhead faced an extreme test and performed magnificently. But it wasn't enough. The catastrophic scenario it was designed to prevent didn't happen. Something no one had imagined did.

Four months into the forty-month plan, the ground surface was actively moving again. The central hoist tipped one and a half inches, the natatorium and Treadwell Club sank to the northwest, and the floor under the pool tables settled an inch. Power poles leaned to the west.

For over two decades, the singular achievements of Treadwell had set precedents and surpassed production records for hard-rock gold mining. Unfortunately, being unique meant there were no past mistakes to learn from. Treadwell's mistakes were one-of-a-kind, too, and they would prove fatal.

THIRTEEN

❖

The Cave-In:
Rumblings Become a Roar

*No one realized the enormous potentialities of the
running tidewater.*

—LIVINGSTON WERNECKE, TREADWELL GEOLOGIST[1]

APRIL 21, 1917: Mayme Kelly had a date for afternoon tea with Mrs.
Mugford and Marion was invited to come along. There were other,
more interesting ways for a restless sixteen-year-old girl to spend a
Saturday, but Marion couldn't do a lot of them, because Mayme kept a
close rein on her stepdaughters. Most of the children went to the movies
at the clubhouse. But not the Kelly kids. A few years back Raymond came
home and asked about Theda Bara kissing a man, and that was the end of
movie time for the Kellys. Then there was the body cast, from hip to neck,
that Marion had worn for the five years since her polio struck. Though
unseen under specially made dresses, the white plaster carapace defined
the shape of her spine and of her life. She could walk, but no more foot
races or ice skating, and now no movies. Her friends regularly reported
to her on the most recent episode of *The Perils of Pauline*.

Saturdays were boring. Lucky Raymond was in high school in Seattle.
It was Honey's turn for piano lesson with prissy Professor Wells from

Victoria, British Columbia. Going to the Mugfords' was bearable for two reasons: Mrs. Mugford baked delicious cakes, and Marion's friend Kari Anderson lived next door. The year before, Kari had married handsome Charles Preston, the chief electrician of Treadwell, and they now had a baby boy, Charles Jr. Kari was only three years older than Marion, but she probably had more boyfriends and had gone to more dances in Douglas and picnics out on nearby islands and down at Taku Inlet than Marion ever would in her whole life. Those Anderson girls, Kari and her older sister Lydia, had such fun roller skating, hunting, climbing Mount Jumbo, and sneaking out at night.

In the warm April sun, Mayme and Marion set off down the board-walk toward the Mugfords', who lived at the end of the walk near the Glory Hole, on a bluff reached by a long wooden stairway. Along the boardwalks, they passed the natatorium. A ten-man repair crew was rush-ing around, trying to shore up the swimming pool and realign the tram tracks that had been torn up and twisted from a series of major ground upheavals all around that spot. The people of Treadwell were used to the ground shifting and slumping—it had been happening for years—but 1917 had been the worst. The day before the tea date with Mrs. Mugford, the Treadwell ladies were enjoying their designated day in the swimming tank, when suddenly the water in the tank was sucked out in one great whooshing gulp through a crack that opened up in a corner of the pool. The attendant shouted and the women scrambled out of the building.

All that week, cracks and fissures appeared around the natatorium, and the foundation timbers split and shattered. The week before, while carpenters repaired damage from earlier slumping, the ground around the building dropped five feet, several inches at a time, while boards cracked and broke. The rail tracks for ore cars that ran by the site dropped three feet, and all the trains stopped.

When Marion and Mayme got closer, they were shocked to see that the workmen had a locomotive hooked up to cables and were pulling down parts of the beachfront gymnasium. Crashing timber and mount-ing rubble was a frightening and foreboding sight. Philip Bradley Jr. and some school chums were having a great time on the beach, using scrapwood from the building wreckage to make fires inside the sand volcanoes they built.[2]

The day before the cave-in, the building that housed the natatorium and swimming pool was sinking. (Courtesy of the Juneau-Douglas Museum, 90.42.034.)

The Kellys arrived at the Mugfords' and started up the wooden steps. Marion had a good sense of balance, even with that heavy shell she wore. She remembered their conversation:

"Mama, I feel the steps shaking!"

"You're just imagining it. Don't mention it when we get up to Mrs. Mugford's because you will just make her worry more."[3]

At the Mugfords' they sipped tea and talked of the Preston baby, who was two months old now. They couldn't avoid discussing the latest rumors about the condition of the mine, the mounting talk of negligence and poor management, and the accusations that greed was at the bottom of it all. But the superintendent had stated just the day before that there was no cause for alarm.

"Subsidence" (that's what the company called the constant caving) had been going on for years, he said; the engineers had correctly predicted what was happening, and the management had it all under control.

The afternoon visit ended pleasantly, although Marion never did get a chance to see Kari. That night Marion and Honey went to bed as usual, and the adults went to the Saturday-night movies at the clubhouse. The movie goers emerged at eleven PM into a mild evening.

The new April moon, invisible in the night sky, gave no hint of the formidable power it wielded. An extraordinary convergence was under way: a new moon at its perigee, the closest it comes to the earth and simultaneously lined up with the sun and earth. This exceptional configuration produced a *proxigean spring (leaping) tide* which could cause the high tide to rise 20 percent above its normal reach.[4]

Someone heard the ominous sound of rushing water nearby. Behind the collapsed natatorium, they discovered a newly formed creek scouring out an ever-enlarging hole. Jack Wilson, the tour guide who also acted as fire and police chief, notified the mine officials.

Once the tide worked a small channel across the sand, there was no stopping it. The stream moved over the slumped ground and then plunged underground to the caved area. Backed by the rising flow of Gastineau Channel, the cascade poured sand and debris into a hole that was fifteen feet wide, thirty feet deep, and widening by the moment. Something big was happening and no one was quite sure what.

Mine geologist Livingston Wernecke rushed to the site, inched his way out on the tram trestle that was precariously strung over the hole, and shone a light down into the widening cauldron. He watched a mass of mud and water, thirty feet down, accumulate and then slide away with a deep rumble. As the muck was gulped down, the lower regions underground belched a blast of air that had the musty odor of the deep reaches of the mine. Stunned but curious townspeople gathered up on the bank above the whirlpool to watch. Kari Anderson Preston stood on the porch of her house, directly above the chasm, terrified, clutching her infant son, as a roiling pit grew beneath them. Frantic parents rushed home to wake up children and take them to safety, not knowing what might happen. Onlookers gathered in nervous knots, unbelieving, terrified, but unable to turn away from the drama. As the torrent poured into the crater, a mass of mud and water would accumulate for a time and then slide back down with a great deep growl. Above the rumble, a shrill alarm whined out continuously into the night. The company whistle gave the signal to evacuate the mines. Two hundred miners were still on shift. Others had been brought up earlier.

Harry Snyder had anticipated a catastrophe at the next high tide; he was home when the alarm sounded, and immediately took off on a run through Treadwell a mile down to the Ready Bullion. As he passed the Mexican mine shaft house, it exploded with timbers flying in all directions. Immense air pressure had built up underground as millions of gallons of water rushed through the riddled earthen pockets.[5]

In all the mines, hoist operators ran the cages up and down to every level, halting at the various stations, bringing frightened miners to the surface, as rock continued to fall from the underground walls, and water collected in the shafts.

Wernecke went down to investigate, along with the shift boss and the assistant superintendent, to make sure that all miners were out. Stopping to check the 1,250-foot level, Wernecke felt fresh incoming air and heard a distant rumble in the adjacent 700 Foot mine. He ran back to the shaft just in time to see the cage going to the surface. He yelled to the cager, "Hurry back, the mine is caving!"

The cage went by him down to the sixteen hundred-foot level, picked up two other miners, and returned after only three or four minutes, but by then the "rumble had become a roar and rocks were dropping from the backs and sides of the [walls of the stopes]."[6]

As the cage began its ascent, a sheet of rock, water, and sand hit the occupants. At the nine hundred-foot level, the pump tender, still at his post, dove through a four-inch sheet of water into the cage. After giving the three-bell emergency signal to surface quickly, the cage shot up the shaft. At five hundred feet, above the floodwaters, the cage suddenly halted, dropped twenty-five feet, and stopped with a jolt. The carbide lamps on the miners' helmets went out. Attempts to light matches failed because everything was wet. Five minutes passed in dark, damp still-ness. Then the cage slowly moved upward. At one thirty AM, the shaking men stepped from the cage. An hour and forty-five minutes had passed since the alarm sounded. The mine was evacuated and all men but one accounted for.

At one fifteen AM, the small group standing vigil watched as the ground around the natatorium and fire hall slipped sideways, then with "cracks, groans, and noises of shattering boards" dropped straight down into the innards of the mine. The oil tank near the central hoist collapsed

On the brink of the Cave-in - Treadwell Mine April 22nd 1917.

The natatorium disappeared into a vortex that opened up between the Treadwell Club on left and the bunkhouse on right. (Courtesy of the Kelly Family Collection.)

and twisted. The incoming tide reached flood stage, and the volume of the water rushing into the cave-in became "a mighty river, the size of the Yukon River at White Horse rapids."[7] This ominous thundering sound, unlike the familiar rhythm of the stamps, was heard a mile away in downtown Douglas.

Water flooding the mines continued a patterned dance. The hole filled for a time, the water slacked, "and then, with a roar, a volume of water would increase again as if some dam had given away." This went on for an interminable hour.

Meanwhile, a dozen Treadwell children congregated upstairs in the two-story home of Dave Landsburg, the night-shift underground superintendent. The children were brought there by distraught parents who feared that their own homes or any buildings nearer the cave-in site were in danger.

Charlotte Mahaffy, daughter of the company metalsmith was there, spirited away from her house where the backyard extended to the edge of the Glory Hole. The children "waited out the dragging hours in darkness." For thirteen-year-old Charlotte:

> Each hour seemed like an eternity. . . . I sat by the window staring out into the moonlit night. We heard commotion—clanging and banging and the undercurrent of hustling and bustling. We sensed disaster. We did not know that miners were being brought from the bowels of the earth or that our parents were frantically evacuating their homes.[8]

Kari Anderson Preston watched from her front door as raging waters cut away at the cliff in front of her house. Her husband, Charles, was at his job keeping the electricity going to run the hoists getting the men out of the mine. About midnight, Kari bundled up her infant son and ran down the back boardwalk to her brother-in-law, Sammy Stone, whose big, secure family house was two doors away from the Kellys'.[9]

Finally, at two fifteen AM, after another eruption at the cave-in site, a two-hundred-foot geyser of saltwater shot out the top of the central shaft. The spouting display went on for a full five minutes before it stopped, like fireworks announcing a finale. After a harrowing three and a half hours, the mine was full. In those forty-five miles of mine shafts and drifts underlying the town to a depth of twenty-three hundred feet, those ancient geologic pockets that gave up ten million tons of gold-bearing ore were filled with three million tons of seawater.[10]

By seven AM, the sky with its hidden moon had faded into a bland predawn gray. The savage tide was at its ebb and the channel water flowed by, no longer a threat.

At daybreak, Mrs. Landsburg set her candlelit dining room with a light breakfast for the youngsters left in her charge—mostly boys, and still no parents.

The Preston cottage, perched at the edge of the cave-in. Kari Anderson Preston stood on the porch clutching her infant son, as the whirling flood waters clawed a cliff at her feet. The bunkhouse and the Treadwell Club held their ground. (Courtesy of the Alaska State Library, Winter and Pond Collection, P087-0364.)

Just before five that Sunday morning, Philip and Hank Bradley woke in the Mansion to the sound of their mother clapping from an open window to draw attention of the men outside. She asked how things were going. Only then did the boys learn that the unthinkable had happened. The mine caved. Their father had been out all night, walking the town, assessing the catastrophe. The boys dashed to the cave-in scene and climbed to a boardwalk high up on the hill where a row of cottages looked down on the scene. Where the natatorium had been the day before, there was now a hole some

The Mugford cottage, where Marion and Mayme had tea the day before the cave-in, hangs on a precipice. The ruptured tank on the left sent a blanket of oil out onto Gastineau Channel. (Courtesy of the Juneau-Douglas City Museum, 89.50.002.)

When the mines were full, a 200-foot-high saltwater geyser shot out of the top of the hoist in the upper left. The Glory Hole (upper right) had become an oily lake. (Courtesy of the Alaska State Library, Winter and Pond Collection, P87-0362.)

two hundred feet across, sides vertical and rising above a lake of oily channel water. One edge of the hole was just at the end of the no. 4 bunkhouse, where the miners were dragging out their trunks and gear. The place where the Bradley brothers had built their sand volcanoes the day before was all gone, along with the natatorium, the gym, and two other buildings. Down-bent ends of pipe and tram track on either edge of the cave-in marked the line of the street. The uphill wall of the hole formed a new high cliff. On one side of the chasm, Charles Preston's house clung, doomed, the screen door flapping. On the other side teetered the Mugford cottage, the stairway gone. Closer to the channel, a partly collapsed fuel tank sent thousands of barrels of oil streaming out into the channel on the ebb tide.

Over in Treadwell Heights, Marion and Honey woke up and noticed something strange about the morning—the stillness. No sounds of pounding stamp mills or screeching ore cars. If it wasn't Fourth of July or Christmas, why was the town shut down? And what was all the loud talking in the streets? Mayme came into the girls' room and announced matter-of-factly, "The mine caved in."

How could that be? They hadn't heard any noise. They ran to the window and saw a great commotion down in the plaza, men with packs on their backs, women carrying household goods, children with arms full of their clothes and treasures, all heading toward the town of Douglas. People dragged trunks and furniture out on the dock and lined up for any boat that came along. The harbor was full of boats of all sizes. Sightseers were everywhere, scrambling down the narrow-gauge track to the beach, until the guards set up a security cordon. There was not much to see. The front page of the *Daily Alaska Dispatch* reported that the only place of interest was where the cave-in occurred. "It could be compared to a fatal bullet hole in a human body, so small was it in proportion to the mines it destroyed. The [now flooded] Glory Hole could be compared to where the bullet came out, the internal injuries could only be seen in the mind."[11]

The Kelly girls heard about the kids huddling at the Landsburgs' and Kari's perilous dash to safety with her baby in her arms. Thirteen families, all friends of the Kellys', were homeless and had gone to Douglas to find shelter. There was no hotel space in Juneau because the Territorial Legislature was in session. Yesterday—was it really only twenty-four hours ago?—Marion had tried but was unable to get together with Kari for tea and gossip. Now what a story they could share. Kari had starred in it, and Marion had slept through it all.

Mayme wanted to leave Treadwell right away, go to Juneau and take the first steamer south. But Willy said, "No. We are staying." He knew the damage was done, and there would be no more caving. His job in the machine shop would continue to service the Ready Bullion mine, the only one of the four Treadwell mines that survived.

By noon Sunday, the day after the cave-in, every person had been account-ed for except one miner, a man named Alex Tassel. The underground workers had been evacuated hours before the final disaster, and Tassel's stope boss saw him in the Mexican mine and shouted, "Get to the shaft and get out of here!" The cageman and the stope boss both said they saw Tassel on top, and others reported sighting him in the town of Douglas in the frantic confusion following the disaster. But Tassel did not return home to his wife and four children. He did not turn in his tag or pick up his check. The company insisted that he had survived and skipped town. Their reason for this cold-hearted stance was based on an incident the year before, when Tassel ran off due to marital problems.

Tassel's wife filed an insurance claim asserting that Alex was killed in the mine tragedy. Bolstering the family's story, the Mexican mine hoist operator revealed that "just before a severe air blast blew the head frame out of the shaft, he thought he heard a signal for the cage at one of the lower levels." The cage operator tried to answer, but when the overhead supports broke, he was helpless to rescue a possible victim.[12]

Based on this information, Alex was presumed dead. A twelve-man coroner's jury deliberated twenty-four hours and confirmed the finding. The coroner issued a death certificate and the family received an insur-ance payment. Mary and Alex had been married for fifteen years and had four children, ages three to fifteen years old. The Tassel children's teacher later wrote, "The mining company gave their mother [money] so the children could be raised without want."[13] She was entitled to $3,000 plus $600 for each child. The company staunchly maintained that the miner had skipped town. The story the Alaska Treadwell Gold Mining Company wanted history to record was that an alert and responsible management carried out a timely and efficient evacuation and although the horses and mules perished, no miners' lives were lost in the dramatic and disastrous cave-in.

Treadwell citizens were streaming to the boats emptying the town, but the Kellys resolved to stay. The *Douglas Island News* headlined the superin-tendent's prediction that the mines "will reopen soon." He was wrong.

FOURTEEN

———⬥———

A Town Brought Down

*[The cave-in] left Treadwell and Gastineau
Channel very much chastened and subdued.*

—DOUGLAS ISLAND NEWS, APRIL 1918

T HE TOWN TOOK LITTLE COMFORT in the superintendent's reassurance that Treadwell would "continue to be the scene of considerable activity for an indefinite period to come." The three flooded mines were beyond rehabilitation at this point, and the work to be done was to "put the mills and plants generally in condition for their inactivity."

Willy Kelly knew he still had a job, because the machine shop, foundry, cyanide plant, and mercantile interests would continue to support operations of the surviving Ready Bullion mine. The machine shop and foundry also supported the Alaska-Juneau Mine across the channel, where Charles Preston, Kari Anderson Preston's husband, was in demand as an electrician. The superintendent, dismissing the exodus underway, claimed that the majority of families who hastily departed on the first boats going south were "preparing to go even before the 'happenings' of a week ago Saturday night." And, he continued, those other "foreigners" (miners) who left, were of "little account" and their departure "of little consequence."[1]

Optimists pointed to modern San Francisco, which now, ten years after the earthquake, had become a greater city than ever before. So people of Douglas Island should believe that "the brightest pages in the history of [Treadwell were] yet to be written," and that another Bradley mining miracle could bring back a period equal to "the good old days."[2]

But Philip Bradley gave a different message to the management in San Francisco, where he lamented that there was little hope for ever bringing back the Treadwell, the 700 Foot, or the Mexican mines.

⎯⎯⎯◆⎯⎯⎯

In the aftermath of the cave-in, those who stayed had a new reason to pull together as a community. The United States had entered World War I sixteen days before the cave-in. The town of Treadwell, helpless in the path of the flooding tide that drowned the mines, rallied with increased fervor to meet the advancing tides of war.

From the day the United States declared war on Germany, the women of Gastineau Channel, white and Native, began knitting socks, mittens, sweaters, and scarves to send to men in the armed forces. Tlingit women made dozens of pairs of moccasins, which were sent through the Red Cross to hospitals in France. Mabel Bradley gathered a group of twenty-five ladies at the Mansion to roll bandages and knit.[3] In every kitchen, cooks saved fruit pits and nut shells to be ground up to make gas-mask filters. While out picking blueberries to consume at home, families gathered sphagnum moss to send overseas to be used for bandages.

The company fire departments suspended planning for the annual Firemen's Ball and instead sponsored boxing events, evenings called "smokers," to raise money. Matrons sponsored dances, and groups of closely chaperoned young women hosted local troops on their way to the front.

Honey Kelly and her teenage friends collected phonograph records for boys on the navy subchaser 309 anchored off Douglas.[4] Tobacco Fund ads in the local paper urged people to adopt a soldier and "keep our boys in the trenches supplied with smokes."

When the Alaska soldiers passed through Juneau on their way to shipping out, General Manager Bradley invited them to stop at the Treadwell bunkhouse and boardinghouse as guests of the company. Honey's boyfriend, John, was among them. Just months before, at the

"Goodbye Juneau, Hello France." The Fort Seward army boat SS Peterson *takes Gastineau Channel boys off to fight in World War I. May 10, 1918. (Courtesy of the Michael and Carolyn Nore Collection.)*

St. Ann's School Valentine's Benefit, Honey received accolades for her patriotic reading, "When Will the War End."[5] The Gastineau Channel citizens gave a great sendoff to the draftees who left on the army boat the *Peterson*. The Bradley boys accompanied their father to Juneau and marched in a parade. They sang patriotic songs all the way down to the dock, where every available boat then followed the *Peterson* down the channel out to Stephens Passage.[6]

The residents of Treadwell and Douglas threw themselves into the war effort, raising money and planting gardens as patriotic things to do. Bradley served as food administrator for Alaska, appointed by his federal counterpart, Herbert Hoover, himself a former mining engineer. Conservation of food and fuel was promoted in the newspaper, on posters, and from pulpits. Schoolchildren pledged to do their part:

> I will help my parents save wheat, meat fats and sugar. I will help save sugar by not eating more than half as much candy as I have

been eating. I will be careful of my shoes and clothing in order that they may be worn for a long time. I will not waste food or anything that may be useful to my country.[7]

Philip Bradley joined the national cadre of "Four Minute Men," who took their finely honed morale-boosting speeches to captive audiences at churches, theaters, and labor meetings. He also started a newsletter, "For The Boys Over There," to keep track of the soldiers from the Gastineau Channel and to send them news from home.

As president of the Red Cross for the Alaska Natives on Douglas, teacher Hanna Breece noticed her students "were becoming thin, and looked wan and hungry." She questioned their mothers and learned "they were eating only fish, no bread, 'because the people of the United States are at war the poor little children there need bread.' Agents of the government were amazed at how heavily the Alaska Natives on Douglas Island subscribed to liberty bonds. The amount they contributed was not huge, but it was very large in proportion to their numbers and means."[8]

Local patriots were disturbed by the story that young sons of wealthy parents in the States were coming North in droves to work in the Alaska canneries, where the wealth now was in Alaskan "silver," the salmon. Those young men sought out-of-the-way places for the purpose of escaping conscription. On the northbound boats, the steamship men scornfully labeled them "rah-rah boys" and "flag cheaters."[9]

The canneries provided good income for local youth, too. Raymond, Marion, and Honey Kelly, accompanied by their mother, went to nearby Admiralty Island to work at the Freshwater Bay Cannery of Alaska Pacific Fisheries, where they made fifty cents an hour. Raymond, just eighteen, needed school funds because he had been accepted for Reserve Officers Training Corps at Gonzaga College in Spokane, Washington. But Mayme abruptly left the cannery and brought the children home before the summer was over because a supervisor was acting improperly toward the teenage girls.

News came from across the Atlantic that former Treadwell miners from the Balkan countries had gathered to go to the Macedonian front to fight for liberation of Serbia. Then word came that Honey Kelly's boyfriend, John, had been killed. Lydia Anderson's French suitor, the

Count, who had been ready to give up his French citizenship to marry her, lost his legs on the battlefield.

❦

On the first anniversary of the cave-in, the local paper gave passing reference to last year's "subsidence which left Treadwell and Gastineau Channel very much chastened and subdued." The tone of the newspaper was a radical departure from the prideful hubris that had once been Treadwell's hallmark. There was still cause for pride, as the Ready Bullion mine achieved another superlative accomplishment after escaping the cave-in and flood: The mine reached a record-breaking drilling level of twenty-eight hundred feet.[10]

That year, the Fourth of July took on a somber and patriotic tone. The parade was led by the Red Cross flag, followed by Old Glory. American sailors from subchaser 30 carried flags of the Allied Nations, Britain, France, Italy Belgium, Serbia, and Japan. In place of the traditional Goddesses of Liberty, four young girls dressed as American Red Cross nurses moved slowly among the crowd and collected $268. Instead of a baseball game, all were exhorted to come to a dance to raise more funds to support the war effort. "So come one come all and help us make the eagle scream."[11]

In the war economy, Treadwell became a mother lode for other valuable metals, as the demand for used machinery and scrap was high. The Bradley boys, Phil Jr. and Henry, helped pull nails from the collapsed bunkhouses, and watched at the wharf as huge salvaged boilers from the steam plant were loaded on a strange freighter marked for delivery in Kobe. Tons of the specially designed and engineered mining tools that made Treadwell famously profitable were chopped into scrap for shipment. A special railroad track was built to move another mammoth boiler from the central power plant to the dock so it could be shipped to Camas, Washington, for a paper and pulp mill. Equipment was sold "at prevailing prices to excellent advantage . . . to India, California, Idaho, Washington, Wisconsin, Illinois, British Columbia and Alaska."[12]

Soon the security forces on the island declared that no one could come to the docks, thus halting the forays of curious boys and putting an end to a traditional pleasant pastime of Treadwell residents—meeting the incoming steamships.

Another favorite island pastime had been halted with the coming of Prohibition. The Territory of Alaska voted themselves Bone Dry ahead of the United States, and on December 31, 1917, all eight Douglas saloons closed their doors. Customers headed out onto the cold street into several feet of snow. "Treadwellites and Douglas residents formed battle lines behind snow banks on opposite sides of Front Street. Snowballs flew, aimlessly and harmlessly, given the state of the warriors. Each side claimed total victory, and headed for home marching unsteadily to the strains of 'Sweet Adeline' and 'Let Me Call You Sweetheart.'"[13]

The Bries' saloon, where Irving Anderson had peddled Prohibition materials at his mother's request and traded a newspaper for a glass of hot celery juice, became Douglas Island's premier soda fountain.

As the autumn of 1918 arrived, the people of Gastineau Channel faced a danger closer to home and more threatening than the march of war. The Spanish influenza pandemic had spread rapidly worldwide, killing millions, more than had fallen in battle.

In this remote northern area, accessible only by boat, people grew anxious that passengers on northbound steamers would bring influenza up from the States. In October, disaster struck. But it came from a different direction and a different threat.

The luxurious *Princess Sophia* of the Canadian Pacific Line was a favorite with channel residents heading south. Built for the run from Vancouver, British Columbia, to Alaska, she made a round trip every two weeks. The late October run always carried a full load. The Yukon River was frozen, the cannery season was over, and miners and workers who did not want to wait for the spring breakup journeyed south. On October 23, 1918, the *Princess Sophia* started south from Skagway. Thirty miles north of Juneau, in the fierce winds and uncharted rocks of Lynn Canal, the steamer struck Vanderbilt Reef, and the bow stuck fast. Word went out over the ship's wireless and all available boats from Douglas, Treadwell,

and Juneau rushed to her aid. As night fell, the captain felt no immedi-
ate danger to the boat and passengers. Rescue boats took shelter among
islands, ready to come back at daylight. The steamship sat on the reef
another day while the weather and the seas worsened. A Taku-driven
blizzard set in, and high tides pivoted the ship and tore a hole in the hull.
The wireless operator sent out a desperate call: "We're taking water and
foundering. For god's sake come and save us." At daylight the storm had
passed, and the rescue ships arrived to find only the top twenty feet of
the *Princess Sophia*'s mast and rigging and part of the funnel visible above
the oil-slicked water.

Every boat available on Gastineau Channel searched the area. The
Treadwell Company boats were sent out, along with the Alaska Natives'
fishing boats and recreational motor launches. The army boat the USS
Peterson, which had brought in troops to break the 1908 Treadwell strike
and then just a few months ago had taken the local boys off to war, joined
the rescue effort. Bodies, furniture, and clothing floated to the surface.
None of the 343 passengers had survived. The only sign of life was an
oil-soaked English setter found on a beach in Tee Harbor, eight miles
from Vanderbilt reef.

Back in the Kelly cottage in Treadwell, Honey wondered why passengers didn't ask to be put aboard rescue ships when the slings were
available; but then she concluded they must have felt safe. At school
Honey heard stories that the passengers drowned or were suffocated by
bunker oil.

In the weeks after the disaster, debris from the wreck, including more
bodies, furniture, and clothing continued to wash up on Douglas Island
beaches. Local businessmen recovered and organized personal belongings,
stored valuables, and tried to return them to families.

Like the SS *Islander* that had sunk seventeen years before, the *Princess
Sophia*, it was thought, had held a great deal of gold aboard because it
had been bringing out the last Yukon miners and businesspeople. Divers
and beachcombers found no locked safe or bags of gold, though Honey
noticed that the daughter of one of the undertakers came to school with
new gold bracelets and rings.

Despite the spreading threat of influenza, the residents of Juneau,
Douglas, and Treadwell broke their quarantine to help clean and prepare

bodies for their voyage south. Many victims were buried in Juneau in Evergreen Cemetery. The SS *Princess Alice*, originally sent to help with the rescue, became "The Ship of Sorrow," carrying dozens of bodies to Vancouver. The mournful vessel arrived in the Canadian harbor at the very moment the whistles were blowing to announce the signing of the Armistice. The war was over.

The sinking of the *Princess Sophia* was the worst maritime disaster in Alaska's history. Like the *Titanic*, the *Sophia* was loaded to capacity and the passenger list included many famous citizens. Those lost included Yukon's financial, political, and social titans of the day. Some said, "When the *Sophia* sank the North went down with her."[14]

Both sides of Gastineau Channel announced the Armistice by ringing the church bells and blowing mine and firehouse whistles. But the influenza quarantine meant no public gatherings or celebrations. The Kellys' uncle Bobby Coughlin and Jack-of-All-Trades Wilson were named special watchmen to enforce the quarantine: no social gatherings at homes, churches, or schools. Theaters and pool halls were closed. Parents were instructed to keep their children off the streets. The Juneau-Douglas-Treadwell cross-channel ferry service was cut from nine trips a day to four. People getting off the ferry were arrested for not wearing the five-by-seven-inch masks, made of four layers of fine gauze with tie strings at each corner. Soon everyone on the streets sported the "bug catchers."[15]

In November 1918, there were one hundred cases of influenza in the Juneau area. Forty died that fall. In Douglas, the Sisters of St. Ann had finished a new hospital just before the Treadwell cave-in. They feared it would close; instead it quickly filled with flu victims. The island was grateful for the Sisters' competence, though Mrs. Bradley, who always had reservations about the Catholics, decried the way the nuns' robes swept germs with them wherever they went.[16]

Across the channel from Douglas, the Alaska-Gastineau Mine lost 20 percent of its workforce. Flu deaths far outnumbered mining deaths.

In Treadwell, the hardest-hit family was the Prestons: Charles, Kari, and their son, Christopher, were all quarantined for weeks. In November, the local paper reported they "were doing nicely and within a short time expect to be entirely well again. On November 16, Charles was out for the first time since the quarantine."[17] Earlier, the paper warned all flu sufferers with a prescient caveat: "Take precaution. It is the after affects that generally prove fatal as patients who thought they are [*sic*] entirely well left home too soon."[18]

The quarantine ended in time for Thanksgiving. Movie houses and pool halls reopened. Churches held special services of thanksgiving for the end of the war. Newspapers emphasized the positive: "Since there was plenty to eat and no suffering of any kind other than the prevailing sickness which now is on the wane, everyone has cause to be thankful."[19]

The celebration and feasting turned to grief at the Preston household. On Thanksgiving afternoon, Charles, Treadwell's electrical superintendent, just out of quarantine, was working across the channel in the Alaska-Juneau Mine. He stood on a platform near a high-tension wire, with his helper twenty feet away holding tools ready to pass to his boss. In a brief moment, Charles, who was intimately familiar with all the electrical connections, inexplicably got caught in the wire. For the ten seconds it took to shut off the current, he hung on the wire as twenty-three thousand volts of electricity surged through his body. Deeply burned from neck to foot, Charles was rushed to the hospital, where he lived for two days, in and out of consciousness, "talking to his wife and recognizing friends." He died November 30.

Lydia Anderson, Kari's older sister, who had finished nurse's training in Victoria, British Columbia, traveled north on the SS *Princess Mary* to be with Kari. On December 6, "the remains of Charles Preston were sent South on the *Princess Mary* for burial in his family plot in Pacific City, Washington. The body was accompanied by Mrs. Preston and her son Christopher, and her sister, Miss Lydia Anderson. Prior to Mrs. Preston's departure, she disposed of many of her household effects consisting of a splendid quality of furniture which was purchased by friends and neighbors on the Island."[20] The last of the Anderson family was gone from Treadwell.

December 1918 brought the gloomiest Christmas ever, with snow, ice, wind, and nothing going on because of lingering influenza concerns. So many people had left that when the steamship *City of Seattle* arrived with seven days' mail and packages, it did not amount to half of the previous year's Christmas deliveries.

Treadwell residents moved to the city of Douglas. The head of Treadwell's boardinghouse left to go into the hotel business. The cow barn where Karl Anderson tended the superintendent's cows and the Kinzie boys got squirted with milk was torn down and burned. Railroad tracks from the sawmill through the Native village were ripped up. Three big mills were torn down, including the 700 Foot and the two that framed the Kellys' house, the giant 300 and the 240. The basketball team of the Haines Alaska Native Brotherhood came to Treadwell to acquire some abandoned floorboards and floated them north to build a gym floor.

Treadwell Heights 1918

Treadwell was quiet in the winter of 1918. People had moved away, buildings and machines had been taken apart and shipped out, and only a few boats docked at the wharf. (Courtesy of the Juneau-Douglas Museum, 90.42.032.)

The 1919 Fourth of July baseball game had to be moved because potholes eight feet in diameter and nine feet deep appeared on that grand field built on the accumulation of almost four decades of mine tailings.

The Firemen's Ball, for twelve years the social event of Gastineau Channel, was a casualty, too. The *Douglas Island News* wistfully recalled "the nights when the Treadwell Club became a little bit of fairyland transported to the earth and the dance floors were crowded with beautifully gowned women and handsome men. But then came that fateful day in April when the bottom dropped out of things. Since that time the dances have been only sweet memories." However, the Treadwell Fire Department decided that the ball would be revived, and in 1919, a "very nice dance with beautiful decorations" occurred at the natatorium in Douglas. The strictly informal affair hosted a small crowd who hoped that the Treadwell firemen would make the affair an annual one in the future as it had been in the past.[21]

That year, Willy Kelly's younger brother, Uncle Milton "Google Eyes" Kelly, who had left Treadwell in 1913, died in Alameda, California, of a stomach ailment at age thirty-five. He had been a foundry worker, Treadwell Club Band drummer, and among the most sought-after bachelors on the channel.[22]

In February 1920, Mayme Kelly lay in St. Ann's hospital, gravely ill from her years of struggle with heart and kidney disease. Outside a Taku wind blew for several days. The *Douglas Island News* tracked its fierceness, noting

> a velocity seldom equaled in Treadwell. The breeze whined, whistled and shrieked and set everything moveable in motion. It rattled the windows and finding the cracks and crannies of the houses even made its presence felt within the homes of the island. On the ferry wharf both doors were blown off the old coal shed and the door of the warehouse blown. Wires blew down and business was at a standstill. Finally, the wind blew itself out and snow fell with a light wind from the southeast.[23]

On February 5, in the midst of the Taku and fifteen years almost to the day of their birth mother's death, the Kellys' stepmother, Mayme, died. And like Nell's, Mayme's obituary graced the front page of the

Douglas Island News: "known and liked by practically everyone on Douglas Island, ... her death will be felt by family ... friends and the Catholic church will ... feel the loss of a faithful worker for the church she loved ... On account of the inaccessibility of the road to the Kelly home at Treadwell, the remains may be viewed at St Ann's Hospital."[24]

Honey and Raymond were away at school in Spokane. Marion stood outside Our Lady of the Mines Church and watched the wagon leading her stepmother's funeral procession, just as she had watched her birth mother's casket fifteen years before, being pulled by sled along the snow to the Catholic section of the Douglas cemetery.

William Kelly was a widower again. The Kelly daughters rallied to take care of their father. Honey came home from boarding school in Spokane and enrolled in Juneau High School. It was a new era for the Kellys and the country. Women's suffrage was the law of the land (Alaska had granted it seven years earlier). The flapper age had arrived. Skirts were getting shorter and the girls were getting bolder. The next summer Honey was selected Goddess of Liberty for the Fourth of July parade in Juneau. Twenty-one-year-old Raymond, who had become an accomplished orator at Gonzaga University in Spokane, was invited to give the Independence Day address on Douglas:

> At some time in our lives ... there will be a day which stands alone, as a day to be remembered. Today is such a day in my life. Little did I dream as I sat in the audience year after year ... and listened to the speaker ... that at some future time there would be accorded to me the opportunity, the privilege, and the pleasure of addressing [this] gathering upon the anniversary of our country's independence.[25]

That same summer, Philip Bradley Jr. graduated from Culver Military Academy in Indiana. Kari Anderson Preston came up from Seattle with her toddler for a summer visit with friends.

Marion Kelly took a job at the First Territorial Bank in Douglas. Always the caretaker, she wanted her beloved father to be happy. She played Cupid, bringing home the young nurse whom she was convinced had saved Willy's life when he was in St. Ann's Hospital with pneumonia the year before. It worked, and in October 1922, Willy, now forty-eight, married

Doris Lund, a twenty-eight-year-old widow with two children. The townspeople gave the newlyweds the traditional "chivaree," a noisy mock serenade, banging pots and pans with wooden spoons in front of the cottage. As a special touch, friends hung the bell from the Treadwell School on the Kellys' porch and rang it all night.

As the Kelly family was opening a new chapter, Treadwell was closing another. On December 18, 1922, the Ready Bullion mine shut down. The last operating mine of the Treadwell complex closed and the world-famous town ceased mining gold. "The passing [of the mine] was so quiet that the local newspapers carried no big stories."[26]

At the same time, the Alaska-Juneau Mine across the channel hit its highest output, and the Kelly family also increased production. Following in the footsteps of Superintendent Philip Bradley, who added twin girls to

Willy Kelly married Doris Lund, adopting her two children, Vera and Joe (rear). They later had twin girls, Patricia (left) and Eileen. Honey is on left. Soon after, the Kellys left Treadwell. (Courtesy of the Kelly Family Collection.)

Treadwell's population in 1915, Willy and Doris produced twin girls, Patricia and Eileen, born March 14, 1924, the same year the Bradley family left Treadwell.

Now that her father was settled, Marion considered her own options for independence after years under the strict rule of a stepmother or a convent school. Intrigued by an ad in the local paper, Marion took the SS *Humboldt* to San Francisco and enrolled in Mrs. Munson's Secretarial School. Honey stayed in the North to become a teacher in a one-room schoolhouse in Haines, then at Point Agassiz near Petersburg. The next year, Raymond married in Spokane, and Marion eloped in San Francisco.

The Kelly family had lived a quarter century of adventure and heartbreak in Treadwell. They celebrated six births and mourned three deaths—a mother, a stepmother, and a stillborn girl. They rode out the boom and bust of the world's largest hard-rock gold mine. In 1925, Willy moved his new young family south to open a store in Valley, Washington, near Spokane.

The Kellys were gone from Treadwell.

FIFTEEN

⸺◈⸺

Reduced to Ashes

"There's a big fire in Douglas."

O N THE MORNING OF SUNDAY, October 10, 1926, the men of Douglas Island, always crazy for baseball, waited for the newsboy to deliver the *Alaska Daily Empire*. The new radio station KFIU did not broadcast on Sunday. The St. Louis Cardinals and the New York Yankees were in the final game of the World Series. Babe Ruth had already set several records.

At the same time, the Douglas Island women watched for reports from the Women's Christian Temperance Union's national convention in Los Angeles. The WCTU pledged to rally an army of one million to fight the Association Against the Prohibition Amendment, who declared that the war on demon rum was a failure. In Juneau and Anchorage, candidates for Alaska territorial delegate debated the "graft and corruption in the politics of this Territory." One candidate proposed a "fair literacy test for voters which would protect the white Alaskans against illiterate Indians mass voting." (The Natives had been given the vote the previous year.)[1]

Roberta Fraser, daughter of Treadwell foundry worker Robert Fraser, set out for Sunday school from her home above the old Treadwell boardinghouse. The family had stayed in town after the cave-in ten years earlier. The foundry continued uninterrupted, casting and repairing parts for the Alaska-Juneau Mine and other businesses.

Parts of Treadwell still showed signs of life, glimmers of what the town used to be. The assay office tested gold that anyone brought in. Even though the Treadwell Company had no mines, it did have money and was always looking for the next prospect. The wharf was usually busy, but not today. Ships regularly tied up to load salvage metal or take away parts of mines and mills to seed budding enterprises elsewhere. The Treadwell Club—now available for rental to anyone—looked shabby. The Mansion loomed over the plaza, no bustle of children, cooks, or governesses, engineers, financiers, or dignitaries. Tom Popovich, a miner who had lost his arm in an accident underground, was the lone resident. F. W. Bradley took a liking to him and set him up as caretaker of the Mansion back in 1922, when the Ready Bullion closed and Treadwell went quiet. Russ Cahill, the head of the foundry—now the biggest operation in town—lived next door in the Little House, the assistant superintendent's commodious residence.

Roberta walked along the remains of the train trestle, watching her footing because the tracks were broken or missing in many places. When she looked up, she saw smoke and flames billowing over the town of Douglas. She ran back to her mother, who was getting ready to go to church, and breathlessly announced, "There's a big fire in Douglas." In the island tradition of going to your neighbors' aid, Roberta and her mother hurried toward the fire site to do whatever they could.

⎯⎯◆⎯⎯

The fire had started around eight AM from sparks falling on an abandoned house in the Indian Village. No one noticed until a half hour later, when the empty building burst into a mass of flames, throwing embers in all directions.

The wail of three alarms brought all Douglas hose companies. Every able-bodied man, woman, and child rushed to the scene with all available hoses and tools. Fanned by the first Taku of the season with fifty-mile-per-hour winds, the fire gained headway and the flames spread. Everything in the town was dry fuel. Flying embers sparked dozens more fires that sprang up around the main conflagration. Firemen spread out in all directions, as much as the firefighting apparatus allowed.

People in a panic pulled clothes, furniture, and personal treasures out of their houses. Roberta and her mother looked for ways to help. The frantic townspeople handed them bags of clothes and stacks of household goods to move out on the tracks or the beach, away from the fires.

That wild and tricky Taku, the unpredictable hell wind, joined in a dance with the fire fiend, and spun the inferno around. First, a wind from the east drove the fire toward the main section of Douglas and whipped the blazing frenzy for three hours. Suddenly at eleven AM, the whirling dervish veered the opposite direction and carried the fire toward Treadwell.

Roberta ran back to her house. Now the family had to save their own belongings. Treadwell people scrambled to rescue their most cherished items: a Bible, an ornate gold-framed christening certificate. Someone moved a piano to the beach, the keyboard already scorched. The manager of the Treadwell grocery store and meat market carried his stock to the shoreline.

Piles of treasured belongings packed out of houses and stacked on the tracks caught fire. The unstoppable flames moved toward Roberta's house. "This fire is going to just keep burning," her dad shouted. "Take your two sisters, go up on the high trestle and over to the foundry. There's a dock there and a boat can get you out." Roberta took as much as she could carry from her house, even the violin that she seldom played. A fishing boat took the girls safely to Juneau, but the Fraser home burned to the ground. The family lost all its possessions, everything they had brought from Scotland, even their photographs and Grandmother's heirloom tea set.

A decade earlier, before the mines caved in, Treadwell had taken pride in its vigilance and fire preparedness. The mining company had laid a six-to-eight-inch saltwater line running from Treadwell to Douglas. But after the cave-in, the people were gone, and there was nobody to tend to those things, no one to start the pumps. Treadwell's famed fireboys were only a memory.

The fire raged all day and into the evening. Moving down the main road to Treadwell, the flames engulfed Our Lady of the Mines Catholic Church, St. Ann's Hospital, and the Alaska Native Brotherhood Hall. Like a forest fire, the extreme heat exploded wood of every kind—trees,

October 10, 1926. Started by a spark and driven by a Taku wind, a fire raged through Douglas and Treadwell while the people of Juneau watched the rising wall of flames and smoke. (Courtesy of the Alaska State Library Photograph Collection.)

buildings, boardwalks. Rolling into Treadwell, the fire devoured the superintendent's mansion, the Treadwell stores, and the original mine office. From downtown Douglas to the site of the cave-in, a distance of two miles, only six homes remained standing. Thirty-eight residences went up in flames.

Even the dynamite, strategically located and detonated to stop the flames, had little success. The coast guard cutter USS *Unalga* pulled alongside the beach and poured a stream of water onto the Treadwell dock and warehouse and saved it.

The Treadwell wharf with the saltwater pumphouse on one end was saved. The mill from the 700 Foot mine and the foundry escaped the

flames. The passenger ferry *Teddy* ran back and forth all day between Juneau and Douglas. People looking over from the Juneau side of the channel were sure the main section of the city of Douglas was doomed. Great volumes of black smoke rolled up like an erupting volcano and covered everything recognizable on Douglas.

The Native Village on the beach between Douglas and Treadwell was totally destroyed, and 125 people from forty-two Native families were homeless, able to save only the clothes on their backs. Many brought their belongings out onto the beach, but an incoming tide washed everything away before the boats could get there. Sparks ignited the feather

The fire roared through Treadwell's wooden buildings and burned them to the ground. (Courtesy of the Alaska State Library Photograph Collection, P01-1729.)

beds piled along the sand, and the wind-scattered feathers looked like a snowstorm.

A rescue home for the Alaska Natives was set up in the Douglas natatorium, the scene of the attempted revival of the Treadwell Fireman's Ball seven years before. The shivering survivors received beds, blankets, hot coffee, and sandwiches. Another Douglas merchant opened his doors

Treadwell Store & Office Bldg after Fire of Oct 10-'26.

The concrete office building, built in 1915, remained standing. (Courtesy of the Alaska State Library Photograph Collection, P01-1796.)

and offered the homeless "a large kettle of wieners, a great quantity of hot coffee and sufficient bread to go around."[2]

Similar to the 1917 cave-in that closed the mines, the catastrophic fire destroyed the town but caused no fatalities. The only fallen firefighter was Treadwell's foundry superintendent Russ Cahill, who escaped from the flames and then suffered a mild heart attack. He was rushed to St. Ann's Hospital in Juneau, where his wife was already confined with their new daughter born three days earlier.

By noon the day after the fire, the determined citizens of Douglas had formed the Douglas Relief Committee. Headlines announced "Citizens Unite for Rehabilitation—Plans Outlined at Meeting."[3] The city of Douglas began to rebuild immediately.

Treadwell had neither the resources nor the will to try.

This great enterprise, an early-twentieth-century saga, an industrial romance of technology, wealth, and a country club on the northern frontier, was finished. "Treadwell: An Alaskan Fulfillment" was a smoldering pile of ashes.

EPILOGUE

※

The Place, the People, the Gold

The Place

In 1928, two years after Treadwell's final fire, the Alaska-Juneau (A-J) Mine bought all the Treadwell property: the powerhouses at Nugget and Sheep creeks, the 240 powerhouse, and the foundry. Dismantling of the town continued, and the warehouses were moved across the channel to the A-J dock. Two years later, the 1930 Census showed Treadwell with a population of sixteen.

The temperate rainforest of Douglas Island returned and grew over the ruins of the old mining town. In 1973 the property was purchased from the A-J by the Alaska Electric Light and Power Company (AEL&P) together with the City and Borough of Juneau. The men who founded AEL&P in 1896 were all affiliated with the Treadwell mines. John and Adam Corbus, Robert Duncan, and John Malony recognized that the electricity generated at the Treadwell's power plants and Sheep and Nugget creeks might be used more widely to enhance people's lives, and for years AEL&P bought electricity from the mines. (A century later, the Corbus family continues to direct the electric company. The hydro plants on Sheep and Nugget creeks are no longer in operation but remain historically significant as artifacts of the Treadwell mining complex.)

In sharing the purchase of the Treadwell property, the City of Juneau wanted to use a section as a park, and the Glory Hole as a dump site for old cars.

On the Treadwell lands, the shafts and tunnels of the mine workings have been closed off, covered over and seeded with grass. The rusted hulks of machinery and some mining equipment have been moved out and are on display throughout Juneau, including an ore car and miners' cage and a cauldron from the foundry. A modern addition to the original artifacts is a life-size bronze statue of a hard-rock miner poised with his trademark tool, the pneumatic drill. This statue greets cruise-ship passengers when they dock and reminds them how this remote outpost first became a destination port. Treadwell put Juneau on the map.

⸺⊰◆⊱⸺

A bridge now connects Juneau with Douglas Island. In the early 1900s, Gastineau Channel residents cherished the indispensable passenger ferries that crisscrossed the waterway many times a day— the *Lone Fisherman*, *Flosie*, and *Alma*. Even then, Mike O'Connor, Douglas Island merchant and promoter, envisioned the bridge connecting Juneau to Douglas that was finally built in 1935. The City of Douglas became part of the City and Borough of Juneau in 1970. Today, the local businesses are promoting a second bridge for "recreation opportunities, traffic flow and access to more land, affordable housing . . . and more industrial-zoned land."

A group of modern entrepreneurs interested in Douglas Island development is Goldbelt, Incorporated, a Native corporation. Goldbelt has tens of millions of dollars in assets, owns land in West Douglas, and wants to develop the area for residential housing, cultural resources, and light commercial facilities. Goldbelt was organized under the terms of the 1971 Alaska Native Claims Settlement Act (ANCSA), the largest single federal settlement of Native American claims. Through ANCSA, descendents of Alaska's original inhabitants received forty-four million acres of land and $966 million in cash divided among more than two hundred community corporations and thirteen regional corporations.[1]

⸺⊰◆⊱⸺

A path that winds through the site of the former town of Treadwell has been adapted for the high-school cross-country team. Now, instead of ore cars screeching along elevated tracks to get the ore to the mill, loping teenagers pant up the trails to shave seconds off their running time in hopes of winning the next meet. On the flat area made of sandy tailings near the old Indian Village, an all-season recreation facility as large and cavernous as the old 300 Mill now houses the Treadwell Ice Arena. The popular complex hosts hockey and figure skating, improving on a century-old tradition started with the winter flooding and freezing of the plaza in front of the superintendent's Mansion.

In summer 2006, an adventure tourist attraction was added for the one million cruise-ship passengers who now come up the Gastineau Channel every year. A zip line from the hoist house at the top of the Mexican mine down to the shoreline site of the old foundry allows tourists to fly through the canopy of giant spruce trees and get a bird's-eye view of the ruins of Treadwell.

People are surprised to learn that even after extensive tests—including the cyanide tailings dump, that barren patch where nothing grows—the Treadwell property does not qualify as a Superfund site. The lode was relatively clean and naturally low in sulfites and did not leach acid. Ninety-six percent of the mercury used in amalgamation was recovered. Dungeness crab thrive in the waters along with the millions of tons of tailings dumped there during the operations of the mines. "There is a healthy sealife population in Gastineau Channel."[2]

Treadwell boasts two official hiking trails. Adventuresome trekkers can follow a twelve-mile-long maintenance path that parallels the historic Treadwell Ditch, a series of streams, flumes, and culverts that captured and harnessed the island's waters for running the mines. This trail winds past log dams, trestles, and trickling water in culverts covered with rotten logs. A second route, the Treadwell Mine Historic Trail, is a two-mile loop, accessed either on St. Ann's Street at the end of the city bus line or down on the beach. Beginning from the bus line, the trail leads straight down the road to the site of Willy Kelly's house. Starting from the beach, the path follows the story of the technology. It begins at the primitive "shrine" of the original five-stamp mill and ends at the bronze plaque facing the skeletal remains of the great Treadwell wharf, site of the machine shop where Willy Kelly worked. Philip Bradley Jr., one of the Treadwell kids, crafted the description on the plaque and dedicated it in 1981. It reads:

> This Commemorative marker is placed on the site of the Treadwell
> Town Plaza and on the site also of the now-filled cove at the

mouth of Paris Creek where gold first was found on Douglas Island.

Higher on this creek at a place later lost to Glory Hole mining, the Treadwell lode was discovered and staked in May of 1881. This was first developed and mined by John Treadwell 1882–1889, then was worked by the Alaska Treadwell Gold Mining Company and affiliates until it finally closed in 1922.

F.W. Bradley of San Francisco headed all work 1899–1933. His Superintendents included R.A. Kinzie, P.R. Bradley, R.G. Wayland, and L.H. Metzgar. Geologists were O.H. Hershey and Livingston Wernecke.

Shaft depth reached more than 2800 feet. Five mills dropped 960 stamps. Gold production totaled some 3.3 million ounces. Daily payroll exceeded more than a thousand men. Life here was good.

The People

John Treadwell

After selling his share of the mines, John Treadwell returned to Oakland, California, where he married Frederika Josephine Graner on December 17, 1889. John and his brother James pursued numerous investment ventures. They opened the Tesla coal mines in 1890 in Alameda and made it the biggest coal producer in the state, mining eighty thousand tons annually. The Treadwell brothers were well-known millionaires in California. The family's North Oakland estate was a showplace, complete with villa and coach house, lush landscaping, and a view across the bay. From the terrace they witnessed San Francisco in flames following the earthquake of 1906. (In a gamble that would later ruin him, John partnered with his brother and started a California trust company that went bankrupt following the earthquake.) The Tesla mines closed in 1911. The family was forced to sell the Oakland estate, which became the campus of the California College of the Arts.

In 1914, while living in New York City, John Treadwell filed a voluntary petition of bankruptcy listing his liabilities as $2.93 million and his assets as zero. He died alone on November 6, 1927, in the Great Northern Hotel in New York, where he had lived since 1914. He was eighty-five. Little is known about Frederika, except that she died on May 23, 1950, and the couple had no children.

Sixty-seven years after his death, in 1994, John Treadwell became inductee number ninety-one in the National Mining Hall of Fame. (Frederick W. Bradley was inductee number two.) Treadwell earned his place because he "prospected, explored, developed and operated Alaska's first successful large-scale, low-grade gold mine. He played a major role in stimulating the economy of the Territory and its wilderness, as well as of the nation, through one of the most advanced operations of the American mining industry in the late 1800s."[3]

The Kellys

When he left Treadwell in 1925, Willy Kelly took his third wife, Doris, and their twin daughters, Patricia and Eileen, plus Doris's two children, Vera and Joe, to Valley, Washington, near Spokane. The Kellys had a small drugstore there, a struggling business from the start. Doris was about to begin a well-paying job as pharmacist at a nearby hospital when the hospital burned down. The sheriff foreclosed on the store. The family moved to Spokane, where Raymond, by then a promising lawyer and active in politics, found his father a job with the Works Progress Administration. Willy died in 1940, at age sixty-five. Doris worked as a nurse in Spokane until her death in 1970 at age seventy-six. One of the twins, Patricia, was the author's godmother. She died in 1968, at age forty-four, following the birth of her thirteenth child. The other twin, Eileen, went to business school then moved to San Francisco to live with Marion. Eileen married and had three sons and a daughter. She lives in Pasadena, and is the only surviving member of the original Kelly family of Treadwell.

When Marion Kelly got on the SS *Humboldt* in Treadwell in 1924 and headed for San Francisco, she never looked back. Her polio had left her with scoliosis. Her right leg was weakened, not from the polio, but because in corrective surgery the doctor had operated on the wrong leg—her good leg. But that didn't stop her.

Always making the most of her steamship adventures, she met her first husband on that emancipation trip from the hard times and strict upbringing in Treadwell. In the San Francisco Bay Area, after her training in Mrs. Munson's Secretarial School, she worked three decades as a legal secretary for the State of California. She got in a lot of dancing, enjoyed San Francisco's nightlife, and vacationed in the California desert, never chancing another Alaska Taku wind.

She weathered two marriages, breast-cancer surgery—the kind that could have saved her young mother's life in 1905—and continuing physical challenges. Through it all, she carried her father Willy's voice from those workouts for the Treadwell Fourth of July footraces: "Pick yourself up and go. Just go. Keep going." She kept going, with grit and gusto.

After retirement at sixty-five, she became an accomplished oil painter. Few of her paintings had Alaska themes; most were copies of Old Masters. The effects of post-polio syndrome plagued her, including muscle weakness and fatigue, but she insisted on using a walker and never a wheelchair. Up until her death in 1993 at age ninety-two, she enjoyed dining out at the latest trendy San Francisco–area restaurants, where she ordered martinis and prime rib.

Raymond Kelly stayed in Spokane after college and law school and became a superior court judge and teacher at Gonzaga University School of Law. He married Helen King, whom he had met through Father Michael O'Malley, a Jesuit who came to Spokane after serving as pastor at Our Lady of the Mines Church in Douglas. Raymond and Helen had five sons and one daughter, the author. As lawyer, judge, and state legislator, Raymond remained the same articulate orator who gave the 1921 Fourth of July speech in Douglas. When he died in 1977, at age seventy-seven, the *Spokane Daily Chronicle* referred to the slight stature he inherited from Nelly, his mother, by lauding him as "the diminutive Irishman who was considered a giant among judges."

Raymond's oldest son, Raymond Jr., had a son, Ray III, who married a woman of Tlingit and Tsimshan descent. Their son, Raymond Kelly IV, bearer of an Alaskan pioneer name, also carries a deeper regional lineage in his name Xóots K̲oowu Hítz (Brown Bear's Nest or Den House) Teik̲weidí (Brown Bear Clan) Saanya Kwaan people (of Cape Fox, Saxman Village) Eagle (Ch'aak') Moeity, Tlingit (Lingit) Nation.

Honorah (Honey) Kelly remained a true Alaskan. After finishing her teacher training in Spokane, she returned to Alaska to teach in Haines and in a one-room schoolhouse in Petersburg, where her students carried rifles to school because along the way they encountered bears. Honey married Archie Archbold, a U.S. Forest Service manager who became assistant superintendent of the Tongass National Forest. They lived at the ranger station in Petersburg, and later moved to Ketchikan.

In Ketchikan, Honey worked for *Alaska Sportsman* magazine, and she herself was the feature in a 1951 story of her derby-winning salmon, which, at fifty-five pounds, was over half her weight.

In 1965, Honey and Arch retired to the Santa Barbara sun that he loved. Shortly after the move, Arch had a stroke and suffered significant memory loss. To help him learn to read again and to bring back his memory, Honey began writing stories for Arch to study with his speech therapist. The stories were simple, like children's stories, about each of them growing up and about their life together in Alaska. Her story "Growing Up in Treadwell" started the journey of this book.

Honey poured out stories on hundreds of handwritten pages. What began as speech therapy for Arch grew into a healing reverie for Honey, who missed her Alaska home and friends. In 1978, Archie died and Honey stopped writing. She longed to take one more trip to Alaska with her sister, Marion, to reprise the Kelly girls' adventures there, but she died a year after Archie.

The Kellys' favorite uncle, Bobby Coughlin, their birth mother's brother, remained on Gastineau Channel. On his death in 1955, at age sixty-six, the *Juneau Empire* (September 23, 1955) acknowledged him as "one of Southeast Alaska's most active figures in territorial and community affairs and private business" for over fifty years.

The Andersons

The Anderson family left Treadwell in 1916 because Gus saw ominous signs of an imminent mine cave-in. Disaster struck Treadwell eight months after they left. The family settled in Seattle, where Frederika, the stalwart Swedish pioneer wife and mother, died of cancer in 1923.

Gus Anderson remained the gruff patriarch as he took turns living with his adult children, often declaring, "I'm head of the house." By agreement, Gus generally stayed only two weeks at a time with each household. Into his nineties, he spent hours outside under a hot sun in his ubiquitous long underwear splitting wood from giant Douglas fir trees that fell in his granddaughter's yard. For his ninety-fifth birthday he visited a neighborhood tavern for a game of bowled duck pins, his favorite recreation. He died in 1962 at the age of ninety-eight.

Kari Anderson Preston, who dashed to safety clutching her baby son and narrowly escaped the Treadwell cave-in, only to lose her husband the next year in a tragic accident, moved to Seattle and trained as an accountant. She married again, and lost her second son to appendicitis when he was four. Her Treadwell-born child, Chistopher, graduated from the Naval Academy and had a career in the service. In her later years, widowed again and blinded by a stroke, Kari still looked back on her life as "blessed." She died July 30, 1990, at age ninety-two.[4]

Lydia Anderson honed her nursing skills in the Canadian Navy and cared for the sick and injured in two world wars. She married in 1923, had two children, and was active in the Ladies of the Golden North, an auxiliary of the Alaska-Yukon Pioneers who were associated with the gold rush. When she died January 12, 1996, at age one hundred, her obituary described her as "independent, ramrod-straight and determinedly healthy . . . she knew her purpose and scoffed at adversity."[5]

Irving Anderson went back to Gastineau Channel and worked in the Alaska-Juneau Mine to pay for dental school. He became a dentist, he says, "no thanks to the model of our Alaska dentist." He overcame his stuttering. The arm he broke on his first day of school remained crooked, but he perfected the tennis skills first taught him in Treadwell by Lydia's boyfriend "the Count."

Irving retained his interest in sailing, raising flowers like the ones he loved on his walks up in the meadow behind Treadwell, and getting his hands on gold—not the brick, but working with gold-leaf artistry in his dental practice. This book owes a lot to Irving, who poured out hours of colorful, heart-filled details about his life in Treadwell, his memories undimmed by a recent stroke. Outliving his siblings and most of his friends, he was the last of his family to die, at age ninety-four, in 1998.

The Kinzies

After Robert A. Kinzie Sr. left Treadwell, he moved the family to Santa Cruz, California, and became the president of the Santa Cruz Portland Cement Company. He designed and built the first oceangoing bulk cement carrier.

He continued to wear his trademark tweed suit with knee-high riding boots and to be an avid fan of the California Golden Bears football team. In the 1890s, he had been a tackle on the team and the quarterback, Eugene Kennedy, later became his brother-in-law and assistant superintendent at Treadwell.

Robert Sr.'s family remembers him not as Treadwell's "anti-union martinet" with the military bearing but as a kind and generous man who made Christmas special. After presents were opened, he would line up all sixteen grandchildren by height and give each a $100 savings bond. He then presided over dinner, which ended with everyone standing and singing "Hail to California."

Robert Sr. died in 1955 at age eighty-three. The Hearst Memorial Mining Building on the University of California campus in Berkeley features a staircase with a balustrade engraved with names of the one hundred most influential American engineers. His name is among them.

Veronica Kinzie, the intrepid Treadwell hostess, remained a gentle, gracious lady in San Francisco social circles. Known to her grandchildren as "Darling," she always dressed in blue, and had a 1936 blue Cadillac La Salle to match. Well into her eighties, she enjoyed discussing current events over a bourbon old-fashioned with orange rind and a cherry with stem.[6] She recalled her fourteen years in Treadwell as "the most interesting and happiest life ever, though admittedly, "not one happy picnic."[7]

Robert Jr. followed in his father's footsteps and became chief chemist and manager of Santa Cruz Portland Cement Company. He lived to witness the return of Halley's Comet in 1986, just as his grandfather had predicted as they watched the comet arc across the night sky in 1910. Back then, at the beginning of the century, earthbound photographers for the first time were able to capture fuzzy images of the phenomenon. This time around, the European spacecraft *Giotto* captured direct images of a comet nucleus.[8] Robert Jr. died in 1988 at the age of eighty-five.

The Bradleys

After the Treadwell mines flooded and closed, Frederick Worthen Bradley continued applying his skills across the channel at the Alaska-Juneau Mine, profitably processing high volumes of low-grade ore, helping southeast Alaska retain the title of lode-mining capital of the world. In recognizing his accomplishments, the American Institute of Mining and Metallurgical Engineers noted that "President Bradley mines gold so efficiently that he earns dividends for Alaska Juneau investors from dirt which contains only 90¢ worth of gold to a ton."[9]

F. W. continued to build his fame and wealth as a risk taker with the "keenest intuition in mining and money matters." He enjoyed solving problems in mining that other engineers considered too hard. Bradley collaborated with Bernard Baruch in New York and William H. Crocker of Crocker National Bank in California. The lifelong friendship and admiration between Bradley and Crocker contributed to the wealth of both.[10]

As a precaution against one of his ventures turning bad and using up his money, he made gifts to his family to protect them. "I had a good husband," his wife, Mary, said. "He left me $12 million."[11] F. W. was careful about promoting his sons, who were mining engineers. He did not put them in high positions in mines where he was president, because they would be resented by older members of the staff.[12]

Bradley became president of the American Institute of Mining Engineers in 1929, and received the Saunders gold medal in 1932, recognizing that he "had reached the pinnacle of the mine engineering profession." He died at his California home on July 6, 1933. Banker William Crocker noted his longtime associate's fifty-year career and hailed Bradley as "a real friend, a real man and a splendid citizen, in addition to being one of the greatest mining experts this country has ever known."[13]

In 1939, the people of Douglas Island changed the name of the island's highest peak from Mount Jumbo, the name given it by an unknown optimistic prospector, to Mount Bradley, after the man who brought a real bonanza to the island.

In 1988, F. W. was named the second inductee to the Mining Hall of Fame. He earned this honor as "one of the finest enterprising mining engineers the industry has known." He had established a record for low-cost gold mining at the Spanish Mine in Nevada County, California and then broke his own record at the Alaska-Juneau Mine after the Treadwell cave-in.[14]

The Bradley family was a mining dynasty. Three of F. W.'s four sons, and both of Philip Sr.'s sons, graduated from the College of Mines at the University of California. Phil Jr. worked underground at the A-J in 1924 and wrote his graduate thesis about the struggles and success of the mine. He spent fifty years as a mining operator and engineer in Alaska, Canada, Latin America, and Southeast Asia. He founded the California Mining Association and served on the California Mining Board for thirty-two years. His memoir, an oral history, was the first in the series *Western Mining in the Twentieth Century*, produced by the Bancroft Library at the University of California at Berkeley.[15] Unfortunately, many of the Bradley family's files, scrapbooks, and photos were destroyed when Phil Jr.'s home burned in the horrific 1991 Oakland hills firestorm, the worst in the area since the 1906 earthquake and driven by a Santa Ana wind as fierce as a Taku.

Treadwell remained a favorite topic of reverie for Phil Jr., and he had fond memories of all the families he knew there, including the Kellys. It was Phil Jr. who composed the text on the commemorative plaque installed in 1981 near the site of the superintendent's Mansion on the Treadwell Historic Trail. Fifteen years later, at age ninety-four, he proclaimed through his tears that "Treadwell was . . . the damndest most beautiful place for a youngster to grow up in. Gee, what a piece of luck that I just have to be thankful for almost every day." Taking note of the longevity of his Treadwell-raised peers, he joked that mining towns must not be as unhealthy as "those environmentalists" claimed. Phil Jr. died in 1999 at the age of ninety-six.

The Miners and Families

People from Treadwell took their places in the history of the region and the country. After the mines closed, the families of the Slovenian and Montenegrin miners stayed in the area and, along with the Alaska Natives and Filipinos, provided community and political leaders throughout the state. A majority of miners went across the channel to work at the Alaska-Juneau Mine, which was also under the leadership of F. W. Bradley. Mines throughout the country welcomed Treadwell veterans: Russell Wayland became general manager of Homestake Mine in South Dakota; others went to Inspiration Copper Mine in Arizona, or Bunker Hill and Sullivan Silver Mines in Idaho. Earl Beistline became dean of the School of Mines at the University of Alaska; Ed Stanyer became head electrician at University of Washington. Frances Cashen was the first Alaska-born woman to join a Catholic sisterhood (Sisters of St. Ann). Thomas Judson served in the Territorial House of Representatives and was elected to several terms as mayor of Juneau. John Dapcevich was a six-term mayor of Sitka. Walter Fukuyama's family was pulled into a darker chapter of the country's history when they were relocated to the internment camp at Minidoka during World War II.[16]

The Alaska Mining Hall of Fame, which honors people with "exemplary ties to Alaska mining history," includes many Treadwell notables: John Treadwell, F. W. Bradley, Earl Pilgrim, Livingston Wernecke, and Earl Beistline.

The Unions

In the 1930s there was agitation to form a union at the Alaska-Juneau Mines to improve working conditions. The Alaska Mine Workers Local No. 1 (AMW) was formed and launched a forty-five day strike. The streets roiled with brawls, tear gas, streaming fire hoses, and arrests of unarmed union people. Reminiscent of Treadwell, strikebreakers marched to the mine under the protection of the U.S. marshals.

According to an anonymous striker-turned-poet, the marshals

Started right in slugging every unarmed union man,
    And if these fought in self-defense they slammed them in the can
    With tear gas bombs and hose turned on they slugged with might and main
    And a union man unconscious on the ground they'd slug again.

After a while the smoke cleared off and things appeared to
quiet,
    But twenty-seven union men were in jail that night.
    Against unarmed men and women the prune sellers started
the fight.
    Yet union men must rot in jail for causing a bloody "riot."[17]

The strike was a demoralizing failure, with punitive repercussions,
and the AMW disbanded. But the experience galvanized the workers'
resolve to form a stronger organization. In December 1938, the A-J employees regrouped and elected the International Union of Mine, Mill,
and Smelter Workers, the Mine Mill, as their collective-bargaining agent.
"The company, now forced to recognize the union and listen to its demands, signed an agreement incorporating most of the standard union
benefits as well as wage increases."[18]

At one point, the Mine Mill was kicked out of the Congress of Industrial Organizations (CIO) for being too radical, in the spirit of the old
Western Federation of Miners from which it arose. Another testament
to the impact of the WFM was *Salt of the Earth*, a 1953 film about a Mine
Mill strike that is the only Hollywood movie ever banned by the U.S.
Congress. Several decades later, when the Library of Congress wanted
to display the top fifty Hollywood films, *Salt of the Earth* was the third
film chosen.

The Tlingit

The Taku Tlingit of Douglas gained recognition and political power in
1934 as a federally recognized tribe, the Douglas Indian Association (DIA),
with a membership of 350. Their waterfront village on Douglas Island
was condemned by the City and Borough of Juneau and burned in 1964
to make way for a boat harbor. Many of the village residents were away at
their summer fish camps when this happened. John Morris, a descendent
of Chief Aanyaalahaash, was home on military leave and witnessed his
family cottage set on fire and other residences "burnt with everything
that was left in them, personal things including gillnets, fishing floats and

lines. The money promised for reimbursement or relocation never came."[19] The DIA continues to seek legal redress for the loss of their lands.

The DIA is pursuing another protracted federal case to reclaim nearby Mayflower Island, the home of the pavilion that hosted dances and concerts in Treadwell days. The island is sacred to the Tlingit and their history records a shaman being buried there.

The Tlingit remain stewards of their ancestral lands and advocates for the protection of subsistence hunting and fishing rights. Most early missionaries believed that in order to survive, the Natives needed to be absorbed into the dominant society. Now maintaining Native identity is highly valued. Tlingit language is preserved by the elders, and there are programs to revive it. The Sealaska Heritage Institute maintains a thriving language-revitalization program. The traditional culture continues through potlatches, memorials, and burial practices. Clan ceremonies remain strong, and clans fiercely protect their ownership of crests, names, and songs, all honored by a biennial celebration in Juneau.[20] The "savage" art noted in the 1896 steamship brochures is now priceless and, in historic and contemporary forms, studied and sought after by collectors and museums around the world.

The Gold

The possibility of gold on the Treadwell site continued to lure prospectors of every era, particularly when the price of gold rose dramatically. Miners even staked claims on the gravels and mine tailings and extracted some gold from the Treadwell leftovers.

The SS *Islander*, which sank off Douglas in 1901, is still being tracked for the possible $6 million in gold rumored to be in the purser's safe. When parts of the ship were raised and beached in 1934, only $75,000 worth of nuggets and dust were found. The purser's safe contained a "handful of U.S. $10 and $20 gold pieces and a stack of rancid U.S. and Canadian paper currency." Dozens of salvage operations have been attempted, driven by the "lure of the vast shipwrecked treasure" and the conviction that "tons of gold bullion lay undisturbed on the bottom of Lynn Canal, still ensconced in the Mail and Storage Room."[21]

Over the years, modern-day prospectors continued to lust after the gold known to be held captive in the depths of the Treadwell mines. The mine workings below sea level are held in a watery suspension, a brackish mix of saltwater and freshwater that rushed in on the night of April 21, 1917. The worksites are preserved because there is no oxygen. If it was ever pumped out, a time capsule would emerge, along with still more treasure held in the untouched parts of that legendary vein of gold.

As early as 1934, a group had the idea of drilling from the Juneau side of the channel, then sinking shafts and tunnels to start mining under the flooded area. Later, almost a century after John Treadwell took a risk and paid $400 for the claim to this site, a Canadian company, Echo Bay Mining, risked millions of dollars to keep exploring the Treadwell. They drilled from the mainland, reaching forty-eight hundred feet into the mine, where they found that the ore deposit did indeed continue below the cave-in, and that a significant amount of gold was still there.

However, today as in the past, corporate mining of low-grade ore has to produce a profit for stockholders. Now, strict regulations and environmental concerns focus on the quantity of water needed for the processes. Disposal of the sandy waste product, the tailings, is a major obstacle in the permitting process, with 127 million tons of mine tailings already spread about the area. In 1900, it was a simple matter: Treadwell had a permit from the War Department for "reclaiming tidelands" with millions of tons of tailings. Today the debate continues over whether disposal should be considered "reclaiming" or defined as "disturbance."

In Treadwell's heyday, townspeople celebrated the incessant pounding of the stamp mills and pointed with pride to the massive pit above the town. People tolerated the chemical haze and the muddy waters, ignoring the barren hillside. Today, community response to the prospect of another mine in their midst is usually "We don't want to see it, hear it, or smell it." Echo Bay's 1996 survey of the Gastineau Channel community showed 10 to 15 percent of local residents were opposed to mining under any circumstances, while 15 to 20 percent wanted it under any circumstances. In 1996, after investing over $100 million in trying to get permits, Echo Bay abandoned efforts to resume mining in the Juneau area.[22]

For four decades the Treadwell Mining Company achieved world fame and record profits, with the price of gold set at $20.67 an ounce.

Treadwell gold is still down there, and the price of gold, moving with the market, has gone above $1,000 an ounce. As a measure of how things have changed, the Gastineau community has determined that, even at that price, reintroducing mining was not worth it. They rejected the 1996 Bureau of Land Management's finding that building a dam to impound millions of tons of mine tailings was the "highest and best use" of Sheep Creek Valley near Juneau.[23]

This sounded like the early days of Treadwell, when the land, the flora and fauna, and the minerals were all there to be appropriated to improve the material well-being of the owners, stockholders, and workers. But unlike early boosters who touted the blasting, pounding, grinding, wealth-producing Treadwell mines as the "Alaskan Fulfillment," modern-day Juneau conservationists lamented the prospect of the loss of wildlife and habitat in that four-hundred-acre emerald valley. Their twenty-first-century belief in preservation echoed the pre-Treadwell ethic voiced by the 1879 explorer of Gastineau Channel, poet and naturalist John Muir. Decrying the nineteenth-century exploitation of nature, Muir's many writings affirmed that "all existence had intrinsic value and did not need a utilitarian context."

For Muir, the real treasures in the Juneau Gold Belt were not the metals and the minerals that could be extracted to provide work for some and wealth to a few. There was the promise of even greater returns for "thousands of tired, nerve-shaken, over-civilized people." Muir placed the highest value on the wild places: "Everybody needs beauty as well as bread, places to play in and pray in, where nature may heal and give strength to body and soul alike."[24]

Afterword

I PERSISTED IN RESEARCHING AND WRITING this book when I realized it was more than a family memoir. At first, I was captivated by the country-club aspects of a gold-mining camp. But the whole story had the elements of great drama, too—a boom-and-bust saga in the early-twentieth-century era of industrial romance. And speaking of romance, in 1964, I married Geoffrey Macaulay Bellman, the great-grandson of Charles Peabody, who founded the Alaska Steamship Company in the 1890s. In piecing together my research, I discovered that Peabody first came up the Gastineau Channel in 1894, on his flagship the SS *Jefferson*, named for the county of his residence in Washington State. In 1905, that same boat transported the body of my grandmother, Ellen Cecile Coughlin Kelly, age twenty-nine, from Treadwell to Oakland, California, for burial.

Since I am an environmental professional and a political progressive, some suspected I was using this book to formulate a diatribe on how mining irreparably harms ecosystems, corporations exploit labor, and racial and cultural prejudice runs deep. My research confirms that pollution, exploitation, and prejudice were all part of the Treadwell story. But I found that in writing this book I had to stop myself from going too far in the other direction, in romanticizing this frontier story.

My best source for tracing the day-to-day lives of the people who lived in Treadwell was the local weekly paper, the *Douglas Island News*, an unabashedly pro-company publication. Another author, starting with other sources that delve deeply into labor history or best practices in hard-rock mining, or the complete cast of characters in the town, might tell the Treadwell story with a different emphasis. Was it just another glaring example of creating wealth for a few through the back-breaking and life-threatening toiling of undervalued workers? And can it be lauded as brilliant engineering and technology to leave an underground honeycomb of huge, wide-open untimbered spaces? And like the voyage of the *Titanic*, was Treadwell a rush to fame and profit that discounted some simple facts of nature?

I was struck by the similar messages given by the *Titanic* engineer and the Treadwell geologist. Both cautioned, "Slow down, pay attention to the threats." But while the industrial masters of the *Titanic* and the Treadwell claimed to have conquered nature, the downfall of each was triggered by an immutable threat in predictable natural cycles: For the *Titanic*, an iceberg floated down in the spring thaw—and sank the world's most famous unsinkable ship. In Treadwell, a new moon in close position to the earth exerted extraordinary pull on a high spring tide—and flooded the largest hard-rock gold mine of the era.

Treadwell Timeline

Archaeological evidence indicates indigenous people living in southeast Alaska nine thousand years ago

1794	Captain George Vancouver explores coastline of Alaska.
1867	United States purchases Alaska from Russia for $7.2 million.
1872	The General Mining Act signed into law by President Ulysses S. Grant to promote the development and settlement of publicly owned lands in the western United States.
1878	John Muir explores Alaska.
1880	Gold discovered by Joe Juneau and Richard Harris in Silver Bow Basin behind town that became Juneau.
1881	Gold discovered by Pierre Erussard on Douglas Island.
1881	John Treadwell buys Erussard's gold claims for $400.
1882	John Treadwell forms Alaska Mill and Mining Company; sets up five-stamp test mill on Glory Hole, becomes first superintendent.
1882–1890	Treadwell Ditch constructed to harness seventeen miles of local streams to bring hydropower to mines and mills.
1884	Congress passes the first Organic Act, which provides essentials of government for Alaska, a temporary capital at Sitka, district court, governor, district attorney, U.S. marshal, and other offices.
1887	Tourist steamships visit Alaska with Treadwell as featured attraction.
1883	Five-stamp test mill replaced by 120-stamp mill.

1882	The Chinese Exclusion Act, signed by President Chester Arthur, bars Chinese laborers from entering the United States and denies them naturalization.
1886	Juneau-area miners cast eighty Treadwell Chinese mine workers adrift in the Gastineau Channel in spite of John Treadwell's attempt to protect them.
1887	Mill at Treadwell mine expands to 240 stamps.
1885	Three hundred tons of ore are milled daily.
1889	Investors, including the Rothschild brothers, incorporate as the Alaska Treadwell Gold Mining Company and purchase the mine for $4 million. John Treadwell sells his interest for $1.4 million. Thomas Mein is new superintendent.
1890–1898	Robert Duncan is Treadwell superintendent.
1891	Alaska Mexican Gold Mining Company incorporates and starts the Mexican mine in an area seven hundred feet south of the Treadwell mine.
1893	The Panic of 1893 causes a serious depression in the United States that set off a series of bank failures and a run on the gold supply.
1894	The Alaska United Gold Mining Company incorporates to mine two other adjacent properties in Treadwell: the 700 Foot mine, in the seven-hundred-foot strip between the Treadwell and the Mexican mines, and the Ready Bullion mine, a half mile south. These four mines become the Treadwell complex, all mining from the same lode.
1897–1899	Klondike Gold Rush.
1899	William Kelly marries Ellen Cecile Coughlin in Oakland, California, and moves to Treadwell to work as a machinist; son Raymond born.
1899	Eight hundred eighty pounding stamps operate in five mills.
1898–1901	John P. Corbus is Treadwell superintendent.
1900	Frederick Worthen Bradley becomes Treadwell consulting engineer.
1901	Marion Kelly born.
1901	SS *Islander* sinks off west side of Douglas Island.
1901–1904	Joseph MacDonald is Treadwell superintendent.

1903	Honorah Kelly born.
1904–1914	Robert Kinzie is Treadwell superintendent.
1904	Treadwell mines featured at Lewis and Clark Exposition in Portland, Oregon, celebrating that the price paid for Alaska has been more than repaid by value of gold from Treadwell.
1905	Ellen Kelly dies, leaving three young children.
1906	San Francisco earthquake destroys headquarters of the Alaska Treadwell Gold Mining Company.
1906	Treadwell Glory Hole surface mining ceases; all operations moved underground.
1907	William Kelly marries Margaret (Mayme) Sullivan.
1907	August Anderson hired as Treadwell hoist operator.
1907	Western Federation of Miners establishes Douglas Island Union no. 1.
1907	Treadwell management supports establishment of Alaska Labor Union No. 1 for English-speaking mine workers.
1907–1908	Miners strike, soldiers come from Fort Seward near Haines. Kelly baby dies at birth.
1909	Alaska-Yukon-Pacific Exposition in Seattle features exhibit of gold and book *Treadwell: An Alaska Fulfillment.*
1909	Pillars in Treadwell mine begin caving.
1909	All buildings in Treadwell painted company colors, red with green trim.
1910	Mexican mine explosion kills thirty-nine miners.
1910	Halley's Comet passes over United States. Robert Kinzie Jr. sees it just after his baby sister has died.
1911	F. W. Bradley becomes president of Alaska Treadwell Gold Mining Company.
1911	Marion Kelly struck with polio.
1911	Fire driven by Taku wind destroys half of Douglas; town rallies to rebuild.
1912	The Second Organic Act of 1912 creates the Territory of Alaska.
1912	The unsinkable SS *Titanic* sinks in mid-Atlantic; 1,522 passengers and crew are lost; 705 survive.

1913	Extensive caving in mines shakes town violently; geologist Livingston Wernecke begins thorough inspection of all mines.
1913	Alaska's first territorial legislature convenes. First bill is unanimous vote for women's suffrage.
1914	Superintendent Kinzie forced to resign; family leaves Treadwell.
1914	Philip Bradley becomes superintendent, moves family into the mansion.
1914	F. W. Bradley begins process to consolidate ownership of three companies, with Treadwell as lead.
1914	World War I begins. Some miners leave to fight for homelands.
1914	The Treadwell complex reaches peak production with four mines feeding five thousand tons of ore a day to 960 stamps in five mills.
1915	Massive three-hundred-foot cave-in collapsed levels 700–1,000 in Treadwell mine.
1915	Earl Pilgrim arrives from University of Washington to spend summer as miner.
1915	Treadwell mines set world records for low-cost mining, processing five thousand tons of ore a day.
1915	Twin girls born into Superintendent Bradley's family.
1916	Profits are down, ore deposits leaner.
1916	Anderson family moves to Seattle.
1916	Kari Anderson marries Charles Preston, Treadwell's chief electrician, and remains in Treadwell.
1916	Territorial delegate to U.S. Congress introduced first bill to grant statehood to Alaska.
1916	Geologist Wernecke establishes forty-month plan to stabilize and shore up mines.
1917	Bulkhead completed between Ready Bullion and other three mines.
1917	United States enters World War I.
1917	Catastrophic caving and flooding of the Treadwell, Mexican, and 700 Foot mines. Hundreds of townspeople leave.

	Ready Bullion mine saved by bulkhead and continues producing.
1917–1918	Russell Wayland is Treadwell superintendent. Philip Bradley becomes consulting engineer and general manager.
1918	"Bone Dry Law" goes into effect after Alaska opts for Prohibition.
1918	SS *Princess Sophia* sinks north of Douglas Island; all 343 passengers lost.
1918	Worldwide influenza pandemic.
1918–1922	Lou Metzger is superintendent.
1920	Mayme Kelly dies.
1922	Ready Bullion mine shuts down.
1922	William Kelly marries Doris Lund, adopts her two children.
1924	The P. R. Bradley family leaves Alaska to return to California.
1924	Willy and Doris Kelly have twin girls.
1925	The Kellys leave Treadwell and move to Washington State.
1926	Taku-driven fire destroys most of Treadwell.
1928	Treadwell complex properties sold to Alaska-Juneau Gold Mining Company.

Acknowledgments

My aunt Marion Kelly Gallagher inspired me with her memories of life in Treadwell. The guidance and support of dozens more people helped me bring together the full story. Many of those who contributed are no longer here, including my father and aunts and the other Treadwell children I interviewed: Irving Anderson, Robert Kinzie, Jr., Philip Bradley, Jr., Roberta Fraser Johnson, and Mamie Feusi Jensen. Margaret Metzger Fordon is still living. This book also honors the memory and legacy of two recent Douglas Island residents and historians. Rick Urion generously provided his extensive file of digitized historical photos, and Willette Janes shared her research, her energy, and her friendship.

Telling the Treadwell story required images as well as words. I received patient assistance from Sandra Johnston at the Alaska State Library, Addison Field at Juneau Douglas Museum, Scott Willis at Alaska Electric Light and Power Company, and Michael and Carolyn Nore. The Anderson and Kinzie families provided unique pictures from their personal albums. Paulette Simpson secured photos of existing artifacts and ruins.

A host of reviewers helped shape this book. I benefitted from the work of Julie Van Pelt, Kathy Bradley, Waverly Fitzgerald, Frank Basler, Fritz Wolff, and particularly the editorial astuteness of Dorothy Craig. Kay Powers gave me insight into labor history. Evelyn Myers and Dr. Rosita Worl added to my understanding of the Tlingit culture. David Stone stressed the importance of mining in the development of Alaska. Deborah Rudis provided detail on pollutants left at Treadwell.

I kept at this project because of encouragement I have received over the years from the University of Washington Non-Fiction Book Writing course, Robert DeArmond, Dr. Terrence Cole, Claire Rudolf Murphy, Barbara Sjoholm, Theo Pauline Nestor, Glen Lindeman, Elisabeth Dabney, Jane Lindsey, and my Wednesday Writers' Group, which includes Debra Daniels-Zeller, Kathy Gehrt, Wendy Hinman, Elsie Hulsizer, Sharon Morris, and Janice Schwert. My friends and family accepted "I'm working on the book" as the predictable response to any inquires and suggestions about my life. My husband, Geoffrey Bellman, offered me everything he had from his deep reservoir of wisdom, experience, and love to help me realize my goal of getting the Treadwell story published.

Endnotes

Prologue

1. U.S. Census Office, 1893, 19.

Introduction

1. Charlotte L. Mahaffy, *I Remember Treadwell*, 2nd ed. (Juneau: Gastineau Channel Historical Society, 1992), 5.
2. *Douglas Island News*, November 20, 2007.
3. The Ditch captured the waters of several creeks—Fish, Eagle, Cowee, Lawson, Paris, Ready Bullion, and Bullion—originally to power waterwheels, then steam plants.
4. *Douglas Island News*, May 5, 1906.
5. For additional detail about the process, see the website "History of the Treadwell Mines Alaska," http://www.juneau.org/parkrec/museum/HTM/Treadwellmine/default.html (accessed September 21, 2009).
6. W. W. Shorthill, "The Treadwell Club," *Alaska-Yukon Magazine*, September 1907, 88–89.
7. T. A. Rickard, *Through the Yukon and Alaska* (San Francisco: Mining and Scientific Press, 1909), 44.
8. Alice Henson Christoe, *Treadwell: An Alaskan Fulfillment* (1909), booklet developed for the 1909 Alaska Yukon Pacific Exposition.

One

1. Jeremy Mouat, *Roaring Days: Rossland's Mines and the History of British Columbia* (Vancouver: University of British Columbia Press, 2005), xii.
2. Robert Campbell, *In Darkest Alaska: Travel and Empire Along the Inside Passage* (Philadelphia: University of Pennsylvania, 2007), 236.
3. Campbell, *In Darkest Alaska*, 259.
4. John Muir, *Travels in Alaska* (1915; repr., San Francisco: Sierra Club Books, 1998).

5. Septima Collis, *A Woman's Trip to Alaska*, quoted in Campbell, *In Darkest Alaska*, 88.

6. Pierre Berton, *Klondike: The Last Great Gold Rush 1896–1899*, rev. ed. (1972; Toronto: Anchor Canada, 2001), 5.

7. Pacific Coast Steamship Company brochure, 1907.

8. Campbell, *In Darkest Alaska*, 65.

9. Earl Redman, *History of the Mines in the Juneau Gold Belt: A Collection of Stories Telling about the Mines, the Prospectors, Their Golden Dreams, and How They Tried to Achieve Them* (Juneau: self-published, 1988), 238–242.

10. U.S. Bureau of the Census, "Commerce in Alaska," 1890, 261.

11. U.S. Bureau of the Census, 1910, 49.

12. U.S. Bureau of the Census, 1910, 49.

13. Berton, *Klondike*, 99.

14. Stephen Haycox, *Alaska: An American Colony* (Seattle: University of Washington Press, 2002), 189.

15. Berton, *Klondike*, 102.

16. Berton, *Klondike*, 95.

17. Claire Rudolf Murphy and Jane G. Haigh, *Children of the Gold Rush*, (Seattle: Alaska Northwest Books, 1999), 11.

18. Berton, *Klondike*, 7.

19. Berton, *Klondike*, 355.

20. Murray Morgan, *One Man's Gold Rush* (Seattle: University of Washington Press, 1967), 173.

21. Berton, *Klondike*, 393.

22. Stephen Haycox, *Frigid Embrace: Politics, Economics, and Environment in Alaska* (Corvallis: Oregon State University Press, 2002), 36.

23. Berton, *Klondike*, 393.

24. David Stone and Brenda Stone, *Hard Rock Gold: The Story of the Great Mines That Were the Heartbeat of Juneau* (Juneau: Juneau Centennial Committee, 1980), 34–36.

25. Haycox, *Frigid Embrace*, 25.

Two

1. Stone and Stone, *Hard Rock Gold*, 10.

2. R.N. DeArmond, *The Founding of Juneau* (Juneau, Glastineau Channel Centennial Association, 1980), 116–117.

3. Campbell, *In Darkest Alaska*, 206.

4. DeArmond, *Founding of Juneau*, 117.

5. U.S. Bureau of the Census, 1890, p. 49.

6. DeArmond, *Founding of Juneau*, 146.

7. Katherine G. Aiken, *Idaho's Bunker Hill: The Rise and Fall of a Great Mining Company 1885–1981* (Norman: University of Oklahoma Press, 2007), 18.

8. Aiken, *Idaho's Bunker Hill*, 42.

9. Livingston Wernecke, "Surface Subsidence and Water Conditions, Ventilation and Bulkheading in the Treadwell Group of Mines," A thesis submitted for the degree of Engineer of Mines, University of Washington, 1917, 90.

10. Conversation with David Stone.

11. Wernecke, "Surface Subsidence," 28ff.

12. "History of the Treadwell Mines Alaska," http://www.juneau.org/parkrec/museum/HTM/Treadwellmine/default.html (accessed August 5, 2009).

13. Stone and Stone, *Hard Rock Gold*, 18.

14. *The Treadwell Mine: The History of Alaska's First Major Gold Mining Operation, 1881–1917*, VHS, directed by Rick Urion (Juneau: Alaska Digital Images, 2007).

Three

1. Berton, *Klondike*, 393.

2. Father Aloysius Ragaru, S.J. Letter 1902, Southeast Alaska Mission Collection 2/1, Jesuit Oregon Province Archives, Gonzaga University, Spokane, Washington, 15.

3. Margaret Crawford, *Building the Workingman's Paradise* (New York: Verso, 1995), 2.

4. Linda Carlson, *Company Towns of the Pacific Northwest* (Seattle: University of Washington Press, 2003), 187.

5. Sande Anderson, "Kennecott: Alaskan Utopia," http://crm.cr.nps.gov/archive/24-09/24-09-6.pdf (accessed August 5, 2009). See also: *Kennecott Kids: Interviews with the Children of Kennecott* (Anchorage: Alaska Support Office, National Park Service, 2001).

6. Crawford, *Building the Workingman's Paradise*, 32.

7. Independence Mine, http://www.dnr.state.ak.us/parks/units/indmine.htm (accessed September 22, 2009).

8. Crawford, *Building the Workingman's Paradise*, 37–45.

9. Crawford, *Building the Workingman's Paradise*, 39.

10. en.wikipedia.org/wiki/Pullman_Company. Accessed October 15, 2009.

11. Crawford, *Building the Workingman's Paradise*, 7.

12. Crawford, *Building the Workingman's Paradise*, 84.

13. Haycox, *Frigid Embrace*, 50.

14. Crawford, *Building the Workingman's Paradise*, 6.

15. Carlson, *Company Towns*, 213.

16. Carlson, *Company Towns*, 5.

Four

1. *Oakland Enquirer*, March 11, 1899.

2. *Douglas Island News*, March 1899.

3. *Douglas Island News*, May 10, 1901.

4. Elva Galloway Hall, "Home Life on Douglas Island," *Alaska-Yukon Magazine*, September 1907, 55.

5. http://www.the shipslist.com/ships/lines/Alaska.htm (accessed October 16, 2009).

6. "The Islander Story," http://www.nickmessinger.co.uk/islander.html (accessed August 5, 2009).
7. *Douglas Island News*, March 1, 1905, 1.
8. Conversation with Marion Kelly.
9. Margaret Cantwell and Mary George Edmond, *North to Share: The Sisters of Saint Ann in Alaska and the Yukon Territory* (Victoria, B.C.: Sisters of St. Ann, 1992), 28.

Five

1. Earl Redman, *History of the Mines*, 30.
2. The information and quotes in this chapter come from the author's interviews with Irving Anderson over several months in 1996.
3. *Douglas Island News*, August 1912.
4. Conversation with Irving Anderson.

Six

1. This chapter is based on Earl R. Pilgrim, "The Treadwell Mines in 1915," *Alaska Journal* 5, no. 4 (Autumn 1975):194–204.
2. Rickard, *Through the Yukon and Alaska*, 38.
3. Chart of bell signals, courtesy of Willette Janes.
4. Treadwell Company Rules, *Daily Alaska Dispatch*, March 12, 1916, 6.
5. Rickard, *Through the Yukon and Alaska*, 30.
6. Ella Higginson, *Alaska: The Great Country*, 2nd ed. (New York: Macmillan Company, 1917), 126.
7. Higginson, *Alaska: The Great Country*, 126.
8. *Douglas Island News*, February 11, 1907.
9. Redman, *History of the Mines*, 36.
10. Pilgrim, "Treadwell Mines," 201.
11. *Douglas Island News*, August 26, 1914.
12. For the total operation of the mines at Treadwell between 1883 and 1922, there were fewer than two hundred deaths. Redman, *History of the Mines*, 37.

Seven

1. *Daily Alaska Dispatch*, August 10, 1901.
2. Conversation with Frank Cashen.
3. Aloysius Ragaru, 1903, *Southeast Alaska Missions Collection* 2/1, Jesuit Oregon Province Archives, Gonzaga University, Spokane, Washington.
4. Taped comments sent from R. A. Kinzie Jr. to Marion Kelly, 1985.

5. T. A. Rickard, *After Earthquake and Fire* (San Francisco: Mining and Scientific Press, 1906), 28.
6. *Douglas Island News*, April 18, 1906.
7. Memoir of Mrs. R. A. Kinzie, recorded by her grandson, Peter Buckley. Undated.
8. Conversation with Margaret Metzger Fordon.
9. Redman, *History of the Mines*, 21–22.
10. Christoe, "Treadwell: An Alaskan Fulfillment," 23.
11. Mahaffy, *I Remember Treadwell*, 41; and Trevor Davis, *Looking Back on Juneau: The First Hundred Years* (Juneau: Miner Publishing Company, 1979), 15.
12. Conversation with Philip Bradley, Jr.
13. *Douglas Island News*, February 2, 1910.
14. Taped conversation with R. A. Kinzie Jr.
15. *Douglas Island News*, October 30, 1913.
16. Conversation with David Stone.
17. Conversation with Irving Anderson.
18. Ed Andrews was one of southeast Alaska's early commercial photographers.

Eight

1. Jeremy Mouat, *Roaring Days: Rossland's Mines and the History of British Columbia* (Vancouver: University of British Columbia Press, 1995), xii.
2. Howard Zinn, *A People's History of the United States* (New York: Perennial Classics, 2003), 331.
3. Aiken, *Idaho's Bunker Hill*, 35.
4. Richard O. Boyer and Herbert M. Morais, *Labor's Untold Story* (Pittsburgh: United Electrical, Radio & Machine Workers of America, 2005), 14.
5. William Dudley Haywood, *The Columbia Encyclopedia*, 6th ed. 2008. *Encyclopedia.com*. (October 17, 2009). http://www.encyclopedia.com/doc/1E1-HaywoodW.html.
6. James C. Foster, "The Treadwell Strikes, 1907 and 1908," *Alaska Journal* no. 6 (Winter 1976); 2.
7. James C. Foster, "The Western Federation Comes to Alaska," *Pacific Northwest Quarterly*, October 1975, 167.
8. Foster, "The Western Federation", 165.
9. Foster, *The Treadwell Strikes*, 5.
10. Foster, *The Treadwell Strikes*, 5.
11. Foster, *The Treadwell Strikes*, 5.
12. Foster, *The Treadwell Strikes*, 5.
13. Eugene Pottier, "The Internationale," *Songs to Fan the Flames of Discontent*, trans. Charles H. Kerr (Chicago: Industrial Workers of the World, 1971). Referred to by workers as "The Little Red Song Book."
14. Foster, *The Treadwell Strikes*, 166.
15. Foster, "Western Federation," 7.

16. Redman, *History of the Mines*, 32.

17. Foster, "Western Federation," 10.

18. *Douglas Island News*, February 1908.

19. *Douglas Island News*, February 1908, 11.

Nine

1. Pacific Coast Steamship Company brochure, 1887, 19.

2. Wallace M. Olson, *The Tlingit: An Introduction to Their Culture and History*, 5th ed. (Auke Bay, Alaska: Heritage Research, 2004). See also *Douglas Island News*, December 14, 1898.

3. Olson, *The Tlingit*, 13. The early camp was at Groundhog Bay.

4. Haycox, *Alaska: An American Colony*, 19.

5. Haycox, *Alaska: An American Colony*, 175. See also: Olson, *The Tlingit*, 77.

6. Rickard, *Through the Yukon and Alaska*, 43.

7. Diary of Bertha Roene, ca. 1899. Courtesy of Wilette Janes.

8. Victoria Wyatt, "Alaskan Indian Wage Earners in the Nineteenth Century: Economic Choices and Ethnic Identity," *Pacific Northwest Quarterly* 78 (1987): 43–49.

9. Olson, *The Tlingit*, 5.

10. Trade routes from the coastal fisheries to inland tribes were known as grease trails in reference to the importance of the eulachon trade.

11. *Quest for Justice: Reclaiming Lingit Aani for T'aaku Kwaan*, undated draft (Douglas, Alaska: Douglas Indian Association).

12. Diary of Bertha Roene.

13. Haycox, *Frigid*, 1.

14. Olson, *The Tlingit*, 77.

15. Charles Replogle, *Among the Indians of Alaska* (London: Headley Bros, 1904).

16. Olson, *The Tlingit*, 82.

17. Aloysius Ragaru, 1903, *Southeast Alaska Missions Collection* 2/1, Jesuit Oregon Province Archives, Gonzaga University, Spokane, Washington, 3–4. Also noted in John Muir, *Travels in Alaska*.

18. Replogle, *Among the Indians*, 50.

19. Richard L. Dauenhauer, "Two Missions to Alaska," in *An Alaska Anthology: Interpreting the Past*, ed. Stephen W. Haycox and Mary Childers Mangusso (Seattle: University of Washington Press, 1996), 76.

20. Dauenhauer, "Two Missions," 77.

21. Replogle, *Among the Indians*, 142. Reverend Replogle had as many as twenty-six Indian children living with him at one time.

22. Ragaru, *Southeast Alaska Missions Collection*.

23. Campbell, *In Darkest Alaska*, 146.

24. Diary of Bertha Roene.

25. Muir, *Travels in Alaska*, 204.

26. Conversation with Irving Anderson.

27. Ann Chandonnet, "Southeast Sagas: Chief Aanyalahaash." *Juneau Empire*, August 29, 2003.

28. Charlotte L. Mahaffy, Manuscript 4-22-15, Alaska State Historical Library.
29. Olson, *The Tlingit*, 82.

Ten

1. Conversation with Marion Kelly.
2. Conversation with Irving Anderson.
3. Memior of Mrs. R. A. Kinzie, 17.
4. *Douglas Island News*, July 5, 1910.
5. *Douglas Island News*, July 7, 1903; *Douglas Island News*, June 30, 1916.
6. *Alaska Daily Empire*, July 5, 1914.
7. Harry Snyder Collection, Alaska State Historical Library, PCA 38, vol. 1, p. 21. See also *Douglas Island News*, July 5, 1911.
8. The fire-hose race remains the featured Fourth of July event on Douglas Island today.
9. In 1921, Raymond Kelly, honor student and debater at Gonzaga University in Spokane, Washington, came back to Douglas Island as the orator for the Fourth of July.
10. *Douglas Island News*, July 15, 1908.
11. *Douglas Island News*, July 4, 1916.

Eleven

1. Conversations with Marion Kelly.
2. *Douglas Island News*, January 30, 1920.
3. Redman, 27.
4. *Douglas Island News*, February 1904.
5. Redman, 30.
6. *Douglas Island News*, July 24, 1912.
7. *Douglas Island News*, September 1, 1916.

Twelve

1. Stone and Stone, *Hard Rock Gold*, 13.
2. Frank Carpenter, "Gold Mining at Treadwell is a Romance," *Daily Alaska Dispatch*, March 19, 1916.
3. David Stone, pers. comm.
4. Redman, *History of the Mines*, 35.
5. Livingston Wernecke, "Surface subsidence and water conditions," *Alaska Treadwell Gold Mining Company, Alaska Mexican Gold Mining Company, Alaska United Gold Mining Company; Report of the President to the Boards of Directors* (San Francisco: Mining and Scientific Press, 1916), 38.
6. Wernecke, "Surface Subsidence and Water Conditions," 83–90.
7. Harry Snyder Collection, PCA 38.

Thirteen

1. Livingston Wernecke, *Report on the Caving and Flooding of the Treadwell Mines on April 21, 1917*. For P. R. Bradley, Consulting Engineer, April 30, 1917.
2. Philip R. Bradley Jr., "A Mining Engineer in Alaska, Canada, the Western United States, Latin America, and Southeast Asia," an oral history conducted in 1986 and 1988 by Eleanor Swent, Regional Oral History Office, The Bancroft Library, University of California at Berkeley, 1988.
3. Conversation with Marion Kelly.
4. Moon Tides: How the Moon Affects Ocean Tides, http://home.hiwaay.net/~krcool/Astro/moon/moontides (accessed August 5, 2009).
5. Harry Snyder Collection, PCA 038 vol II, no. 72.
6. Wernecke, "Report on the Caving and Flooding," 5.
7. Wernecke, "Report on the Caving and Flooding," 5.
8. Mahaffy, *I Remember Treadwell*, 34.
9. Conversation with Irving Anderson.
10. Stone and Stone, *Hard Rock Gold*, 24.
11. *Daily Alaska Dispatch*, April 24, 1917.
12. Redman, *History of the Mines*, 46.
13. Jane Jacobs and Hannah Breece, *A School Teacher in Old Alaska: The Story of Hannah Breece* (New York: Knopf, 1997), 192.

Fourteen

1. *Douglas Island News*, April 27, 1917.
2. *Douglas Island News*, May 4, 1917; *Alaska Daily Empire*, May 4, 1917.
3. *Douglas Island News*, September 23, 1918.
4. *Alaska Daily Empire*, July 14, 1918.
5. *Douglas Island News*, February 25, 1918.
6. Bradley, *An Oral History*, 45.
7. *Douglas Island News*, October 5, 1918.
8. Jacobs and Breece, *Story of Hannah Breece*, 192.
9. *Douglas Island News*, April 1, 1918.
10. *Douglas Island News*, July 16, 1918.
11. *Douglas Island News*, June 21, 1918. See also July 5, 1918.
12. *Daily Alaska Dispatch*, August 3, 1917. See also: Wernecke, "The Treadwell Subsidence," 40.
13. Harry Snyder Collection, PCA 038 Part II no. 154.
14. Ken Coates and Bill Morrison, *The Sinking of the Princess Sophia: Taking the North Down With Her*, 2nd ed. (Fairbanks: University of Alaska Press, 1993).
15. *Douglas Island News*, October 22, 1918.
16. Bradley, *An Oral History*.
17. *Alaska Daily Empire*, November 13, 1918.
18. *Alaska Daily Empire*, October 15, 1918.
19. *Douglas Island News*, November 27, 1918.
20. *Alaska Daily Empire*, December 11, 1918. See also December 12, 1918.

21. *Douglas Island News*, August 29, 1919.
22. *Douglas Island News*, January 30, 1920.
23. *Douglas Island News*, February 10, 1920.
24. *Douglas Island News*, February 10, 1920.
25. Author's files.
26. Redman, *History of the Mines*, 48.

Fifteen

1. *Alaska Daily Empire*, October 11, 1926.
2. *Douglas Island News*, October 11, 1926.
3. *Alaska Daily Empire*, October 11, 1926.

Epilogue

1. Haycox, *Frigid Embrace*, 97–99. See also http://justice.uaa.alaska.edu/rlinks/natives/ak_ancsa.html (accessed October 15, 2009); http://www.litsite.org/index.cfm?section=History-and-Culture&page=ANCSA-at-30&cat=Articles&viewpost=2&ContentId=849 (accessed October 12, 2009).
2. Deborah D. Rudis, *Metal Concentrations in Sediments and Select Biota in Gastineau Channel, Juneau, Alaska*. U.S. Fish and Wildlife Service, Southeast Alaska Ecological Services, Juneau Alaska. April 1996; http://alaska.fws.gov/fisheries/contaminants/pdf/Gastineau%20Channel%20Metals.pdf (accessed October 20, 2009); also conversation with Deborah Rudis, October 22, 2009.
3. National Mining Hall of Fame, http://www.mininghalloffame.org/hallfame.htm (accessed August 5, 2009).
4. Conversation with Judy Kelliher, niece of Kari Anderson, July 27, 2007.
5. Obituary for Lydia Anderson, *Seattle Times*, January 19, 1996.
6. Memoir of Mrs. R. A. Kinzie, 14.
7. R. A. Kinzie Sr., Family notes from Douglas Moore, son of Eugenia Kinzie and grandson of R. A. Kinzie Sr.
8. Giotto Spacecraft, http://hyperphysics.phy-astr.gsu.edu/hbase/solar/giotto.html#c1 (accessed August 5, 2009).
9. *Time*, February 29, 1932.
10. Aiken, *Idaho's Bunker Hill*, 42.
11. Stone and Stone, *Hard Rock Gold*, 77. Also personal conversation with David Stone.
12. Letter written by Oscar Hershey, courtesy of P. R. Bradley Jr. and David Stone.
13. Aiken, *Idaho's Bunker Hill*, 92.
14. National Mining Hall of Fame, http://www.mininghalloffame.org/hallfame.htm (accessed August 5, 2009).
15. Bradley, *An Oral History*.
16. Gastineau Channel Memories, vol. 1 (1880–1959), http://www.juneau.org/parkrec/museum/forms/GCM/index.php (accessed September 29, 2009).
17. Stone and Stone, *Hard Rock Gold*, 69–70.
18. Stone and Stone, *Hard Rock Gold*, 69–70.

19. *Quest for Justice: Reclaiming Lingit Aani for T'aaku Kwaan*, draft (Douglas, Alaska: Douglas Indian Association, undated), 10. Also, personal conversation with John Morris.

20. Goldbelt Alaska Native corporation, http://www.goldbelt.com/our_company/Our_Company.html (accessed October 15, 2009).

21. Princess Sophia, http://www.nickmessinger.co.uk/islander.html (accessed August 5, 2009).

22. Personal conversation with David Stone.

23. David Dorris, Bureau of Land Management's project manager for the 1992 Alaska-Juneau environmental impact statement (EIS) concluded that "the highest and best use of Sheep Creek Valley is as a tailings storage facility." The projected tailings volume was in the range of ten thousand tons per day for fourteen years. The Southeast Alaska Conservation Council objected to the 350-foot dam across the face of Sheep Creek Valley, which would create a 2.5-mile-long tailings storage and treatment facility that discharged thirty to fifty million gallons of polluted water per day into Gastineau Channel, "on top of the taking of that beautiful valley." Personal conversation with Aaron Brakel.

24. Haycox, *Frigid Embrace*, 30, 41–42; Campbell, *In Darkest Alaska*, 58–68. http://www.sierraclub.org/john_muir_exhibit/writings/favorite_quotations.html (accessed October 7, 2009).

SELECTED BIBLIOGRAPHY

Aiken, Katherine G. *Idaho's Bunker Hill: The Rise and Fall of a Great Mining Company 1885–1981*. Norman: University of Oklahoma Press, 2007.

Berton, Pierre. *Klondike: The Last Great Gold Rush 1896–1899*. Toronto: Anchor Canada, 2001. First published 1972 by McClelland and Stewart.

Boyer, Richard O., and Herbert M. Morais. *Labor's Untold Story*. Pittsburgh: United Electrical, Radio & Machine Workers of America, 2005.

Bradley Family Papers. Bancroft Library, University of California at Berkeley. Carton #37 91/30.

Bradley Jr., Philip R. "A Mining Engineer in Alaska, Canada, the Western United States, Latin America, and Southeast Asia." Oral history conducted in 1986 and 1988 by Eleanor Swent, Regional Oral History Office, The Bancroft Library, University of California at Berkeley, 1988.

Brinsmade, Robert Bruce. *Mining Without Timber*. New York: McGraw-Hill, 1911.

Brown, Mary Margaret. *A Century of Service 1858–1958*. Victoria, British Columbia: Sisters of St. Ann, 1966.

Campbell, Robert. *In Darkest Alaska: Travel and Empire along the Inside Passage*. Philadelphia: University of Pennsylvania Press, 2007.

Cantwell, Margaret, and Mary George Edmond. *North to Share: The Sisters of Saint Ann in Alaska and the Yukon Territory*. Victoria, British Columbia: Sisters of St. Ann, 1992.

Carlson, Linda. *Company Towns of the Pacific Northwest*. Seattle: University of Washington Press, 2003.

Carpenter, Frank. "Gold Mining at Treadwell Is a Romance." *Daily Alaska Dispatch*, March 19, 1916.

Christoe, Alice Henson. *Treadwell: An Alaskan Fulfillment*. Booklet developed for the 1909 Alaska Yukon Pacific Exposition, 1909.

Coates, Ken, and Bill Morrison. *The Sinking of the Princess Sophia: Taking the North Down with Her*. 2nd ed. Fairbanks: University of Alaska Press, 1993.

Crawford, Margaret. *Building the Workingman's Paradise*. New York: Verso, 1995.

Dauenhauer, Richard L. "Two Missions to Alaska." In *An Alaska Anthology: Interpreting the Past*, edited by Stephen W. Haycox and Mary Childers Mangusso. Seattle: University of Washington Press, 1996.

Davis, Trevor. *Looking Back on Juneau: The First Hundred Years*. Juneau: Miner Publishing Company, 1979.

DeArmond, R. N. *The Founding of Juneau*. Juneau: Gastineau Channel Centennial Association, 1980.

DeArmond, Robert N., and Sarah Eppenbach. *Centennial Gazetteer: A Guide to Juneau Alaska Place Names*. Juneau: Gastineau Centennial Association, 1979.

Dexter, Julianne Nick. *Gold!!! No Gold*. Escondido, Calif.: Omni Publishers, 1976.

Dodson, Peggy Rouch. *Girl in the Gold Camp: A True Account of an Alaska Adventure, 1909–1910*. Seattle: Epicenter, 1996.

Ducker, James H. "Gold Rushers North: A Census Study of the Yukon and Alaskan Gold Rushes, 1896–1900." In *An Alaska Anthology: Interpreting the Past*. Edited by Stephen W. Haycox and Mary Childers Mangusso. Seattle: University of Washington Press, 1996, 206–221.

Finlay, James Ralph. *The Cost of Mining*. 3rd ed. New York: McGraw Hill, 1920.

Foster, James C. "The Western Federation Comes to Alaska." *Pacific Northwest Quarterly* 66, no. 4 (October 1975).

———. "The Treadwell Strikes, 1907 and 1908." *Alaska Journal* 6 (Winter 1976).

Gregory, James N. "The West and the Workers, 1870–1930." In *A Companion to the American West*. Edited by William Deverell. Malden, Mass.: Blackwell Publishing, 2004.

Hall, Elva Galloway. "Home Life on Douglas Island." *Alaska-Yukon Magazine*, September 1907.

Haycox, Stephen. *Alaska: An American Colony*. Seattle: University of Washington Press, 2002.

———. *Frigid Embrace: Politics, Economics, and Environment in Alaska*. Corvallis: Oregon State University Press, 2002.

Haycox, Stephen, and Mary Childers Mangusso, eds. *An Alaska Anthology: Interpreting the Past*. Seattle and London: University of Washington Press, 1996.

Higginson, Ella. *Alaska: The Great Country*. 2nd ed. New York: Macmillan Company, 1917.

Hinckley, Ted C. "Prospectors, Profits and Prejudice." *America West Journal* 2 (1965): 58–65.

Jacobs, Jane, and Hannah Breece. *A School Teacher in Old Alaska: The Story of Hannah Breece*. New York: Knopf, 1997.

Kelly, Sheila. "A Child's Life in Treadwell." The *Alaska Journal, History and Arts of the North*, 14, no. 2 (Spring 1984):12–20.

———. "Honey and Arch: An Alaskan Love Story." The *Alaska Journal: History and Arts of the North*, 16, Special Edition (1986):204–208.

Lass, W. P. "Cyanide Plant at the Treadwell Mines of Alaska." *Bulletin of the American Institute of Mining Engineers* 61 (1912):183–216.

Mahaffy, Charlotte L. *I Remember Treadwell*. 2nd ed. Juneau: Gastineau Channel Historical Society, 1992.

———. Manuscript 4-22-15. Alaska State Historical Library.

Mighetto, Lisa, and Marcia Babcock Montgomery. *Hard Drive to the Klondike: Promoting Seattle During the Gold Rush*. Elizabethton, Tenn.: Smoky Mountain Books, 2002.

Morgan, Murray. *One Man's Gold Rush*. Seattle: University of Washington Press, 1967.

Mouat, Jeremy. *Roaring Days: Rossland's Mines and the History of British Columbia.* Vancouver: University of British Columbia Press, 1995.

Muir, John. *Travels in Alaska.* 1915. Reprint, San Francisco: Sierra Club Books, 1998.

Murphy, Claire Rudolf, and Jane G. Haigh. *Gold Rush Women.* Seattle: Alaska Northwest Books, 1997.

———. *Children of the Gold Rush.* Seattle: Alaska Northwest Books, 1999.

Musk, George. *Canadian Pacific: The Story of the Famous Shipping Line.* Toronto: Holt, Rinehart and Winston, 1981.

Nadeau, I. A. "The Alaska Yukon Pacific Exposition." *The Coast* 18, no. 3 (1909): 174–176.

Olson, Wallace M. *The Tlingit: An Introduction to Their Culture and History.* 5th ed. Auke Bay, Alaska: Heritage Research, 2004.

Pilgrim, Earl R. "The Treadwell Mines in 1915." *Alaska Journal* 5, no. 4 (Autumn 1975): 194–204.

Pottier, Eugene. *Songs to Fan the Flames of Discontent.* Translated by Charles H. Kerr. Chicago: Industrial Workers of the World, 1971.

Redman, Earl. *History of the Mines in the Juneau Gold Belt: A Collection of Stories Telling About the Mines, the Prospectors, Their Golden Dreams, and How They Tried to Achieve Them.* Juneau: self-published, 1988.

Replogle, Charles. *Among the Indians of Alaska.* London: Headley Bros., 1904.

Rickard, T. A. *After Earthquake and Fire.* San Francisco: Mining and Scientific Press, 1906.

———. *Through the Yukon and Alaska.* San Francisco: Mining and Scientific Press, 1909.

———. *A History of American Mining.* New York: McGraw-Hill, 1932.

Roppel, Patricia. *Striking It Rich! Gold Mining in Southern Southeast Alaska.* Greenwich, Conn.: Coachlamp Productions, 2005.

Sainsbury, C. L. *Dig Deep for Yellow Gold.* Self-published, 1985.

Shorthill, W. W. "The Treadwell Club." *Alaska-Yukon Magazine,* September 1907, 88–90.

Stone, David, and Brenda Stone. *Hard Rock Gold: The Story of the Great Mines That Were the Heartbeat of Juneau.* Juneau: Juneau Centennial Committee, 1980.

Sullivan, Joseph. "Sourdough Radicalism, Labor and Socialism in Alaska, 1905–1920." In *An Alaska Anthology: Interpreting the Past.* Edited by Stephen W. Haycox and Mary Childers Mangusso. Seattle and London: University of Washington Press, 1996, 222.

Tillotson, Marjorie. "History of the Schools in the Gastineau Channel Area." *The Alaska Journal* 6 (1972):252.

Urion, Rick. *The Treadwell Mine: The History of Alaska's First Major Gold Mining Operation,* VHS. Juneau: Alaska Digital Images, 2007.

U.S. Census Office. *Report on the Population and Resources of Alaska at the Eleventh Census: 1890.* Washington D.C.: Government Printing Office, 1893.

Wayland, Russell G. "A Forty Month Program of Operation Proposed for the Treadwell Group of Mines." A thesis submitted for the degree of Engineer of Mines, University of Washington, 1917.

Wernecke, Livingston. "Surface Subsidence and Water Conditions," *Alaska Treadwell Gold Mining Company, Alaska Mexican Gold Mining Company, Alaska United Gold*

Mining Company; Report of the President to the Boards of Directors. San Francisco: Mining and Scientific Press, October 20, 1916.

———. "Report on the Caving and Flooding of the Treadwell Mines on April 21, 1917." For P. R. Bradley, Consulting Engineer, April 30, 1917.

———. "The Treadwell Subsidence." March 4, 1918.

Wyatt, Victoria. "Alaskan Indian Wage Earners in the Nineteenth Century: Economic Choices and Ethnic Identity." *Pacific Northwest Quarterly* 78 (1987):43–49.

Zinn, Howard. *A People's History of the United States*. New York: Perennial Classics, 2003.

Index